DREAM TEAM

SAINTS AND GENTLE SOULS
FROM THE WORLD OF SPORTS

FREDERICK J. DAY

AUTHOR OF *CLUBHOUSE LAWYER*
ILLUSTRATIONS BY VINN TRUONG

iUniverse, Inc.
New York Lincoln Shanghai

DREAM TEAM
Saints and Gentle Souls From the World of Sports

Copyright © 2007 by Frederick J. Day

iUniverse books may be ordered through booksellers or by contacting:

iUniverse
2021 Pine Lake Road, Suite 100
Lincoln, NE 68512
www.iuniverse.com
1-800-Authors (1-800-288-4677)

Because of the dynamic nature of the Internet, any Web addresses or links contained in this book may have changed since publication and may no longer be valid.

The views expressed in this work are solely those of the author and do not necessarily reflect the views of the publisher, and the publisher hereby disclaims any responsibility for them.

ISBN: 978-0-595-45406-8 (pbk)
ISBN: 978-0-595-70071-4 (cloth)
ISBN: 978-0-595-89719-3 (ebk)

Printed in the United States of America

In memory of my father, founder of the Pine Bush Little League, Albany, NY—

What he lacked as an athlete, he made up for as a dreamer.

Ray Kinsella: *It would kill some men to get that close to their dream and not touch it ... they'd consider it a tragedy.*

Doc Graham: *Son, if I'd only gotten to be a doctor for five minutes, now that would have been a tragedy.*

—Field of Dreams.

Contents

1960–1969

1970–1979

1980–1989

2000–2007

Epilogue

Acknowledgments

Blessed Mother Teresa of Calcutta once suggested that God intentionally places certain souls in our way with specific purposes in mind. If so, there are many reasons why God may have arranged for me to meet Ellen Flannery, my friend and basketball teammate. Among the many fruits of my friendship with Ellen, it was Ellen who planted the seed for *Dream Team,* and then nourished that seed and stimulated its growth.

To be specific, on November 1, 2005, in recognition of the Feast of All Saints, Ellen sent a message asking if I had composed a "dream team" of saints. I responded that my dream team of saints consisted of Arthur Ashe, Joe Delaney, Roberto Clemente, and Mickey Mantle. Shortly thereafter, it occurred to me that I had committed a grave injustice in leaving Harold McLinton off my list. And along with Harold McLinton, why not Pee Wee Reese? Before long, the concept for *Dream Team* emerged. Along the way, Ellen provided continual feedback and encouragement, and helped greatly in refining the concept. She also introduced me to Dream Teamer Toni Stone, among others.

There were others whom God seems to have placed in my way as friends and unerring sources of ideas for *Dream Team.* The Rev. Ed Ifkovits, S.J., parochial vicar at St. Aloysius Catholic Church in Washington, D.C., provided the inspiration for research into the "one-day wonder," Al Travers. Ed also introduced me to Lutz Long, Junius Kellogg, "Big Pete" Schneider, and other gentle souls. My friend, scriptural advisor, and history guru, EJ "Mr. D" Dvorscak, provided me with an abundance of useful reference books. Without these books I would have been unaware of the unselfish contributions of tennis enthusiasts Jim and Gloria Smith, among others. From Florida, my friends Melissa and Randy Keefer provided a constant stream of information on Annie Oakley, Effa Manley, Maddy English, and other notable women who stand tall in the history of sports. Similarly, my stepfather Bill Pollock, a golf enthusiast and all-around sports whiz, introduced me to the charitable works of Payne Stewart and several other athletes. My wife, Bic, also made invaluable contributions in helping *Dream Team* find its way to publication. My mother, Betty Pollock, and my sisters, Patty, Barb, Kathy, and Marzie, were enthusiastic supporters and willing reviewers. My goddaughter and favorite shortstop, Megan Shaffer, graciously recounted the story of her friend and former teammate, Shelby Njoku, and reviewed draft *Dream Team* narratives. The Schneider clan, Cathi, Jim, Pete, and Mike, provided intimate glimpses into the life of their father, Big Pete, and offered heart-warming anecdotes about that very special man.

My friends, Ron Vincoli, CJ Nitkowski, and Ha Pham, reviewed *Dream Team* drafts, made helpful suggestions, and offered encouragement. My friend, Leo Marquez, helped out with *Dream Team* research. Also, my weekly meetings with the "Knights of Panera" helped to stimulate thoughts about all the good people in sports. With their enthusiasm and expertise, Kristin Oomen, Laura McGinn, and Dr. Traci Vujicich of iUniverse helped greatly to move *Dream Team* forward to publication. Finally, I am indebted to my friend and college roomie, Roy Peter Clark, whose wonderful book, *Writing Tools*, helped to shape the approach and manner of expression in *Dream Team*.

I thank them all. I thank, especially, the good Lord for having placed these special people in my way.

Preface

o o o o o o o o o o o o o o o o o o o o o o o o o o o o o o o o o o

The very fact that God has placed a certain soul
in our way is a sign that God wants us to do
something for him or her.

—*Blessed Mother Teresa of Calcutta (1910–1997).*

Once, as former pro football running back Curtis Martin was walking to his automobile in the Foxboro Stadium parking area after a game, a vehicle pulled up next to him. A young boy stuck his arm out one of the vehicle's windows and handed Martin an envelope. The vehicle carrying the young boy then pulled off, leaving Martin to ponder the contents of the envelope. Upon opening the envelope, Martin found an invitation to the child's birthday party, complete with the date of the party, the address, and directions.

On the day of the party, the doorbell at the boy's home rang. To the astonishment of the young boy, standing at the front door was Curtis Martin—in full party mode.

If Martin's act of kindness was unprecedented, it was certainly not out of character. "The main reason I play football," Martin once said, "is to light up the face of a sick child or someone less fortunate, for that makes my heart sing."

Sportswriter Paul Gallico once commented that sportswriters are often cynics because they "learn eventually that, while there are no villains, there are no heroes either." But, Gallico warned, "until you make the final discovery that there are only human beings, who are therefore all the more interesting, you are liable to miss something." *

If Gallico is correct in his assertion that there are no heroes, it is undeniable that a select few of the participants in amateur and professional sports have, like

Curtis Martin, established themselves as human beings capable of heroic, almost saintly, deeds.

On August 5, 1936, at the Berlin Olympics, Lutz Long of Germany and Jesse Owens of the United States competed in the broad jump. Owens captured the gold medal, Long the silver. The two became fast friends. After Owens returned to the States, he and Long kept in contact through letters. When World War II broke out, Long was inducted into the German army. Owens and Long continued to correspond until Long was sent to North Africa. Long feared that he would not survive. In his last letter to Owens, Long wrote of a premonition about his death. He also asked a favor of Owens—if Long were to die during the war, he wished that Owens would locate Long's son, Karl, when the war was over. "Tell him," Long wrote to Owens, "how things can be between men on this earth."

Through the stories of athletes, some prominent and others not so prominent, *Dream Team* seeks to tell "how things can be between men (and women) on this earth." *Dream Team* is the story of former major-leaguer Gabby Street helping a young African-American woman, Toni Stone, learn the game of baseball when he could easily have ignored her. *Dream Team* is the story of baseball player-turned-teacher Madeline "Maddy" English giving a speech in her hometown of Everett, Massachusetts, and then running outside to play catch with some young girls who were in the audience. It is the story of tennis player Arthur Ashe reaching for "the purest joy in life" by trying to help others.

Above all, *Dream Team* is the story of individuals who took the time to do something for the souls whom God placed in their way.

---

* Wagenheim, Kal. *Clemente!* Chicago: Olmstead Press, 2001.

How Dream Team is Organized

Many of the good works and humanitarian deeds portrayed in *Dream Team* took place against the backdrop of unique political or historical events. The story of German Lutz Long, for example, would not be complete without reference to the doctrine of Aryan supremacy being espoused by Hitler and the Nazi party in the 1930s. Similarly, the nobility inherent in Pee Wee Reese's public support for Jackie Robinson can be fully appreciated only with an understanding of the prevailing social climate in the United States of the 1940s. It seems appropriate, therefore, to organize the *Dream Team* narratives according to historical eras. For this reason, the narratives are grouped by decade beginning, first, with the period from 1890 to 1899 and proceeding decade-by-decade to 2007.

After deciding to organize the *Dream Team* narratives according to decades, the next step was to assign each individual who is the subject of a narrative to a specific decade. This process suggests a level of precision that is not mirrored in real life. To illustrate, the narrative on former Supreme Court justice Byron R. White is included in the decade 1960–1969 because his finest hour arguably occurred in 1961 when, as a Department of Justice official, he faced down both the governor of Alabama and the Alabama Ku Klux Klan. Necessarily, there is an element of arbitrariness in placing White's narrative in the decade 1960–1969, instead of 1930–1939, when he excelled as an athlete, or in the decade 1980–1989, when he wrote some of his most prominent Supreme Court dissents.

For virtually all of the *Dream Team* members portrayed in this volume, the placement of their individual narratives involves a similar subjectivity. In general, however, I assigned individual narratives to specific decades based on three considerations: the individual's period of prominence in his or her athletic endeavors; the period in which the individual made his or her most distinguished contributions to society; or the date of the individual's death.

Author's Note: The *New American Bible*, with revised Psalms and New Testament (1988, 1991), Catholic Book Publishing Co., New York, NY, served, generally, as the source for the verses from the Book of Psalms and the Book of Proverbs that are quoted in this volume.

1890–1899

1890–1899

The *New York Times* of 1890 reported, day after day, the devastating effects of the flu epidemic sweeping through the eastern United States at the time. The epidemic would claim the life of Father Michael McGivney, baseball player and founder of the Knights of Columbus, in August 1890.

After a concerted effort by conservationists, the federal government set aside a vast area of Wyoming and Colorado in 1891 to become Yellowstone National Park, the country's first national park. In 1892, the flood of immigrants arriving from Europe and elsewhere forced the government to open up Ellis Island, located in New York harbor, for processing new arrivals to the United States.

A growing credit shortage in 1893 created panic, resulting in a depression. Over the course of the Depression, fifteen thousand businesses, six hundred banks, and seventy-four railroads failed. There was severe unemployment and wide-scale protesting, leading to sporadic outbreaks of violence. Labor leader Eugene Debs led the Pullman Rail Strike of 1894. The strike was a response to the action of the Pullman Rail company in cutting worker salaries, but refusing to lower the rents paid by railroad workers living in Pullman houses. In 1895, famed American rifle sharpshooter Annie Oakley toured the United States with James A. Bailey of Barnum and Bailey circus fame. Oakley gave 131 shooting exhibitions in 190 days, and covered more than nine thousand miles during the tour.

The Spanish-American War broke out in 1898. At the time, Cuba, Puerto Rico, the Philippines, and Guam were among the few remnants of the Spanish empire. Spanish rule in Cuba was particularly oppressive, with many Cubans being held in concentration camps. In February 1898, an explosion in the harbor at Havana sank the American battleship USS *Maine*. A total of 266 United States sailors lost their lives. The cause of the explosion would never be determined. However, American journalists William Randolph Hearst and Joseph Pulitzer, and other prominent Democrats, used the incident to stir up sentiment for waging war against Spain. "Remember the *Maine*" became a popular refrain.

The United States declared war against Spain in April 1898. The U.S. held a decisive naval advantage. The two countries signed a peace treaty in December

1898. As a result, Spain granted Cuba its independence, and the United States gained the former Spanish colonies of Guam, the Philippines, and Puerto Rico.

MICHAEL McGIVNEY

Born on August 12, 1852, in Waterbury, Connecticut, Michael McGivney was a five-foot-ten-inch, fleet-footed athlete, with a special fondness for baseball. While still a youth, McGivney realized that he had a calling to the priesthood. He enrolled at the Seminary of Sainte Hyacinthe in Quebec, Canada in September 1868. McGivney transferred to the Seminary of Our Lady of Angels in Niagara Falls, New York after his second year at Sainte Hyacinthe. His primary motivation for changing seminaries was the lure of the athletic program available at Our Lady of Angels. Priestly calling or not, McGivney was born to play ball. While studying in Niagara Falls, he played left field and batted cleanup for an amateur team known as the Charter Oaks. In December 1877, he was ordained as a priest. Thereafter, whenever there was a parish festival, McGivney made sure that the schedule of events included a baseball game. He died on August 14, 1890, at the age of thirty-eight.

The probate court for the city of New Haven, Connecticut faced a dilemma in January 1882. Catherine Downes, impoverished mother of six children and step-mother to eight more, had lost her husband, Edward, to brain fever. The court required Catherine to find guardians capable of posting a financial bond for each of her teenage sons. By court order, any of the boys who lacked a guardian would be turned over to foster care.

Catherine was able to find guardians for all but nineteen-year-old Alfred. The court convened a hearing for Alfred on February 6, 1882. The judge opened the proceedings by asking if anyone present was willing to serve as Alfred's guardian. Father Michael McGivney, twenty-nine years old and a parish priest, stood up and agreed to be guardian. With that act, McGivney ensured that the Downes family would remain intact.

McGivney displayed a rare ability to relate to people, whether serving as a teenager's guardian, visiting prisoners, saying Mass, or playing left field. He was happiest when he was engaged in the ordinary duties of being a priest. However, it was his role as founder of the Knights of Columbus, a Catholic fraternal organization, for which he gained his greatest recognition. McGivney was disturbed by the conspicuous lack of religious zeal among Catholic men; most were content to leave religious observances to the women in their families. McGivney felt the need for an organization that would foster a stronger bond between young men and the Church. At the same time, he hoped to establish a financial institution that could provide monetary support for poorer families, especially those whose breadwinners took sick or had died. The Knights of Columbus came into being in 1882, with McGivney providing both the impetus and the business acumen.

Inspired by Father McGivney, the Knights continue to this day to promote the traditions of the Catholic faith and serve the needs of the poor.

◆   ◆   ◆

Defend the lowly and fatherless; render justice to the afflicted and needy.
—Psalm 82, verse 3.

May 20, 1872

Mohawks	Runs	Outs	Charter Oaks	Runs	Outs
Grace, catcher...........	1	2	Hanlon, first base..........	2	3
Kearns, pitcher............	2	1	Don Levy, right field.......	3	1
Russell, first base..........	1	2	Ring, shortstop.............	3	2
Hall, second base.........	1	1	McGivney, left field........	3	2
Barrett, third base........	0	2	Pope, catcher..............	3	1
O'Connor, shortstop....	0	3	Growney, center field.....	3	1
Delaney, left field........	0	1	Welch, third base..........	1	2
Kernan, center field......	0	2	Splain, pitcher.............	2	2
Lee, right field............	1	1	O'Grady, second base...	3	1
Totals...................	6	15	Totals......................	23	15

Umpire: T.E. Donnelly. Scorers: Messrs. Byrnes and Kelly.

ANNIE OAKLEY

Annie Oakley was born on August 13, 1860, in Darke County, Ohio. She survived a difficult childhood to gain worldwide fame as a rifle sharpshooter. Oakley was one of seven daughters in a family of eight children. Oakley's father died in 1866, exposing the family to severe financial hardship. By the age of seven, Oakley was trapping quails, squirrels, and pheasants to provide food for her family. At the age of ten, she passed up the opportunity to go to school in order to work as a seamstress and help support her family. Later, she went to work as a child caretaker for an abusive family which, for two years, held her under prisonlike conditions. When Oakley finally freed herself, she became a professional market hunter, selling game birds and furs. She won her first shooting competition when she was fifteen years old. Oakley joined Buffalo Bill Cody's Wild West vaudeville show when she was twenty-five and gave shooting exhibitions throughout the United States, England, and France. In one exhibition before twenty thousand people, Oakley shot forty-nine out of fifty live pigeons, solidifying her reputation as the best shooter alive. She died on November 3, 1926, at the age of sixty-six.

Annie Oakley, nicknamed "Little Sure Shot," earned millions with her shooting exhibitions but never lived lavishly. The poor and downtrodden were never far from her thoughts. "If I ever spend one dollar foolishly," she said, "I see tear-stained faces of little helpless children, beaten as I was." From the day that Oakley began earning money from her exhibitions, she sent money home every month to her mother. When traveling, she would mail school supplies and clothes to her nieces and nephews. She provided funds to help more than twenty young women pursue higher education. During her travels, both in the United States and in Europe, Oakley put on free shooting exhibitions to raise money for children's hospitals and orphanages. When live birds were used in her shooting competitions, Oakley arranged to have the birds she shot rounded up and cooked as meals for hospitals and orphanages.

In 1915, Oakley settled in Pinehurst, North Carolina, where she gave shooting lessons to women without charge. Oakley told the women that her compensation would come from seeing them become shooting enthusiasts. When the

United States entered World War I in 1917, Oakley spent months traveling at her own expense to Army camps throughout the country so that she could give trick-shooting performances to entertain soldiers. She told reporters, "I am the happiest woman in the world because I had the opportunity to 'do my bit' in a way which was best suited to me."

After two of her sisters died of tuberculosis, Oakley gave charity exhibitions to raise money to fight the disease. She also melted the gold medals that she had accumulated during her career and contributed the money to a tuberculosis sanitarium near Pinehurst. She helped to educate women about guns and encouraged women to participate in outdoor sports and recreational activities.

Annie Oakley defied convention and encouraged other women to do the same. In her unique way, she opened doors for many. At a time when women in the United States were not allowed to vote, Oakley rose to the top in a male-dominated sport. She routinely competed against, and defeated, men in shooting competitions—and did it in a way that left both adversaries and fans spellbound. She exhibited a personality that inspired men as well as women. Upon witnessing Oakley in competition, one reporter wrote, "Miss Annie Oakley possesses one of the gentlest and kindest dispositions that one could ever wish to own. Her pleasant manner and her soft, cheery voice are only excelled by her accuracy of aim and adroitness with the rifle."

◆   ◆   ◆

Lavishly they give to the poor, their prosperity shall endure forever.
—Psalm 112, verse 9.

References

Michael J. McGivney

    Brinkley, Douglas and Julie M. Fenster. *Parish Priest: Father Michael McGivney and American Catholicism.* New York: William Morrow, 2006.

Annie Oakley

    Flynn, Jean. *Annie Oakley: Legendary Sharpshooter.* Springfield, NJ: Enslow Publishers, Inc., 1998.

    Macy, Sue. *Bull's-Eye: A Photobiography of Annie Oakley.* Washington, D.C.: National Geographic Society, 2001.

1900–1909

1900–1909

In the U.S. presidential election of 1900, William McKinley defeated William Jennings Bryan. A year later, anarchist Leon Czolgosz shot and killed McKinley, elevating Vice President Theodore Roosevelt to the presidency. In 1900, Harvard University tennis player Dwight Filley Davis, winner of the 1899 U.S. intercollegiate tennis championship, organized and played in a three-day tennis competition between the United States and Great Britain. Davis commissioned a silver bowl to serve as the trophy for the competition, later to become known as the Davis Cup.

In 1902, Stanford University and the University of Michigan played in the first ever post-season football game, with Michigan winning forty-nine to zero. The game was the forerunner of the modern-day Rose Bowl. The era of aviation began in 1903 when Orville Wright successfully piloted the first heavier-than-air craft at Kitty Hawk, North Carolina.

The first Olympics ever held in the United States took place in St. Louis in 1904. American athletes placed first in twenty-one events. In October 1905, baseball's New York Giants, led by manager John McGraw, defeated Connie Mack's Philadelphia Athletics, four games to one, to win the World Series. A little known outfielder, Archibald "Moonlight" Graham, played in one regular season game for the 1905 Giants, before quitting baseball to pursue a career in medicine. Many years later, Graham's story would become a focal point of the movie *Field of Dreams*.

President Theodore Roosevelt became the first American ever to be awarded the Nobel Peace Prize in 1906. The honor was in recognition of Roosevelt's efforts in ending the Russo-Japanese War. In that same year, Roosevelt visited Panama to inspect sites being considered for construction of the Panama Canal. In doing so, he became the first president to travel outside the United States while in office. In 1908, Henry Ford introduced the Ford Model T automobile. In 1909, the National Association for the Advancement of Colored People, more commonly known by the acronym NAACP, was established.

DWIGHT FILLEY DAVIS

Dwight Filley Davis was born in St. Louis, Missouri, in 1879. He entered Harvard University in 1896, where he excelled in tennis. Davis won the U.S. Men's Tennis Championship in 1898 and the intercollegiate singles title in 1899. He sought to use tennis to promote international brotherhood and good will. At his insistence, the U.S. National Lawn Tennis Association invited England to send its best tennis players to Boston for an international match. Davis commissioned the casting of a silver trophy cup, which became known as "Dwight's pot." The first such competition, named the International Lawn Tennis Challenge, occurred in 1900. Led by Davis, the U.S. team won both the singles matches and doubles play, winning the right to keep the pot. The Challenge became an annual event and, in 1905, was expanded to include other countries. After graduating from Harvard, Davis returned to St. Louis to launch a political career. He served as Director of Parks for the city from 1911 to 1915. When the United States entered World War I in 1917, Davis joined the military and participated in the St. Mihiel and Meuse-Argonne operations in Europe. He voluntarily went on intelligence-gathering missions near enemy lines, exposing himself to hostile fire and earning the Distinguished Service Cross. Davis was appointed Secretary of War by President Calvin Coolidge in 1925 and later served as Governor General of the Philippines. He died on November 28, 1945. Following Davis's death, the International Lawn Tennis Challenge was renamed the Davis Cup.

In 1911, when Dwight Davis became the Director of Parks for St. Louis, the city's public parks consisted of stately oak trees, large stretches of grass-covered land, and an abundance of "Keep Off the Grass" signs. Within weeks, Davis and his staff removed the "Keep Off the Grass" signs. "The primary purpose of the park system," Davis announced, "is to grow men and women, not grass and trees."

For Davis, tennis was one of the key components in the effort to "grow men and women." He believed that tennis competitions helped to instill a sense of sportsmanship in youths. Toward that end, he promoted the establishment of municipal, district, state, and national tennis tournaments in St. Louis. He wrote to officials in other Missouri cities and in other states to stimulate interest in intercity and interstate tennis competitions. He also worked to change the character of tennis from a sport played by the elite of society to a sport available to everyone. Under his leadership, St. Louis created tennis courts that were available without charge to all members of the public, the first municipal tennis courts in the entire country. He also used his authority to turn public lands into baseball fields and golf courses.

Later in life, Davis held prominent government positions in Washington, D.C. Whether in St. Louis or Washington, however, he consistently pushed for recognition of three ideas that he considered especially important: (1) parks were for people; (2) tennis belonged in public parks; and (3) tennis competitions promoted fellowship, good will, and sportsmanship.

Shortly before his death in 1945, Davis admitted one regret: if he had known how enduring the International Lawn Tennis Challenge would be, he said, he would have had his pot made out of gold instead of silver.

◆   ◆   ◆

Take the impurities out of silver and the artist can produce a thing of beauty.
—Proverbs 25, verse 4.

ARCHIBALD "MOONLIGHT" GRAHAM

Archibald "Moonlight" Graham was a successful minor league baseball player with the Charlotte Hornets of the North Carolina League in the early 1900s. The New York Giants called Graham up to the major leagues during the 1905 season. However, Graham fell into disfavor with Giants manager John McGraw. McGraw complained that Graham possessed "million dollar legs and a ten-cent brain." Graham made his only appearance in a major league game on June 29, 1905, when he replaced right fielder George Browne in the ninth inning. After that game, Graham retired from professional baseball to focus full-time on academics, without ever having had the opportunity to bat in the major leagues. His "ten-cent brain" notwithstanding, Graham became a medical doctor and ultimately opened a practice in Chisholm, Minnesota. Graham's short-lived major league career provided the inspiration for W. P. Kinsella's novella Shoeless Joe *and the acclaimed movie* Field of Dreams. *Graham died on August 25, 1965.*

Archibald Graham interned in various hospitals in the eastern United States after obtaining his medical degree. After completing his internships, "Doc" Graham turned down several lucrative opportunities in well-established medical facilities to serve the rural community of Chisholm, Minnesota. Graham spent his first six years in Chisholm working at Rood Hospital. For the next forty-four years, he was the resident physician for Chisholm public schools.

Graham became a hero to Chisholm's farming and mining families. The *Chisholm Free Press* called him "the champion of the oppressed" and "the grand marshal of every football, basketball, and baseball game." He devoted his life to establishing a nationally recognized testing and after-care program for heart and blood pressure abnormalities in young children. Graham's charitable works in Chisholm were legendary. Economic conditions in Chisholm were often harsh, as inhabitants suffered through depressions, big and small, and labor strikes. Throughout the difficulties, Graham made sure that no child in his care went without food, eyeglasses, or tickets to ball games.

In the words of the *Chisholm Free Press*, "there were many simple, humble things that made Doc happy."

◆   ◆   ◆

He shepherded them with a pure heart; with skilled hands he guided them.
—Psalm 78, verse 72.

GRAHAM, ARCHIBALD WRIGHT ("MOONLIGHT")

Born: November 9, 1876, Fayetteville, NC
Died: August 25, 1965, Chisholm, MN
5'10½" 170 lbs.

Year	Team	Games	BA	AB	H	2B	3B	HR	RBI	PO	E	A	FA	Gms by Pos
1905	NY N	1	—	0	0	0	0	0	0	0	0	0	—	OF - 1

References

Dwight Filley Davis

>   Kriplen, Nancy. *Dwight Davis: The Man and the Cup*. Boulder, CO: Lexicon V Publishers, 1997.

Archibald "Moonlight" Graham

>   Keith Olbermann, "'Moonlight' Graham Remembered," MSNBC Profile, http://msnbc.msn.com/id/8423741.

>   Veda F. Ponikvar, "His Was a Life of Greatness," *Chisholm Free Press*, 31 August 1965.

>   Ben Walker, "Hollywood Did Not Invent Moonlight Graham," *Pittsburgh Post-Gazette*, 25 June 2005, http://post-gazette.com/pg/05176/528257.stm.

1910–1919

1910–1919

Democrat Woodrow Wilson won the Presidency in 1912 in a landslide victory over Progressive candidate Theodore Roosevelt and the incumbent president, Republican William Howard Taft. Native American Jim Thorpe became known as the world's best athlete at the 1912 Olympics in Stockholm, Sweden. The International Olympic Committee later concluded that Thorpe had competed as a professional athlete and stripped him of all his Olympic medals. The Committee would reverse its decision in 1982 and return the medals to Thorpe's descendants.

In 1913, Walter Johnson of the Washington Senators posted one of the most dominating seasons by any pitcher in the history of major league baseball. Johnson won thirty-six games with a 1.09 earned-run average for Washington, a team whose formal name was the Nationals, but which was universally known as the Senators.

World War I began in June 1914 after a young Bosnian revolutionary, acting with the tacit consent of Serbian officials, assassinated Archduke Francis Ferdinand of Austria. In response, Austria declared war upon Serbia. Anticipating that Germany would join forces with Austria, Russia mobilized its troops on the German and Austrian borders. In August 1914, Germany declared war on Russia and, a few days later, on France as well. When Germany invaded Belgium, in an effort to cross into France, England entered the war on the side of the French.

Golfer and Chicago native Chick Evans won both the U.S. Amateur golf championship and the U.S. Open title in 1916. It would take another fourteen years for that feat to be duplicated, with golfing great Bobby Jones winning both titles in 1930.

Under the leadership of President Woodrow Wilson, the United States remained neutral in the European conflict until 1917. In April 1917, after German submarines sank several American ships, Wilson obtained a declaration of war from Congress. The first U.S. troops went to Europe two months later. By November 1918, Germany had concluded that military victory was out of reach and agreed to an armistice. As part of the peace treaty, the parties agreed to establish Wilson's proposed League of Nations. With U.S. soldiers returning home, the country bestowed a hero's welcome on pilot Eddie Rickenbacker, the "Ace of

Aces." In less than twelve months of combat flying, Rickenbacker downed twenty-six enemy aircraft.

Rutgers University football player Paul Robeson, a future star of the stage, was named All-American in both 1917 and 1918. Walter Camp, long-time Yale University football coach and the man who is recognized as "the father of American football," declared Robeson "the greatest defensive end ever to trod the gridiron."

AL TRAVERS

Aloysius Joseph Travers, barely twenty years old, found himself on the mound at Shibe Park as the starting pitcher for the Detroit Tigers against the Philadelphia Athletics on May 18, 1912. It was a most improbable development. A former schoolboy pitcher at St. Joseph's Preparatory School in Philadelphia, Travers was then a student at St. Joseph's College. Before the game was to begin, the Tigers players declared a strike and refused to play. The strike was in protest of a two-day suspension given to teammate Ty Cobb. American League officials informed the Tigers' management that the team would face a substantial fine if it didn't field a team. In search of replacement players, Tigers manager Hughie Jennings called St. Joseph's College and recruited seven players, including Travers. In front of fifteen thousand fans, Travers pitched an eight-inning complete game against the Philadelphia regulars, giving up twenty-six hits and twenty-four runs. Travers pitched well enough that, after the game, some teams expressed interest in signing him. However, he was intent on becoming a Jesuit priest. Travers died on April 19, 1968.

Al Travers entered the Jesuit Novitiate in Poughkeepsie, New York in the year after his one-day stint as a major league pitcher. As a Jesuit scholastic, he taught grammar at Gonzaga High School in Washington, D.C., and served as moderator of the school band. For the school's May Day procession of 1919, Travers decided the band needed more depth and talent. He recruited members of the Fort Myer Army Band from nearby Arlington, Virginia, and dressed them in Gonzaga High School uniforms. Aided by the Army recruits, the band drew rave reviews. School administrators became somewhat suspicious, however, when they saw some of the band members sporting mustaches. When the truth came out, the school rector reprimanded Travers.

Travers was ordained as a priest in 1926. After his ordination, he taught at high schools in New Jersey and New York, and eventually settled in Philadelphia as a teacher of Spanish and religious studies at St. Joseph's Prep. Travers' ingenuity in recruiting Army band members for the Gonzaga band was indicative of the creativity that characterized his teaching. Former students remember Father

Travers as a caring, kind, and inspirational teacher—and as a "one-day wonder" in the major leagues.

◆   ◆   ◆

Better one day in your courts than a thousand elsewhere.
—Psalm 84, verse 11.

WALTER JOHNSON

Walter Johnson, nicknamed "The Big Train," pitched for the Washington Senators from 1907 to 1927. He was reputed to be both the fastest pitcher and the most beloved man in baseball. In 1913, Johnson won thirty-six games and lost only seven, with an earned run average of 1.09. For his career, he won 416 games, ranking second only to Cy Young among pitchers of all time. In 110 of his 416 victories, Johnson held the opposing team without a run. When Johnson announced his retirement after the 1927 season, The Washington Post *wrote, "Johnson unquestionably leaves the national game with more friends than any other athlete of the sports world." Johnson died on December 10, 1946, at the age of fifty-nine.*

On Saturday, October 4, 1924, Johnson pitched in the biggest game of his career, facing the New York Giants in the first game of the World Series. The Big Train had been in the major leagues for eighteen years. It was his first appearance in the World Series. At the end of nine innings, the game was tied. However, the Giants pushed across two runs in the twelfth inning to win, aided by the sloppy outfield play of Washington rookie Earl McNeely. Johnson pitched all twelve innings for the Senators and took the loss.

After the game, reporters asked Johnson about McNeely's play in center field. "No one should blame the boy," Johnson said. "He was just over-anxious, that's all." The next morning, Johnson woke early to help his wife and mother bring flowers to disabled soldiers at Walter Reed Hospital.

According to *The Washington Post* sports columnist Shirley Povich, "Walter Johnson, more than any other ballplayer, probably more than any other athlete, professional or amateur, became the symbol of gentlemanly conduct in the battle heat." He once lost a game by a score of 1–0 when teammate Clyde Milan, playing center field, let a routine base hit roll through his legs in the ninth inning. Unperturbed, Johnson commented, "Milan doesn't do that very often. Anyway, I should have struck that hitter out."

Johnson was as talented as he was gracious. In an editorial published after his death, *The Washington Post* wrote, "Not more than a handful of men in the whole of human history can be said to have achieved the sort of greatness possessed by Walter Johnson." The *Post* called Johnson "the peer of Shakespeare or of Michelangelo," a man who had achieved "an absolute and unchallenged preeminence within his *métier*."

In 1929, Johnson took over as manager of the Senators. The early spring was unseasonably cold and when the Senators traveled to Cleveland for a series against the Indians in May, they encountered snow. Johnson came down with a bad cold which triggered a kidney problem. When Johnson's fever climbed to 102 degrees, he took a train back home. Upon arrival at Washington's Union Station, Johnson was wheeled off the train and taken to the hospital. Though still feeling the effects of his fever, Johnson insisted on stopping at the room of another patient, a twelve-year-old schoolboy pitcher who had lost a leg in an automobile accident. Johnson assured the boy that, even with the loss of his leg, his future remained bright. "If we can't do the thing we want most," Johnson told the boy, "there is always something else."

◆   ◆   ◆

If you want people to like you, forgive them when they wrong you.
—Proverbs 17, verse 9.

CHARLES "CHICK" EVANS, JR.

Charles "Chick" Evans was born in 1890. He became a caddie at the age of eight and spent much of his teenage years caddying and golfing at the Edgewater Golf Club on Chicago's North Side. Evans developed into an elite golfer when still in his teens. Competing as an amateur, he won the Western Open in 1910. In 1916, he captured the U.S. Open title with a two-under-par score of 286. It was the first time any U.S. Open participant had ever broken par over seventy-two holes. During his golfing career, Evans competed in fifty successive U.S. Amateur championships, winning the event in 1916 and 1920. He played golf with six U.S. presidents and was elected to the World Golf Hall of Fame. Evans died on November 6, 1979, at the age of eighty-nine.

After completing high school, Chick Evans enrolled at Northwestern University in Evanston, Illinois. His college career was short-lived, however. His family could not afford the tuition payments, and Evans was forced to drop out after his first year.

In 1916, after winning the U.S. Open, Evans wrote a series of instructional lessons to encourage others to play golf. The lessons were turned into phonograph records, which earned Evans royalties of five thousand dollars. Evans consulted with his mother on what to do with the money. His mother told him that since the money came from golf, it should go back into golf. Together, mother and son decided to use the proceeds to create a scholarship fund for caddies. Their goal was to make sure that caddies who followed in Chick's footsteps would not have to pass up formal education due to a lack of money.

The first two Evans Scholars enrolled at Northwestern University in 1930. Since that time, more than eight thousand five hundred men and women caddies have attended eighteen different colleges and universities on grants from the Evans Scholars Foundation. Along with funds to cover tuition and housing,

Evans Scholars receive the following advice, written by Chick Evans and passed on through the years:

> You must remember that if you have any trouble you must not become impatient. Don't think about winning. It isn't important. Rather, determine to do everything with your best skill. The result doesn't matter. Most mistakes can be remedied and success often stands jauntily on the very last hole.

◆   ◆   ◆

Though wealth increase, do not set your heart upon it.
—Psalm 62, verse 11.

PAUL ROBESON

Paul Robeson was born in Princeton, New Jersey on April 9, 1898. He was the son of a former slave. As a child, Robeson displayed a gift for both athletics and oratory. From 1915 to 1919, he played football, baseball, and basketball, and hurled the javelin for Rutgers University. Standing six feet two inches tall and weighing two hundred pounds, Robeson earned twelve varsity letters at Rutgers and was named All-American in football during both his junior and senior seasons. Football authority Walter Camp, who started the practice of bestowing All-American honors on collegiate players, called Robeson "a veritable superman." In 1920–1921, while attending Columbia Law School, Robeson played professional football for the Akron Pros of the American Professional Football Association, soon to be renamed the National Football League. Along with his friend, former Brown University star Fritz Pollard, Robeson was one of the first African Americans to play professional football. In 1922, Robeson starred for the NFL's newly-formed Milwaukee Badgers. Robeson quit football after the 1922 season to focus on developing his career as a singer and stage actor. He died on January 23, 1976.

By 1928, Paul Robeson was well on his way to becoming an internationally renowned singer and actor. In April of that year, he left the United States to take the lead role in the London production of the Jerome Kern–Oscar Hammerstein musical *Show Boat*. Robeson earned rave reviews for his performance and, particularly, for his rendition of the Kern–Hammerstein classic, "Ol' Man River."

For years after his successful run in *Show Boat*, Robeson made London his primary residence. As he accumulated enthusiastic reviews and a host of credits for his work on London's stages, he was content to enjoy the good life and socialize with members of England's high society. In 1933, when asked to participate in a show to benefit Jewish refugees who were fleeing Nazi Germany, Robeson responded, "I'm an artist. I don't understand politics." Though Robeson ultimately agreed to help with the benefit, the emergence of his social conscience remained a work in progress.

By 1936, Robeson had become fully committed to the cause of social justice. In that year, he provided financial backing for *Germany Today*, a journal founded to expose the truth about Nazism. "I, as a Negro, and all my fellow blacks are oppressed," he told the chairman of *Germany Today*. "What Hitler is doing in Germany is the same thing—perpetuating racial hatred." On other occasions, Robeson spoke out against the deplorable conditions confronting the poor throughout the world. "The vast numbers of poor people do not have equality, work, or food," he declared. "People must have that first."

By 1937, Robeson was using his time and talents to help fight the spread of fascism in Spain. "We, as a people," he said, "can no longer be indifferent to international events." Robeson worked tirelessly to raise money for the Aid Spain Committee in England, a pro-democracy organization committed to stopping the aggression of Hitler and Mussolini in Spain. In June 1937, Robeson headed a massive benefit at England's Royal Albert Hall to raise funds for the Spanish cause. "The artist must take sides," he told the audience. "He must elect to fight for freedom or slavery."

In more subtle ways as well, Robeson gave voice to his social concerns. In his formative years as a performer, Robeson happily sang the final verse of "Ol' Man River" using the words penned by Oscar Hammerstein:

> Ah gets weary an' sick of tryin'
> Ah'm tired of livin' an' scared of dyin'
> But ol' man river
> He just keeps rollin' alon'.

By 1937, Robeson came to view Hammerstein's words as sadly out of touch. In December 1937, Robeson appeared at another Albert Hall rally to benefit the Spanish cause, this one attended by an audience of more than twelve thousand. Singing "Ol' Man River" at that benefit, Robeson unveiled a dramatic revision of the final verse:

> But I keep laughin' instead of cryin'
> I must keep fightin' until I'm dyin'
> And old man river
> He'll just keep rollin' along.

In January 1938, Robeson traveled to Spain to support the fight against fascism. He toured hospitals and sang for wounded soldiers. He visited sites in Madrid to see the devastation inflicted by the German Luftwaffe. He met with soldiers on the battlefields, conducted impromptu concerts, and distributed food to those in need. "My songs," he told his audiences, "come from the lips of the people ... who suffer and struggle to make equality a reality." In the words of an observer, Robeson "was like a Joan of Arc, totally engaged. Nothing else mattered."

◆   ◆   ◆

The Lord put a new song in my mouth.
—Psalm 40, verse 4.

References

Al Travers

Hal Butler, "Baseball's Wackiest Game," *True* magazine, July 1971, 16.

Bill Ring, "Priest, Famed As One-Day Big Leaguer, Dies," *NC News Service*, 23 April 1968.

Walter Johnson

Thomas, Henry W. *Walter Johnson: Baseball's Big Train*. Washington, D.C.: Phenom Press, 1995.

"Walter Johnson," *The Washington Post*, 12 December 1946, 6.

"This Morning with Shirley Povich," *The Washington Post*, 12 December 1946, 10.

Charles "Chick" Evans, Jr.

Website for the Western Golf Association and Evans Scholars Foundation, http://evansscholarsfoundation.com.

Paul Robeson

Boyle, Sheila Tully and Andrew Bunie, *Paul Robeson: The Years of Promise and Achievement*. Amherst, MA: University of Massachusetts Press, 2001.

Duberman, Martin. *Paul Robeson: A Biography*. New York: The New Press, 1989.

1920–1929

1920–1929

Two men destined to dominate their respective fields made news early in the decade. First, as the result of a January 1920 trade between the Boston Red Sox and the New York Yankees, George Herman "Babe" Ruth brought his potent bat to New York. Secondly, in 1921, Albert Einstein, speaking at Columbia University, delivered the first of many lectures in the United States about his theory of relativity.

In 1922, in a case known as the *Federal Baseball Club of Baltimore*, the Supreme Court found that the playing of professional baseball did not involve commerce between the states. For that reason, the Court ruled that professional baseball was not subject to Federal antitrust laws. Chief Judge Oliver Wendell Holmes, author of the decision, wrote that although baseball involved the transportation of people and equipment across state lines, "the transport is a mere incident, not the essential thing."

Time magazine was introduced as a weekly publication in 1923. That same year, *Runnin' Wild*, featuring a tune named "The Charleston," became a Broadway hit, kicking off the Roaring Twenties and the flapper era. Mocking the attitudes that inspired the prohibition of alcoholic beverages, young women across the country popularized a mode of dance dubbed the Charleston. In 1924, President Calvin Coolidge appointed J. Edgar Hoover as director of the Federal Bureau of Investigation.

Aviator Charles Lindbergh became the first solo pilot to fly nonstop from New York to Paris in 1927. That same year, Babe Ruth hit sixty home runs for the New York Yankees. In 1928, Amelia Earhart became the first woman to cross the Atlantic in an airplane. On October 29, 1929, a date which became known as Black Tuesday, over sixteen million shares of stock traded at losses. When the stock markets continued to plunge, the United States soon found itself in the throes of the Great Depression.

MOSE J. "CHIEF" YELLOWHORSE

Mose J. "Chief" Yellowhorse, a native of Pawnee, Oklahoma and a full-blooded member of the Pawnee tribe, played major league baseball with the Pittsburgh Pirates for two seasons. He is considered by many to be the first full-blooded Native American to play in the major leagues. Yellowhorse joined the Pirates as a pitcher in 1921, when he was twenty-three years old. His ascent to the Pirates came after a season in which he won twenty-one games for the minor league Arkansas Travelers. Kid Elberfeld, who managed Yellowhorse at Arkansas and who had batted against Hall-of-Famer Walter Johnson, claimed that Yellowhorse was as fast as Johnson. In Pittsburgh, Yellowhorse quickly developed into a favorite of the fans, who would exhort the Pirates to "Put in Yellowhorse!" whenever the team's other pitchers faltered. A heavy drinker, Yellowhorse was not nearly as popular with the Pirates' management. Despite a penchant for late evenings, Yellowhorse enjoyed a successful rookie season, winning five games and losing three. However, he suffered a rupture in his arm in midseason and had to undergo surgery. By the end of Yellowhorse's second season, the Pirates had tired of his drinking habits and dispatched him to the minor leagues. He bounced around the minors from 1923 to 1925 and retired from baseball in May 1926. He died on April 10, 1964, at the age of sixty-six.

Long after he had retired from baseball, Mose Yellowhorse continued to be a fan favorite in Pittsburgh, Sacramento, Little Rock, and virtually every other city in which he had played. On occasion, his former teams would schedule "Chief Yellowhorse Night" and salute him with speeches and gifts before a game. Fans in Sacramento, where Yellowhorse had posted a sterling 22–13 won–lost record in 1923, were particularly fond of the "Chief." Yellowhorse traveled to Sacramento in 1958 to attend a night in his honor. In preparation for the Chief's visit, the owner of the Sacramento team ordered "enough whiskey to intoxicate an army." When Yellowhorse showed up, however, the owner found out, to his great surprise, that the Chief hadn't consumed a drop of whiskey in thirteen years. Yellowhorse had turned his life around. Yellowhorse discussed his decision to stop drinking in an interview with a Sacramento newspaper. "I came to that decision on my own," he said, "and I did it with will power."

When he stopped drinking, Yellowhorse started working with youths. He coached a baseball team composed of full-blooded Pawnee teenagers and took the team to play in games throughout Oklahoma and Arkansas. He worked to establish Little League baseball in Pawnee and in other areas in Oklahoma. For years, he served as director of the annual Pawnee Homecoming celebration, an event which featured tribal singers and dancers. Yellowhorse developed into an elder statesman and a role model, respected for his wisdom and his knowledge of Pawnee traditions. He spent his time counseling young Pawnee men, telling them to carry out their lives in a responsible manner and remain true to their Pawnee heritage. Yellowhorse urged the young men to value their Pawnee heritage more than personal achievements. "Don't make the same mistakes I made," he would tell them.

On January 25, 1964, the Pawnees held a celebration in Yellowhorse's honor. More than seven hundred people attended and participated in a day of singing, dancing, and ceremony. When it came time for Yellowhorse to address the crowd, he told them, "This was your dance, your gathering. I was glad to see each and every one of you take part. When I go home, I will remember every one of you in my prayers."

Less than three months later, Yellowhorse died. The Chief had gone home.

◆   ◆   ◆

What he commanded our ancestors, they were to teach their children.
—Psalm 78, verse 5.

AL SCHACHT

Al Schacht was known as "the Clown Prince of Baseball." His talent lay in making people laugh. Schacht brought a host of endearing qualities to the task, one of which was a painfully honest self-awareness. He was candid in assessing his appearance, telling audiences, "I came into this world very homely and haven't changed a bit since." Schacht broke into baseball as a pitcher with Newark of the International League in 1913, but his career was derailed when he was inducted into the Army in 1917. Discharged after World War I, Schacht signed to pitch for the Washington Senators in September 1919. His best season came in 1920, when he won six games and recorded a 4.44 earned run average. That same year, however, he injured his shoulder in a play at second base. His arm was never the same. Schacht closed out his major league career in 1921, with a record of fourteen wins and ten losses over three seasons. He served as third base coach for the Senators in 1923 and, at the same time, began working on the pantomime routines that would make him a featured entertainer at the World Series and all-star games. For years, he entertained fans at ballparks throughout the country. In 1946, baseball awarded him the Bill Slocum Memorial Award for his enduring contributions to the sport. Schacht died on July 14, 1984, at the age of ninety-two.

Al Schacht learned early to find humor in the absurdities in baseball and in life. He was gifted with the ability to throw a baseball better than most but, at five feet eleven inches tall and 136 pounds, he lacked the physique expected of a ballplayer. Born in the Bronx on the site that would become Yankee Stadium, Schacht experienced great difficulty in persuading team owners to allow him to play. When he showed up for a tryout with the Cincinnati Reds, the manager made it clear that he was expecting a 160-pounder. Schacht replied that he hadn't eaten lunch yet. Obsessed with baseball, he experienced troubled relationships with his mother and his fiancée, both of whom considered a career in baseball to be impractical. Over time, Schacht repaired the relationship with his mother; his fiancée moved on. At the age of twenty-seven, when he finally started feeling like he belonged in the big leagues, he suffered a career-ending injury.

Instead of bemoaning the ironies in life, Schacht learned to laugh. He found that he had a knack for making baseball fans laugh too. Once, before a game, he ate a meal off home plate, because that's what plates are for. Without speaking a word during his routines, Schacht used his humor to help his audiences keep baseball and the world at large in perspective.

When the United States entered World War II in 1941, the War Department asked Schacht to entertain U.S. troops. He readily agreed. In one stretch of two months, he performed 159 stage shows, visited seventy-two hospitals and 230 wards, and traveled over forty thousand miles. Schacht performed for troops in Africa, Sicily, New Guinea, the Dutch East Indies, the Southwest Pacific, the Philippines, and Japan. He found audiences filled with homesick soldiers and sailors. He used his baseball stories and his comedy routines to ease their loneliness. Schacht came under enemy fire many times during his tours, but refused to quit. Having found so many soldiers yearning for a touch of home, Schacht persevered, spreading smiles and laughter wherever he went.

◆   ◆   ◆

Even in laughter, the heart may be sad.
—Proverbs 14, verse 13.

PIER GIORGIO FRASSATI

Pier Giorgio Frassati was born into a wealthy Italian family in Turin, Italy. The son of the publisher of La Stampa, *an influential Italian newspaper, Frassati was a rugged athlete, an experienced skier, and an expert swimmer. He enjoyed sailing, canoeing, cycling, and horseback riding. A member of the Italian Alpine Club, Frassati would set out at sunrise, with ropes, ice axes, and sacks of food, to scale the mountain peaks of Val di Susa and other locations in the Alps. On such trips, Frassati often provoked laughter among his companions by his inept efforts at singing. According to biographer Maria Di Lorenzo, Frassati viewed the mountains as a "bridge between heaven and earth" and "a unique place to meet God and come face to face with the mystery of creation." Frassati died on July 4, 1925, of acute poliomyelitis. He was twenty-four years old.*

Pier Giorgio Frassati dedicated his life to easing the plight of the poor. He freely gave away his money and clothing, keeping little for himself. When traveling by train, he passed up berths in the first and second classes, always sitting in the less-costly third class. Well aware of the Frassati family wealth, friends would ask Frassati why he traveled in third class. Invariably, he would tell them that he traveled third class because there was no fourth class.

As a youth, Pier Giorgio Frassati felt a particular kinship with those who worked as miners in Italy. The miners, illiterate and living in inhumane conditions, were the outcasts of the Italian working class. Frassati dreamed of devoting his life to working with them. He pursued a degree in engineering in the hope of becoming a mining engineer. As Frassati approached the completion of his university studies, his father offered to give him a new automobile as a graduation gift. Frassati asked, instead, for the value of the car in cash. He chose the cash so that he could better help those whom he called "my poor."

◆   ◆   ◆

He makes me sure-footed as a deer; he keeps me safe on the mountains.
—Psalm 18, verse 34.

DICK "NIGHT TRAIN" LANE and ELLA LANE

Born on April 16, 1928, Dick "Night Train" Lane rose from humble origins to become a perennial All-Pro cornerback in the National Football League and a member of the NFL's Hall of Fame. After completing junior college, Lane joined the Army and served in both World War II and the Korean War, rising to the rank of lieutenant colonel. Lane left the Army and settled in California upon completion of his duty in Korea. With few employment prospects, he took a job as a sheet metal worker, but soon concluded that there was no future in sheet metal. Lane collected his high school and junior college newspaper clippings, showed up at the Los Angeles Rams' offices, and asked for a tryout. Impressed with Lane's size and speed, the Rams gave him a chance. Fourteen years later, Lane closed out his football career with sixty-eight interceptions, the third highest total in the history of the NFL. He was also known for his love of jazz. Teammates in Los Angeles tagged Lane with his distinctive nickname because he would listen, over and over, to Buddy Morrow's hit recording of "Night Train." Lane died on January 29, 2002, at the age of seventy-three.

After Dick Lane died, Dorothy Yancy, Lane's niece, spoke of the impact that her "Uncle Train" had on others. "He was like a magnet," she said. "You would fall in love with him the moment you met him."

Lane was an all-star on the field and a friend of children off it. In retirement, he ran Detroit's Police Athletic League, a sports program designed for youths who were at risk. Teens throughout Detroit knew, respected, and loved Night Train. After his death, the United States Senate passed a resolution honoring Lane for his service to the country and his dedication to helping the children of Detroit.

Lane's accomplishments, in and out of football, were considerable. Those accomplishments paled in comparison, however, to the character, love, and courage of his foster mother, Ella. If not for Ella, the baby Night Train would likely never have survived infancy.

Dick Lane was born to a woman who was a prostitute in Austin, Texas. Lane's father, known in Austin as "Texas Slim," was a pimp. Three months after Lane was born, his mother tired of the burdens of caring for a baby. She wrapped baby Night Train in newspapers and placed him in a local trash bin. Sometime later, Ella Lane, a widow and the mother of two children, passed by the trash bin and heard a strange noise. Ella thought the noise was the cry of a cat. Hoping to relieve the cat's distress, she looked into the trash bin and found a baby. Ella took the baby home, welcomed him into her family, named him Richard, and showered him with the love and affection that only a mother can give.

◆   ◆   ◆

Listen to my cry for help, for I am brought very low.
—Psalm 142, verse 7.

References

Mose J. "Chief" Yellowhorse

    Fuller, Todd. *60 Feet Six inches, The (Baseball) Life of Mose Yellowhorse.* Duluth: Holy Cow Press, 2002.

Al Schacht

    Ralph Berger, "Al Schacht," *The Baseball Biography Project*, The Society of American Baseball Research (SABR), http://bioproj.sabr.org.

Pier Giorgio Frassati

    Di Lorenzo, Maria. *Blessed Pier Giorgio Frassati: An Ordinary Christian.* Boston: Pauline Books & Media, 2004.

Dick "Night Train" Lane and Ella Lane

    Randy Kindred, "From A Humble Beginning to Life in the Fast Lane," (Bloomington, IL) *Pentagraph*, 1 February 2002, B1.

    Jack Saylor, "'Night Train' A Hit Back in the 1950s," *Milwaukee Journal Sentinel*, 3 February 2002, 9C.

    "Friends, Family Pay Last Respects," *The Augusta Chronicle*, 3 February 2002, C11.

    "Dick 'Night Train' Lane, Footballer Whose Tackle Was Banned," *The (London, UK) Daily Telegraph*, 7 February 2002, 31.

    U.S. Senate Resolution in Recognition of Richard "Night Train" Lane, *Congressional Record*, 107th Congress, Second Session, 8 February 2002.

1930–1939

1930–1939

As the 1930s began, the United States continued to feel the debilitating effects of the stock market crash of 1929 and the ensuing Great Depression. Nearly two thousand five hundred banks failed. An estimated five million American workers had lost their jobs. With the economy showing no signs of recovering, voters elected Democrat Franklin Delano Roosevelt as president in 1932 in a landslide over incumbent Herbert Hoover. Roosevelt told the country in his inaugural address that "the only thing we have to fear is fear itself." In both 1932 and 1933, the University of Michigan football team, with future U.S. president Gerald R. Ford anchoring the offensive line, won the collegiate national championship.

The effects of the Great Depression extended far beyond the United States. The citizens of Germany suffered more than most, as unemployment hovered near six million. Adolph Hitler found a fertile environment in which to preach his message of German nationalism and vitriolic opposition to bankers, land speculators, and Jewish capitalists. By 1932, the Nazis were the largest single party in Germany. In 1933, Hitler became chancellor of the German Republic. He quickly seized dictatorial powers and took the title of *Führer*, or "leader." In short order, the Nazis enacted repressive measures toward the six hundred thousand Jews holding German citizenship. Hitler moved Nazi troops into the German area west of the Rhine in March 1936, which the1919 Treaty of Versailles had declared a demilitarized zone.

In a climate of increasing Nazi fervor and the imposition of civil restrictions on Jews and other "non-Aryans," Germans played significant roles in two historic sporting events in 1936. In June, German heavyweight boxer Max Schmeling, a decided underdog, beat American Joe Louis by knockout in the twelfth round of a bout at Madison Square Garden. Though Schmeling steadfastly refused to join the Nazi party, Hitler hailed his victory as a symbol of Aryan supremacy. In August, Germany hosted the Olympics in Berlin. With Hitler looking on, African American Jesse Owens won four gold medals in track and field. German Lutz Long placed second to Owens in the broad jump.

Schmeling fought Joe Louis in June 1938 in a rematch at Yankee Stadium. This time, Louis battered Schmeling badly, knocking him out in the first round. Schmeling returned to Germany alone and without fanfare.

In March 1939, Hitler transformed Czechoslovakia into a German protector-ate. It had become increasingly clear that Hitler intended to extend Nazi rule over the entire continent of Europe. On September 1, 1939, the German army invaded Poland. Two days later, Great Britain and France declared war on Ger-many. World War II had begun.

EFFA MANLEY

From 1935 to 1948, Effa Manley was one of the most prominent executives in baseball's Negro Leagues. Caucasian by birth, Manley was raised with six siblings who were all African American. "I was always this little blonde, hazel-eyed, white girl, always with Negro children," she once said. Her unique background enabled her to move effortlessly among both the black and white communities in the segregated world of the 1930s and 1940s. She married businessman Abe Manley, whom she met at a World Series game at Yankee Stadium. In 1935, Abe Manley founded the Brooklyn Eagles baseball team, which became one of eight franchises in the Negro National League. The Manleys moved the team to Newark, New Jersey after the 1935 season. For the next thirteen years, Effa Manley ran the Newark Eagles' front office and functioned as the team's owner. She was widely regarded as one of the most enlightened owners in the Negro Leagues. Manley died on April 16, 1981. In 2006, she was elected to baseball's Hall of Fame, becoming the only woman to be enshrined in the Hall.

According to popular legend, Effa Manley once ordered the manager of the Newark Eagles to start pitcher Terris "The Terrible" McDuffie in a game that many of Manley's women friends would be attending. McDuffie was a talented pitcher with an excellent fastball and good control. He also happened to be particularly good-looking. Manley, the story goes, wanted to show off Terris "The Terrible" to her friends.

The episode, if true, represents one of the few occasions on which Manley allowed her focus to wander. Most often, Manley directed her actions toward achieving more significant objectives—objectives that often involved social change.

In the early days of June 1934, Manley carried a picket sign urging customers to boycott the L. M. Blumstein department store on West 125th Street in Harlem. At the time, the store derived seventy-five percent of its business from black shoppers, but employed no black sales clerks. Manley met with the store's owners to seek a change in hiring practices. At that meeting, she told Blumstein's owners that the only employment options for black women in Harlem "were to work as someone's maid, or become prostitutes." Due to Manley's efforts, those options soon expanded. Within months, L. M. Blumstein opened up thirty-five sales jobs to black workers.

When the Manleys joined the ranks of baseball owners, Effa Manley applied her energy and talents to fielding a winning baseball team. At the same time, however, she worked to improve social conditions. In addition to running the Eagles, Manley served as treasurer of the New Jersey chapter of the National Association for the Advancement of Colored People. She often canvassed the crowds at Eagles' games to raise money for the NAACP. To call attention to the Ku Klux Klan's practice of hanging blacks who were suspected of committing crimes, Manley scheduled "Stop Lynching Days" at the ballpark.

Concerned that Eagles players could not find work during the off-season, Manley began bringing black baseball teams to play in the Puerto Rican winter league. Manley used baseball to help children as well. She often allowed youngsters into Eagles' games for free. In 1942, she founded the Newark Cubs, a youth baseball team, to keep black children off the streets. To foster responsible behavior among children, Manley required all members of the Cubs to sign contracts in which they agreed to: (1) maintain good physical condition, (2) demonstrate good sportsmanship at all times, (3) keep their baseball uniforms clean, and (4) show up for games on time.

Manley demonstrated a special interest in causes that promoted the welfare of New Jersey's African American population. She scheduled baseball games to raise funds for the black Elks Lodges and other black social groups. She raised money to pay the costs of training for black physicians and nurses, and used the proceeds from Eagles' games to buy new medical equipment for black-owned hospitals.

◆   ◆   ◆

Rescue those who are being dragged to death, and from those tottering to execution withdraw not.
—Proverbs 24, verse 11.

LUTZ LONG

Carl Ludwig "Lutz" Long was a German sprinter and broad jumper who competed against African American Jesse Owens in the 1936 Berlin Olympics. In the finals of the broad jump, Long and Owens were tied for the lead after two attempts. Owens won the event on his third and final jump, leaping twenty-six feet, five inches. Long finished second. After the Olympics, Lutz Long fought for Germany in World War II. He died on July 13, 1943, during fighting in Sicily. After Long's death, the International Olympic Committee awarded him the Pierre de Coubertin medal, a highly prized award named in honor of the founder of the modern Olympic games, and reserved for athletes who best demonstrate the spirit of sportsmanship.

In the years since the 1936 Olympics, Jesse Owens' victory in the broad jump competition has become laden with details of questionable authenticity. It is impossible to separate fact from fiction. In one account sometimes repeated by Jesse Owens, Lutz Long gave Owens a tip during the competition that helped Owens clinch the gold. According to a contradictory version, Owens and Long never spoke a word to each other until after the event was over.

No matter how the story of the 1936 broad jump is told, however, Long emerges as a man of integrity and character. The Olympics took place against the backdrop of escalating tensions in Europe. A year earlier, Benito Mussolini, Italy's dictator, had annexed Ethiopia. In Germany, Hitler was spreading the gospel of Aryan supremacy. In the spring of 1936, Hitler's army had moved into the previously demilitarized Rhineland.

The Olympic high jump competition was held on August 3, 1936. In his *New York Times* report, sportswriter Arthur Daley wrote that, in the aftermath of the high jump, "German nationalism and the prejudice that seems to go with it revealed themselves somewhat disagreeably." As Daley recounted events, Hitler watched Cornelius Johnson, an African American, soar to victory in the high jump. Then, when the competition was over, Hitler hastily departed the stadium in order to avoid having to congratulate Johnson.

On August 4, Lutz Long and Jesse Owens faced each other in the broad jump. Owens unleashed his jump of twenty-six feet five inches to claim the gold, with

Long taking the silver. Daley wrote that, after winning the broad jump, Owens was seen "affectionately walking along the track arm in arm" with Long. In a world poised for war, Owens and Long had put their emotions on display, providing a meaningful glimpse into the ideals underlying Olympic competition. And without saying a word, Long had demonstrated his contempt for the theory of Aryan supremacy.

The events of August 4, 1936, forged a lasting friendship between Long and Owens. The two stayed in frequent contact. When World War II broke out, Long was inducted into the German army and ordered to North Africa. Long sent one last letter to Owens before leaving Germany. He wrote:

> My heart tells me that if I am to be honest with you, this is the last letter that I will ever write. If it is so, I ask you to go to Germany when this war is done. Someday find my son Karl and tell him about his father. Tell him, Jesse, what times were like when we were separated by war. Tell him how things can be between men on this earth.

After the war, Owens did meet up with Karl Long in Berlin "to tell him how things can be between men on this earth."

◆   ◆   ◆

The Lord has revealed his triumph for the nations to see.
—Psalm 98, verse 2.

[*Author's Note*: There was undeniable drama in Jesse Owens' gold medal-winning performance in the 1936 Olympic broad jump. In the qualifying round, Owens defaulted on each of his first two runs by running through or stepping beyond the take-off line. To advance to the finals, he had to avoid defaulting on his third and final attempt. As reported in the *New York Times*, on Owens' last attempt, "he sprinted carefully" and "left the ground with a half-foot clearance at the take-off." When talking about the jump in later years, Owens would sometimes tell audiences that, before the last attempt, Lutz Long had placed a towel on the runway at a point six inches in front of the take-off line. In Owens' retelling of the story, Long suggested that, to avoid any risk of defaulting, Owens should begin his leap when he reached the towel. At other times, however, Owens would contradict that story, telling people that he and Long never spoke to each other until after the broad jump competition had ended. Historians tend to discount the story of Long's towel, primarily because the accounts written by two prominent sportswriters who were watching the competition, Grantland Rice and Arthur Daley, did not report any interaction between Owens and Long until after the broad jump was over.]

MAX SCHMELING

Max Schmeling was born on September 28, 1905, in northeastern Germany. He began fighting in amateur boxing tournaments as a teenager. Schmeling possessed a powerful knock-out punch and quickly experienced success in the amateur ranks. He turned professional in 1924. In 1927, Schmeling won the European boxing title, becoming the first German ever to accomplish that feat. He fought Jack Sharkey for the heavyweight title of the world in 1930 at Yankee Stadium. That bout ended in victory for Schmeling after Sharkey was disqualified for punching below the waist. In 1936, Schmeling signed to fight Joe Louis. Initially, Nazi dictator Adolf Hitler was angry at Schmeling for fighting an African American. However, when Schmeling knocked out Louis, the Nazis lauded Schmeling as a hero. In June 1938, Schmeling and Louis met in a rematch, with Louis winning decisively. The match effectively ended Schmeling's boxing career. He would go on to fight a few more bouts but without success. Schmeling died on February 2, 2005, at the age of ninety-nine.

Max Schmeling suffered greatly as a result of his 1938 loss to Joe Louis. In the span of a single round, Louis had landed more than forty punches and knocked Schmeling down three times. Schmeling had to be carried from the ring on a stretcher. It would take more than a year for him to recover from his injuries. Moreover, in the eyes of the Nazis, Schmeling had disgraced Germany by losing to the "Brown Bomber." Since his stunning victory over Louis in 1936, Schmeling had steadily fallen out of favor with Hitler. He had adamantly refused to join the Nazi party. In clear defiance of Hitler, he had continued to work with a fight manager in the United States, Joe Jacobs, who was Jewish. The 1938 loss to Louis was Schmeling's latest and most conspicuous "transgression."

On November 9, 1938, less than five months after the Schmeling-Louis rematch, rampaging Nazi gangs destroyed 191 synagogues and murdered ninety-one Jews as part of the Kristallnacht ("night of broken glass") pogrom. The Kristallnacht was part of a continuing sequence of Nazi-inspired violence directed against German Jews and other "non-Aryans." At the time of the Kristallnacht, Schmeling was staying in a hotel room in Berlin, recuperating from injuries suffered in the Louis bout. Schmeling brought two Jewish children, Henry Lewin and his brother Werner, to his hotel room to shelter them from the Kristallnacht. Leaving word with the hotel management that he was not to be disturbed under any circumstance, Schmeling harbored the two boys for seven days until the danger passed. He then arranged for the boys to be transported to a safe haven in China. It was one of many occasions on which Schmeling risked his life to protect children from the Nazis.

A modest man, Schmeling never publicized his efforts to help others. His autobiography, published in 1977, made no mention of the Lewin brothers. The incident became public knowledge only when Henry Lewin, who grew up to become one of the most prominent property owners in Las Vegas, held an event in Schmeling's honor at the Sands Hotel in 1989.

In the years after World War II, Schmeling became a highly successful businessman in Germany, with a Coca-Cola franchise and other interests. During his lifetime, he gave away hundreds of thousands of dollars to help the elderly and the poor. He also provided financial support for his one-time adversary, Joe Louis. When Schmeling died, he left his entire estate for the benefit of underprivileged boys in East Germany.

◆   ◆   ◆

You are my shelter; from distress you keep me; with safety you ring me round.
—Psalm 32, verse 7.

GABBY STREET

Charles Evard "Gabby" Street was born in Huntsville, Alabama on September 30, 1882. He became an excellent teenage athlete and joined the Cincinnati Reds as a catcher in 1904. For seven seasons, he was a part-time catcher and a full-time student of the game. As a member of the Washington Senators, Street once caught a ball that was dropped from an aperture at the top of the Washington Monument, more than five hundred feet above ground. Ballistics experts estimated that the ball was traveling at a speed of 290 miles per hour when Street caught it. He is remembered more for that feat than for his accomplishments on the baseball field. From 1930 to 1933, Street managed the St. Louis Cardinals. He was named manager of the St. Paul Saints of the American Association in 1935. While in St. Paul, he befriended a teen-age African American girl, Toni Stone, who went on to play for the Indianapolis Clowns and the Kansas City Monarchs of the Negro leagues. Street died on February 6, 1951.

There were many reasons why, in 1936, Gabby Street could have ignored Toni Stone. For Street, St. Paul was just another stop in a long career filled with one baseball town after another. He was from the Deep South and well into his fifties, a baseball "lifer." As manager of the St. Louis Cardinals, Street had worked with the likes of Pepper Martin and Hall-of-Famer Frankie Frisch. If he took the time to encourage a local black girl possessed by the improbable dream of becoming a baseball player, there was little in it for him.

Stone was a gifted athlete, capable of acrobatic moves on a baseball field. Aside from her obvious athletic talent, however, there was little to recommend her. She was uneducated and, for purposes of both baseball and the world beyond, she was the wrong color and the wrong sex. Where others saw a sassy black girl engaged in a foolish pursuit, however, Street saw a ballplayer. In defiance of the prevailing attitudes, he helped Stone refine her skills. He gave her baseball gloves and other equipment. He invited her to attend his off-season baseball camp. He spent hours with her in individual lessons. Gabby Street cared.

◆   ◆   ◆

I stretch out my hands to you.
—Psalm 88, verse 10.

TONI STONE

The only thing Toni Stone ever wanted to do in life was play baseball. She was the child of poor African American parents living in St. Paul, Minnesota. Stone never graduated from high school; her education came on the baseball fields. A five-foot-seven-inch infielder, she played sandlot ball in the 1930s in St. Paul, where her talent caught the eye of former major-leaguer Gabby Street. With Street's help, Stone developed into an excellent player. In the late 1940s, while in her twenties, Stone played for the black San Francisco Sea Lions, a barnstorming semipro team. When the Boston Braves purchased the rights to Henry Aaron from the Indianapolis Clowns of the Negro League, the Clowns signed Stone to replace him at second base. On Easter Sunday of 1953, the Clowns faced legendary pitcher Satchel Paige. Stone hit a ball back up the middle against Paige for a single, the only hit of the game for the Clowns. In addition to the Indianapolis Clowns, Stone played with the rival Kansas City Monarchs. She was inducted into the International Women's Sports Hall of Fame in 1985. Stone died on November 2, 1996, at the age of seventy-five.

Marcenia Lyle "Toni" Stone endured the same indignities and racial epithets that were heaped upon her fellow African American ballplayers. She also encountered discrimination because she was a woman trying to carve out a niche in a man's world. Teammates and opponents would brusquely tell her to go home and cook dinner. Newspaper columnists lobbied against her, stirring fears of a future that would be "a woman's world with men just living in it." Stone responded, "A woman has her dreams too." Well aware that she would be the target of both racial and sexist slurs, Stone took great pains to make sure her conduct was beyond reproach. On the field, she refrained from cursing, spitting, or becoming too vocal. Even so, she found no relief from the barbs and bigotry. Stone took solace in her faith. Once, while the Clowns were in Milwaukee for a doubleheader, the team's manager removed Stone from the first game after she had played only an inning. Between games of the doubleheader, Stone walked to a church near the ballpark. She sat down in the church and cried. "What's wrong?" she asked God. "Do I need to pray harder?" The more the abuse continued, the harder Stone prayed. "Faith is what helps you to meet the challenges of life," she would tell others.

◆   ◆   ◆

How long, O God, shall the enemy jeer?
—Psalm 74, verse 10.

CHARLIE GEHRINGER

Charlie Gehringer played in five games for the Detroit Tigers in 1924. After additional seasoning, Gehringer won the job as the Tigers' regular second baseman in 1926. He remained with the club for sixteen years, hitting over .300 in each of thirteen seasons. In 1937 he led all American League hitters with a .371 average. For his career, Gehringer batted .320. He was elected to the Hall of Fame in 1949 and died on January 21, 1993, at the age of eighty-nine.

When Charlie Gehringer died, a former teammate, Billy Rogell, said, "I guess the good Lord needed a second baseman. And he got the best one he could've gotten." In the rough-and-tumble period preceding World War II, Gehringer was an anomaly—quiet when other players were boisterous; humble when others were outspoken and arrogant; gentle at a time when players were often combative. Hall-of-Famer Mickey Cochrane, a former teammate, said that Gehringer would say "hello" at the beginning of the season, "goodbye" at the end, and in between hit .350. According to *The Washington Post* sportswriter Shirley Povich, "Gehringer didn't know how to strut." Povich found Gehringer to be unique among major league ballplayers, one who was content to let his bat and glove speak for him. When Gehringer won the American League's Most Valuable Player award in 1937, the *Spalding Guide* wrote that "no player is more modest and more deserving of such a compliment."

On one occasion, friends from Gehringer's hometown of Fowlerville, Michigan honored the second baseman by holding "Charlie Gehringer Day" at the ballpark on the day of a Tigers' game. The Fowlerville fans met with Gehringer on the field before the game and gave him a series of gifts, including a set of golf clubs. Not realizing that Gehringer golfed left-handed, the fans had purchased clubs for a right-handed swinger. When presented with the gift, Gehringer expressed his appreciation, never pointing out the mistake. Not wanting to embarrass his friends, Gehringer learned to play golf right-handed. He used right-handed clubs the rest of his life.

◆   ◆   ◆

My mouth has not transgressed as humans often do.
—Psalm 17, verses 3–4.

References

Effa Manley

>   Justice B. Hill, "In Day of Hall Firsts, Manley Stands Out," MLB.com, 30 July 2006, http://mlb.mlb.com/NASApp/mlb/news/article.jsp?ymd= 20060730&content_id=1584100.

>   Overmyer, James. *Queen of the Negro Leagues: Effa Manley and the Newark Eagles*. Lanham, MD: Scarecrow Press, Inc., 1998.

Lutz Long

>   Arthur J. Daley, "Owens Captures Olympic Title, Equals World 100-Meter Record," *The New York Times*, 4 August 1936, 1.

>   Arthur J. Daley, "U.S. Captures 4 Events; Owens Sets Jump Record," *The New York Times*, 5 August 1936, 1.

>   Larry Schwartz, "Owens Pierced A Myth," ESPN Sports Century Biography, http://espn.go.com/classic/biography/s/Owens_Jesse.html.

>   Sumner, Jan. *Legacy of a Monarch: An American Journey*. Denver: Jadan Publishing, 2005.

>   "On the Adolph Hitler-Jesse Owens Legend," 5 March 1995, *The AFU and Urban Legend Archive*, http://tafkac.org/celebrities/jesse_owens _hitler_legends.html.

Max Schmeling

>   Jonathan Gurwitz, "Lost Bout Too Often Defined the Life of a Great Man," *San Antonio Express-News*, 9 February 2005, 9B.

>   Clarence Page, "Two Very Different Men, One Principle in Common," *Newsday*, 11 February 2005, A50.

>   "Schmeling and Wife Were Caring People," *The (Harrisburg, PA) Patriot-News*, 24 February 2005, A15.

Gabby Street

Hubbard, Crystal. *Catching the Moon: The Story of a Young Girl's Baseball Dream.* New York: Lee & Low Books, 2005.

Toni Stone

Martha Ackmann, "Look Who Replaced Hank Aaron," *Indianapolis Star*, 5 March 2006.

Martha Ackmann, "A Woman in the Hall of Fame? Toni Stone Would Be Thrilled," *National Public Radio: Only a Game*, 29 July 2006.

Hubbard, Crystal. *Catching the Moon: The Story of a Young Girl's Baseball Dream.* New York: Lee & Low Books, 2005.

Susan Sward, "Obituary: Toni Stone," *San Francisco Chronicle*, 6 November 1996, B4.

Robert Thomas, Jr., "Toni Stone, 75, First Woman To Play Big-League Baseball," *New York Times*, 10 November 1996, 1.47.

Charlie Gehringer

Pietrusza, David, Matthew Silverman, and Michael Gershman, eds. *Baseball: The Biographical Encyclopedia.* Kingston, NY: Total Sports Publishing, 2000.

1940–1949

1940–1949

As the 1940s began, the United States was drawing ever closer to war. Isolationists in the United States urged neutrality. However, the Nazi occupation of Czechoslovakia and Poland in 1939 made U.S. involvement inevitable. With the hostilities increasing, the 1940 Olympics were cancelled.

In Hollywood, burlesque and theater comedians Bud Abbott and Lou Costello appeared in their first movie, *One Night in the Tropics*, released in 1940. Their classic routine, "Who's on First?" was the highlight of the film.

On December 7, 1941, Japan attacked the United States naval base at Pearl Harbor in Hawaii. The next day, President Franklin Roosevelt announced a declaration of war against Japan. In short order, Japan's allies, Italy and Germany, declared war on the United States. The war would continue until 1945. At the suggestion of Philip Wrigley, owner of the Chicago Cubs, major league baseball owners established the All-American Girls Professional Baseball League. Wrigley feared that the war would cause major league baseball to suspend play and wanted to preserve some form of baseball. The All-American Girls League provided high-caliber professional baseball from 1942 until 1954.

On Christmas Eve of 1944, 802 U.S. soldiers lost their lives when the troop ship *Leopoldville* sank in the English Channel after being struck by a German torpedo. After a bloody battle lasting thirty-six days in 1945, the Marines captured the island of Iwo Jima from the Japanese. In August 1945, President Harry Truman gave the order to drop atomic bombs on Nagasaki and Hiroshima, leading to the destruction of the two cities and massive casualties. Japan formally signed the terms of surrender aboard the battleship USS *Missouri* on September 2, 1945.

Amid much protest, the Brooklyn Dodgers brought African American Jackie Robinson to the major leagues in 1947. On April 15, 1947, the Dodgers opened the regular season against the Boston Braves. Robinson started at first base for the Dodgers, becoming the first black ballplayer to appear in an official major league game. In 1948, Southern Methodist University football star Doak Walker won the Heisman Trophy, edging out North Carolina All-American Charlie "Choo Choo" Justice for the honor. Justice would again finish second in the Heisman voting in 1949, runner-up that year to Notre Dame's Leon Hart. Also in 1949, band leader Benny Goodman popularized the song "All the Way Choo Choo," composed as a tribute to Charlie Justice.

LOU COSTELLO

Lou Costello, born Louis Francis Cristillo, was a gifted athlete who excelled in base-ball and basketball. As a teenager in the 1920s, Costello attended Cornwall-on-Hud-son Military School in New York on an athletic scholarship. Hoping to carve out a career as a performer, Costello left Cornwell-on-Hudson before graduating and settled in Hollywood, California. Costello's first job was as a stuntman. In 1936, he teamed up with straight man Bud Abbott. For two decades, Abbott and Costello formed the most prominent comedy team in Hollywood. Costello died on March 3, 1959, three days shy of his fifty-third birthday.

In the years before his death, Costello, still a monumental figure in the enter-tainment business, lived in Beverly Hills. One day a man named Jack Leonard, who had played ball with Costello during their childhood days in Paterson, New Jersey, called the actor to ask a favor. Leonard, who was then working for *Time* magazine, had a colleague whose two young daughters were dying of cystic fibro-sis. The girls' father hoped to cheer up the girls by presenting them with an auto-graphed picture of a Hollywood personality. Costello immediately invited the girls to his house. The girls, their father, and Leonard spent an entire afternoon with Costello, eating hot dogs in his backyard and roaring with laughter.

◆   ◆   ◆

He who refreshes others will himself be refreshed.
—Proverbs 11, verse 25.

EDDIE RICKENBACKER

Eddie "Rick" Rickenbacker is best known as the "Ace of Aces" of the U.S. Army Air Service during World War I. One of the elite pioneering aviators with the 94th Pursuit Squadron stationed in France, Rickenbacker recorded twenty-six "kills" of German aircraft in less than one year as a combat pilot. Prior to enlisting in the Army in 1917, Rickenbacker had been a champion automobile road racer. He began his road racing career in 1910. By 1913, he was driving for the high-profile Duesenberg racing team. Rickenbacker gained nationwide attention in 1914 when he won the three hundred mile Sioux City Speedway Sweepstakes, earning ten thousand dollars for the Duesenberg team. Rickenbacker served as the Chief Executive Officer of Eastern Air Lines from 1953 to 1963. He died on July 23, 1973, at the age of eighty-two.

During the latter years of his life, Eddie Rickenbacker maintained a home in Key Biscayne, Florida. When in Key Biscayne, Rickenbacker could often be seen throwing food to the seagulls that soared above the waters near his residence. It was Rickenbacker's way of paying back the seagulls.

During World War II, Rickenbacker served as a special civilian advisor to the U.S. military. In October 1942, at the direction of Secretary of War Henry Stimson, Rickenbacker embarked on a tour of U.S. air bases located in combat theaters around the world. Stimson wanted Rickenbacker to evaluate the preparedness of the air bases and to bolster the morale of the American fliers. Along the way, Rickenbacker was to stop on the island of New Guinea to deliver a message from Stimson to General Douglas MacArthur. The message was so secret that it could not be reduced to writing. MacArthur, the supreme commander of Allied forces in the Southwest Pacific Theater, was then headquartered in Papua, a part of New Guinea.

With the message for MacArthur foremost in his mind, Rickenbacker, accompanied by a military aide and six crewmen, left Hawaii in the early hours of October 21, 1942, in a B-17 aircraft. The plane was bound for Brisbane, Australia and, ultimately, a landing strip in Port Moresby, the capital of Papua. En route, the aircraft ran out of fuel, forcing the pilot to make an emergency landing in the South Pacific Ocean, north of Samoa and the Fiji Islands. Rickenbacker and the other men inflated the plane's emergency life rafts and hoped for rescue. After a few days, the men had consumed all of the food that they were able to carry from the plane.

On the eighth day, with the men near starvation, a brown bird descended from the sky, flapped its wings, and landed on Rickenbacker's head. Fearful that any abrupt movement would scare the bird, Rickenbacker raised his hands—ever so slowly—toward the bird. With a sudden grasp, he clutched the bird's legs. After stripping off the feathers, Rickenbacker cut the bird apart and distributed its carcass in equal portions for the men to eat. The men then attached hooks to the bird's guts and caught two tiny fish. Within hours, a squall arose over the ocean, delivering more than a quart of fresh water. The bird, fish, and rain water sustained the men until they were rescued.

Rickenbacker thought the bird to be a seagull, though others maintained that it would have been highly unusual for a seagull to fly so far from land. In any event, after Rickenbacker recovered from the ordeal, he wrote a series of articles about the "seagull episode." In turn, the articles became the basis of a best-selling book. Rickenbacker donated the proceeds of the book, more than twenty-five thousand dollars, to benefit the families of airmen who had died during World War II. Later, Rickenbacker wrote an article titled "When a Man Faces Death," in which he attributed his survival to the presence of God in the life rafts. "Perhaps such things as the control of mind over matter and the transmission of thought waves are tied together," he wrote, "part of something so big we haven't grasped it yet."

◆   ◆   ◆

I say, 'If only I had wings like a dove that I might fly away and find rest.'
—Psalm 55, verse 7.

NILE KINNICK

Nile Kinnick, nicknamed the "Cornbelt Comet," was a talented all-around athlete from Adel, Iowa. As an American Legion baseball player, Kinnick was the catcher for future Hall-of-Fame pitcher Bob Feller, also from Iowa. At the age of fourteen, Kinnick moved with his family to Omaha, Nebraska, where he made the all-state high school football and basketball teams. In 1936, Kinnick enrolled at the University of Iowa, focusing on football. A halfback on both offense and defense, Kinnick could pass with either hand. He developed an uncanny ability to throw precision passes to his teammates while he was in motion. In his senior season, Kinnick led Iowa to a surprising 6–1–1 record, including upset wins over Indiana, Wisconsin, Notre Dame, and Minnesota. At season's end, he was awarded the Heisman Trophy. In December 1941, less than a week before the Japanese attacked Pearl Harbor, Kinnick enrolled in the Navy Air Corps and became a fighter plane pilot. He died on June 2, 1943, after making an emergency landing in his airplane off the coast of Venezuela during a training exercise.

The last football game in which Nile Kinnick ever played came in the summer of 1940, when he joined other college all-stars in a preseason exhibition against the NFL champion Green Bay Packers. Kinnick passed for two touchdowns and kicked four extra points. After the game, Kinnick and teammate Erwin Prasse took a train back to Iowa City. En route, Kinnick said to Prasse, "Erwin, my football career is over." Kinnick then wandered off on his own through the train. When Kinnick did not return, Prasse went looking for his friend and teammate. He found Kinnick in a car full of deaf students, talking to the students in sign language. A quick learner with an inexhaustible curiosity, Kinnick had memorized the finger movements the preceding year while reading a book on sign language.

Early in life, Nile Kinnick developed a sensitivity to the needs of others. As a schoolboy in Iowa, Kinnick rose early every day for three months to help a neighboring family with farm chores, when the head of the family was stricken with pneumonia. Later, as a high school student in Omaha, Kinnick would pass long lines of people begging for coal to heat their homes. The sight would cause Kinnick to ponder the challenges facing America. "Every man's place on earth is important," he would write in his diary.

An inveterate writer, Kinnick used his diary to record his thoughts in 1941 as he prepared to enter military service. "May God give me the courage and ability to so conduct myself in every situation that my country, my family, and my friends will be proud of me," he wrote.

On the morning of June 2, 1943, Kinnick and several other pilots climbed into their F4F Wildcat fighter planes and took off from the deck of the aircraft carrier USS *Lexington*. The pilots were in the final days of training before heading for action in the Pacific. Kinnick's plane began to leak oil in mid-flight. The fuselage of his Wildcat became streaked with oil; engine failure was inevitable. Kinnick had two options, landing on the *Lexington* and jeopardizing the safety of other planes and their crew members, or ditching his plane in the sea and risking his own life. He chose the latter. Almost immediately, rescue boats from the *Lexington* arrived at the location where Kinnick had gone down, but there was no trace of either the "Cornbelt Comet" or his plane.

After Kinnick's death, Kinnick's father wrote a letter to his younger son, Benjamin, who was an Army bomber pilot. In his letter, Nile Sr. said, "Benjamin, tonight, the stars will not shine as brightly as they did before, but they will shine."

Fifteen months later, Benjamin would also die when his plane was shot down over the Pacific during combat.

◆   ◆   ◆

The Lord numbers all the stars, calls each of them by name.
—Psalm 147, verse 4.

CHRIS RUMBURG

Chris Rumburg, a stocky two-hundred pounder, was the starting center for the Washington State football team during the late 1930s. He served as captain of the Cougars during his senior season and, after college, joined the U.S. Army. Rumburg served with the Sixty-sixth Infantry Division in World War II, reaching the rank of lieutenant colonel. He died on Christmas Eve of 1944, along with 801 other American soldiers who were on board the troop transport Leopoldville. *A torpedo fired by a German submarine struck the* Leopoldville *as it was ferrying the soldiers across the English Channel.*

The *Leopoldville*, a Belgian Lines cruise ship leased to the United States, steamed out of Southampton, England on the morning of December 24, 1944, bound for France. World War II was then in its latter stages; in less than six months, the United States and its allies would declare victory in Europe. In December of 1944, however, the Germans still occupied portions of France, including the Brittany coast. The Nazis continued to operate submarine bases from the French ports of Lorient and St. Nazaire.

More than a thousand soldiers from the Sixty-sixth Division, most of them heading for their initial combat experience, were packed on board the *Leopoldville*. When the transport was five miles from the French port of Cherbourg, a German submarine attacked. One torpedo passed by the *Leopoldville* without inflicting damage. A second torpedo scored a direct hit and exploded inside two of the *Leopoldville*'s troop compartments. The compartments quickly flooded.

Though injured, Chris Rumburg focused on saving others. Time after time, he and a fellow officer, Captain Hal Crain, dove into the compartments that had sustained the most damage and dragged men to lifeboats. In a final act of courage, Rumburg took off the life vest he was wearing, gave it to another soldier, and again dove into one of the troop compartments. He became trapped amid the debris and drowned.

Two and a half hours after the torpedo struck, the *Leopoldville* sank, taking Rumburg, fellow hero Hal Crain and hundreds of other soldiers to the depths of the icy English Channel.

◆   ◆   ◆

He reached down from on high and took hold of me; drew me out of the deep waters.
—Psalm 18, verse 17.

[*Author's Note:* The U.S. War Department and its successor, the Department of Defense, never released information regarding the sinking of the *Leopoldville* because of war-time censorship restrictions. The War Department told next of kin only that their relatives had died in combat. Much of what is known about the fate of Chris Rumburg and other soldiers aboard the ship comes from eyewitnesses such as Jacquin Sanders, whose article, "The Tragedy of Troop Ship 'Leopoldville'," appeared in the *St. Petersburg Times* on June 10, 1994. The article remains one of the few public accounts of the *Leopoldville*'s final voyage.]

GLENN DAVIS

According to the Los Angeles Times, *Glenn Davis was the best athlete ever developed in southern California. After a stellar high school career, Davis entered the United States Military Academy at West Point in 1943. He teamed with Felix "Doc" Blanchard to form one of the most potent ball-carrying duos in collegiate history. Davis was known as "Mr. Outside," Blanchard as "Mr. Inside." In 1945, Davis was runner-up to Blanchard in the voting for the prestigious Heisman Trophy. Davis would win the award the following year. After graduation, Davis was commissioned as a lieutenant in the Army and served in Korea. In 1950, he was discharged from the Army and joined the Los Angeles Rams. He played on two championship teams with the Rams before retiring. Davis died on March 9, 2005. He was eighty years old.*

Shortly after Glenn Davis died, his widow received a letter from one of Davis's golfing buddies. In the letter, the writer listed three reasons why he had enjoyed Davis's friendship. First, the friend explained, Davis never took the Lord's name in vain. Second, Davis never said a bad word about anyone. Third, the friend wrote, one day after he and Davis had finished golfing, Davis took off his street shoes and gave them to the gentleman who had caddied for him. Davis told the caddy, "You need a better pair of shoes if you're going to walk more."

Davis loved to give things away, whether shoes or more valuable items. In the late 1990s, when he was in his seventies, Davis put his Heisman Trophy underneath his arm and walked onto the campus of his old high school in La Verne, California. Carrying the trophy into the school building, Davis met teacher Dan Harden. "I have something for the school, and I'd like to leave it here," Davis told Harden.

The transaction lasted only a couple of minutes. Davis wanted no fanfare, leaving strict instructions that the school should not call the newspapers. Davis's motivation was as uncomplicated as the transaction itself. He thought he owed the school thanks.

Davis lived his life according to simple rules: give to others, don't waste time, give thanks.

There was another rule, one that Davis revealed to his stepson, John Slack, during one of Slack's high school track meets. Slack had won the one hundred-yard dash in 9.9 seconds. Afterwards, Davis heard Slack bragging about his time to some friends. Though past his athletic prime, Davis challenged his stepson to a race. Slack pointed out that Davis didn't have track shoes. Davis insisted. The two began sprinting.

Davis—older, wiser, and faster—outpaced his stepson. He then instructed Slack to always let his performance speak for itself.

◆   ◆   ◆

The mouths of the just utter wisdom; their tongues speak what is right.
—Psalm 37, verse 30.

MADDY ENGLISH

Madeline "Maddy" English learned to play baseball by tagging along with her older brother to pick-up games in her hometown of Everett, Massachusetts. When English graduated from high school, a scout from the Chicago Cubs organization suggested that she try out for the All-American Girls Professional Baseball League. English demonstrated a deft touch as a fielder and occasional power at the plate. The League signed her to a contract and, from 1943 to 1950, she played third base for the Racine Belles. English was named to the AAGPBL all-star team three times. An excellent base runner, she once stole seven bases in a single game. After her playing days, English enrolled at Boston University, ultimately earning a master's degree in education. She is a member of the Women in Sports Hall of Fame, the Boston University Athletic Hall of Fame, and the New England Sports Museum Hall of Fame. English died on August 20, 2004, at the age of seventy-nine.

After retiring from baseball, Maddy English devoted her life to education. Upon earning her college degree, she became a physical education teacher at Parlin School in Everett. She remained in that capacity for ten years and then served as a guidance counselor for an additional seventeen years. As both a physical education teacher and guidance counselor, she encouraged her students to "reach for the stars."

English was a natural teacher who cared deeply about others. Well into her career as an educator, she would give speeches to audiences in Everett and then, after the speeches, rush outside, pick up a baseball glove, and play catch with the young girls in attendance. In recognition of her contributions to the community, the city of Everett named an elementary school after her in 2003, the Madeline English School. English is the only former member of the All-American Girls Professional Baseball League to have a school named after her.

◆   ◆   ◆

Attend, my people, to my teaching; listen to the words of my mouth.
—Psalm 78, verse 1.

BYRON NELSON

For professional golfer John Byron Nelson, the year 1945 was magical. He competed in thirty tour events that year and won eighteen of them. Beginning in early March with a victory in the Miami International Four-Ball competition, he went almost five months without losing a tournament. By the time Nelson lost at the Memphis Invitational in August, he had won eleven consecutive events. The streak, which included nineteen straight rounds with scores under seventy, remains the most impressive display of golfing dominance ever. Nelson retired from full-time golf in 1946 at the age of thirty-four. At retirement, he had a total of fifty-two victories in official Professional Golf Association tournaments. He was elected to the PGA Hall of Fame in 1953. Nelson died on September 26, 2006, at the age of ninety-four.

In 1936, Byron Nelson signed a contract worth five hundred dollars to appear in cigarette advertisements over the course of a six-month period. It was a decision that Nelson, who never smoked, would come to regret. Shortly after the advertisements began running, Nelson received an influx of harshly critical letters, many from Sunday school teachers. Almost uniformly, the letters faulted Nelson for not being a good role model for children. Hoping to stop the advertisements, Nelson called the cigarette manufacturer and offered to give back the five hundred dollars. The manufacturer refused the offer, advising Nelson that the advertisements could not be stopped. Nelson then did the next best thing. As he recounted it, "I promised the good Lord if he'd forgive me, I'd never let anyone else down and try to be a good example, and I've worked very hard at doing that."

When Nelson played exhibition matches at local golf courses, he invariably asked two questions before teeing off. First, he would ask, "What's the course record?" And second, "Who owns it?" The reason for asking these questions was not immediately obvious, so one day Nelson explained the purpose for his inquiries. "If the home pro owns the course record," he said, "you don't break it. The home pro lives there. We're just visitors."

In the late 1960s, Nelson worked with the Salesmanship Club of Dallas to establish the Byron Nelson Classic as a charitable endeavor. The Nelson Classic has been held each year since then. The event raises more money for charity than any other golf tournament. In 2006, the Nelson Classic raised $6.33 million. The proceeds of the tournament are used to support the Salesmanship Club Youth and Family Centers, which provide a multifaceted rehabilitation program, including summer camps and other activities, for handicapped children and those at risk.

For all his noble ambitions, good works, and success in golf, Nelson remained a very humble man. "I don't know very much," he told a reporter in 1997. "I know a little bit about golf. I know how to make a stew. And I know how to be a decent man."

Others went further. Pro golfer Ken Venturi, when speaking of Nelson, once said, "You can always argue who was the greatest player, but Byron is the finest gentleman the game has ever known."

◆   ◆   ◆

Those whose steps are guided by the Lord, whose way God approves, may stumble but they will never fall.
—Psalm 37, verses 23–24.

BRANCH RICKEY

Wesley Branch Rickey gained fame as the general manager who brought Jackie Robinson to the major leagues. Rickey got his start in baseball as a catcher and outfielder for the St. Louis Browns, but saw his playing career end after only 119 games. He returned to the major leagues as manager of the Browns in 1913. Over the course of ten seasons as a manager, Rickey experienced only limited success. He became general manager of the St. Louis Cardinals in 1925. In three of the next five years, the Cardinals finished first in the National League standings. Rickey remained with the Cardinals until after the 1942 season, when he was named general manager of the Brooklyn Dodgers. Rickey's tenure in Brooklyn lasted for seven years, during which he successfully integrated the Dodgers and, in the process, transformed the baseball world. Rickey died on December 9, 1965. He was inducted into baseball's Hall of Fame in 1967.

On August 18, 1945, Branch Rickey met with twenty-six-year-old Jackie Robinson in the Dodgers' offices on Montague Street in Brooklyn. "Do you know why you were brought here?" Rickey asked. "You were brought here," Rickey proceeded, "to play for the Brooklyn organization." The meeting turned into a three-hour session. Rickey needed to find out if Robinson could endure the difficulties that were sure to follow. Pulling out a copy of Giovanni Papini's book, *The Life of Christ*, Rickey schooled Robinson on the conduct that would be expected of him.

Rickey read Papini's words to Robinson, "There are three answers men can make to violence: revenge, flight, turning the other cheek." Rickey told Robinson that turning the other cheek was the most difficult option but, for an African American selected to integrate baseball, it would be the only effective response. Rickey explained his point by again referring to *The Life of Christ*. "Your adversary is ready for anything but this," Rickey read. It was a lesson that Robinson took to heart.

If Branch Rickey had been less resolute in his moral convictions, Jackie Robinson would never have made it to Brooklyn. When Rickey's intentions to put Robinson in a Dodgers' uniform became known, opponents quickly surfaced.

Knowing the difficulties that would arise, Rickey's wife tried to talk Rickey out of signing Robinson. "Why should you be the one to do it?" she asked. "Haven't you done enough for baseball?"

As Rickey proceeded with his plan, the other major league teams tried to stop him. At a meeting in January 1947, the owners of the other teams voted fifteen to one against letting Robinson join the Dodgers. Rickey remained determined. Later, when some of the Dodgers' most visible stars objected to having Robinson on the team, Rickey vowed to trade or release any player who refused to accept Robinson as a teammate.

Two games into the 1947 season, as the Dodgers prepared to play the New York Giants at the Polo Grounds in Harlem, National League president Ford Frick urged Rickey to hold Robinson out of the games. Frick feared that the crowds would grow wild and unruly. Rickey again stood his ground, and Robinson played.

For ten seasons, Robinson played and played well.

◆   ◆   ◆

A mild answer calms wrath.
—Proverbs 15, verse 1.

ALBERT B. "HAPPY" CHANDLER

Albert Benjamin "Happy" Chandler was an accomplished high school and collegiate athlete. He excelled in baseball, basketball, and football. With designs on a career in politics, Chandler graduated from the University of Kentucky Law School in 1924. He served in the Kentucky state senate from 1929 until 1935, when he was elected governor of Kentucky. He represented Kentucky in the United States Senate from 1939 until 1945. In 1945, major league baseball owners selected Chandler to succeed Judge Kenesaw Mountain Landis as the commissioner of baseball. During his tenure as commissioner, Chandler paved the way for Jackie Robinson to become the first African American in the modern era to play major league baseball. Chandler died on June 15, 1991.

In August 1945, Branch Rickey, general manager of the Brooklyn Dodgers, brought Jackie Robinson to Brooklyn for a meeting. Rickey's intent was to see if Robinson was interested in playing for the Dodgers. Robinson was receptive, and Rickey signed him to a contract to play with the Dodgers' top farm club, the Montreal Royals. A year later, after Robinson had demonstrated his skills in Montreal, Rickey was confident that Robinson was ready for the major leagues. However, the major leagues were not ready for Robinson. Team owners voted fifteen to one against letting Robinson play.

Troubled by the owners' strong sentiments, Rickey traveled to Happy Chandler's home in Kentucky to seek Chandler's view. When Rickey asked if Chandler would allow Robinson to play, Chandler's response was emphatic. He told Rickey, "I'm going to have to meet my maker some day. If he asked me why I didn't let this boy play, and I answered, 'Because he's a Negro,' that might not be a sufficient answer. I will approve of the transfer of Robinson's contract from Montreal to Brooklyn, and we'll make a fight with you. So bring him on in."

Chandler's stand would cost him his job. In 1951, baseball's owners, offended because Chandler had crossed them, refused to renew his contract as commissioner.

◆   ◆   ◆

The beginning of wisdom is the fear of the Lord.
—Proverbs 9, verse 10.

JACKIE ROBINSON

Jack Roosevelt Robinson was the first African American baseball player to play in the major leagues. He played for the Brooklyn Dodgers from 1947 to 1956. In 1947, he hit .297 with twelve home runs and was named major league rookie-of-the-year. Robinson followed up his rookie season by hitting .296 in 1948. A year later, he hit .342, leading all National League batters. A daring base runner, Robinson led the National League in stolen bases in 1947 and 1949. For his career, he compiled a batting average of .311. Robinson was elected to baseball's Hall of Fame in 1962. He died on October 24, 1972. He was fifty-three years old.

The epitaph on Jackie Robinson's tombstone in Brooklyn's Cypress Hills Cemetery reads, "A life is not important except in the impact it has on other lives."

Robinson was a role model for young ballplayers of his era. His influence, however, extended far beyond the playing fields. A month before Dr. Martin Luther King, Jr. was assassinated, the civil rights leader told a dinner guest that Jackie Robinson was more important to the success of the civil rights movement than King himself. Robinson's sister explained, "Martin Luther King had his dream, but he didn't know how to start it. And then he became aware of Jack, in baseball. And he said, 'This is what I want to do in other areas.'"

In 1947, when Robinson began his major league baseball career, he was subjected to a level of abuse, both verbal and physical, never before experienced by any professional athlete. There were days when Robinson gave serious thought to quitting. More than on any other occasion, his experiences on April 22, 1947, almost caused him to turn his back on baseball. The Philadelphia Phillies were playing the Dodgers at Ebbets Field. For nine innings, Philadelphia's manager—and many of the Phillies' players—yelled racist insults at Robinson. Robinson would later write that the Phillies game "brought me nearer to cracking up than I ever had been."

Robinson thought of grabbing some of the individuals in the Phillies' dugout, smashing their teeth in, and then walking away from baseball. In the end, he didn't smash anybody's teeth in, and he didn't walk away from the game. Robinson attributed his perseverance to the example set by Branch Rickey. He said, "I thought of Mr. Rickey—how his family and friends had begged him not to fight for me and my people.... Mr. Rickey had come to a crossroads and made a lonely decision. I was at a crossroads. I would make mine. I would stay."

In staying, Robinson was able to provide a powerful lesson in forgiveness. The 1947 season was a dismal year for the Phillies. They won only sixty-two games, lost ninety-two, and finished next-to-last in the league. The manager's job was in jeopardy. As the end of the season approached, the manager asked Robinson if he would consent to take a picture with him. "A picture like this in the newspaper," the manager explained, "may save my job." Robinson put aside any feelings of ill will and posed for a picture, shaking hands with the man who had tormented him five months earlier.

After his playing days, Robinson became a crusader for civil rights. He served as chairman of the NAACP's Freedom Fund drive. In 1958, he traveled to Jackson, Mississippi and, with a hostile mob of segregationists milling outside the building, urged his audience to "press on peacefully for rights." In August 1962, two days after two black churches had been burned to the ground in Albany, Georgia, Robinson went to Albany at Dr. King's request and delivered a speech advocating continued nonviolent resistance. In May 1963, shortly after Dr. King's hotel had been bombed, Robinson joined Dr. King in Birmingham, Alabama. With Dr. King at his side, Robinson spoke to a packed church about civil rights.

◆   ◆   ◆

Let me answer my taunters with a word, for I trust in your word.
—Psalm 119, verse 42.

HAROLD "PEE WEE" REESE

Harold "Pee Wee" Reese was born on July 23, 1918. He spent sixteen seasons as the regular shortstop for the Brooklyn Dodgers. At the height of his career, he missed three other seasons, 1943–1945, due to military service in World War II. A superb fielder, Reese served as the team captain for much of his tenure with the Dodgers. For his career, he hit .269, with a career-best of .309 in 1954. He played in seven World Series and was elected to the Hall of Fame in 1984. He died on August 14, 1999.

On Tuesday evening, May 13, 1947, the Brooklyn Dodgers played the Cincinnati Reds at Cincinnati's Crosley Field. Though the game received only modest publicity in the newspapers, there was obvious historic significance. It would be Jackie Robinson's first appearance in Cincinnati as a major league ballplayer. Up to that point, Robinson had only twenty games under his belt in a Dodger uniform. He had done little to distinguish himself. Referring to Robinson, Arthur Daley had written in the *New York Times* on the morning of the Cincinnati game, "The Negro first baseman of the Dodgers hasn't been any ball of fire but he deserves his chance." Many of the Cincinnati fans disagreed, showing no willingness to give Robinson a chance.

The Reds' starting pitcher, Johnny Vander Meer, retired the Dodgers without a run in the first inning. Then the Dodgers took the field for the bottom half of the inning. When Robinson took his position at first base, the fans, as well as some of the Cincinnati players, let loose with a venomous mixture of catcalls, taunts, and racial epithets. Pee Wee Reese, playing shortstop for the Dodgers, was saddened. When the abuse continued, Reese walked over toward Robinson at first base. He greeted Robinson with a smile and perhaps a twinkle in his eye. Reese put his arm around Robinson's shoulders. The significance of the gesture was not lost on the fans; there was a stunned silence in the stands. Pee Wee Reese had taken a stand for decency. The ball game resumed. From that point on, Robinson knew he was not alone.

Reese's courage amazed both his own teammates and other observers. "Think of the guts that took," Brooklyn pitcher Carl Erskine would later say. Author and baseball authority Roger Kahn called Reese's display of support for Robinson "baseball's finest moment."

◆   ◆   ◆

Hide me in the shadow of your wings from the violence of the wicked.
—Psalm 17, verses 8–9.

[*Author's Note*: Former Brooklyn Dodger pitcher Rex Barney provided one of the few first-hand accounts of Reese's display of support for Robinson in Cincinnati. Barney recounted the event for author Peter Golenbock when Golenbock was researching and writing his 1984 book, *Bums: An Oral History of the Brooklyn Dodgers*. Barney told Golenbock that he was warming up on the mound and heard the fans heaping verbal abuse on Robinson. Then, according to Barney, "while Jackie was standing by first base, Pee Wee went over to him and put his arm around him as if to say, 'This is my boy. This is the guy. We're gonna win with him.'" Writer Jonathan Eig, author of *Opening Day: The Story of Jackie Robinson's First Season*, has speculated that Reese's public display of support for Robinson never occurred or, if it did, it happened somewhere other than in Cincinnati. Eig argues that Barney's account is not credible. Reese was supposed to have placed his arm around Robinson when the Dodgers first took the field in the bottom half of the first inning. Eig points out that Barney pitched against Cincinnati on May 13, 1947, but not until the seventh inning. Eig also notes that there were no game-day newspaper accounts of the interaction between Reese and Robinson. Nonetheless, it seems unlikely that Barney would have related the anecdote without any factual basis for it. Even if Eig is correct when he argues that Reese did not join Robinson at first base in Cincinnati, the fact remains that Reese, a Southerner, was one of Robinson's biggest supporters on the field and in the clubhouse. The "Teammates" sculpture of Reese and Robinson, which greets visitors to Keyspan Park in Brooklyn, stands as tangible evidence of the relationship between the two players.]

SAM LACY

Samuel Harold Lacy, an African American, covered developments in sports and society at large for black newspapers from 1934 until his death in 2003. He was born in 1903, grew up in Washington, D.C., and graduated from Howard University. Lacy played semi-pro baseball after college and then turned to journalism. He wrote first for the Washington Tribune, *where he served as managing editor and sports editor. In 1940, he became assistant editor at the* Chicago Defender. *Lacy joined the weekly* Baltimore Afro-American *newspaper in 1944 as a columnist and sports editor. He spent the last sixty-four years of his life working at the* Afro-American. *Through both his columns and his personal deeds, Lacy carved out a role as an advocate for social change. He was one of the principal architects of desegregation in major league baseball. Lacy was inducted into the writers' wing of the Baseball Hall of Fame in 1998. He died on May 8, 2003, five months shy of his one-hundredth birthday.*

If not for Sam Lacy, there would likely have been no Jackie Robinson in major league baseball. In the late 1930s, Lacy began campaigning for the integration of pro sports. When Branch Rickey set out to integrate the Brooklyn Dodgers in the mid-1940s, Lacy was ready. An astute observer of both people and sports, Lacy had identified Robinson, then playing with the Negro League Kansas City Monarchs, as the player best qualified to break baseball's color barrier. Lacy believed Robinson possessed the strength to tolerate the inner pain of hate and discrimination. Along with Wendell Smith of the *Pittsburgh Courier*, Lacy worked to convince Rickey that Robinson could handle the challenge. Then Lacy prayed that he was right.

Lacy knew well the pain of hate and discrimination. As a teenager in the 1920s, Lacy had stood alongside his father at a parade for the Washington Senators when one of the Senators players spit on Lacy's father. Much later, Lacy accompanied black players on their baseball travels throughout the South and experienced, firsthand, the racist attitudes and second-class accommodations. He once traveled with Robinson to Macon, Georgia, for an exhibition game and watched as bigots burned a cross on the front lawn of the boardinghouse where the two were staying. Time after time, Lacy found himself excluded from "white only" press rooms at ballparks. In 1947, a Yankee Stadium attendant refused to admit Lacy to cover the World Series, even after Lacy showed his press credentials.

Lacy did not let the experiences affect his personality. Friend and colleague Michael Wilbon marveled that Lacy "remained so upbeat, so positive, so sweet of disposition, and so free from bitterness."

Lacy tried to eliminate racial barriers wherever he found them. He led the fight for more black umpires in baseball. Well into the 1950s, when black baseball and football players played on the road, they could not stay in the same hotels as their white teammates. Lacy challenged the practice. At Lacy's urging, New York Giants president Chub Feeney pressured white hotel operators to provide rooms for Willie Mays and the team's other black players. Lacy took the same approach in football.

Not all of the black players appreciated Lacy's efforts. Some reveled in the freedom that came from separate accommodations, where curfews were loosely enforced and behavior was not monitored. Lacy had little patience with those who complained. "This is bigger than you," he would tell the players.

When inducted into the Baseball Hall of Fame, Lacy downplayed his accomplishments. "Any person with a little vision, a little curiosity, a little nerve could have done what I did," he said. In 2000, Congress passed a bill naming a post office on Baltimore's West Thirty-fourth Street after Lacy. Appreciative but characteristically humble, Lacy asked the bill's sponsor, "Why?"

◆　　　◆　　　◆

You have tried me by fire, but find no malice in me.
—Psalm 17, verse 3.

DOAK WALKER

In the 1940s and 1950s, Ewell Doak Walker was one of the most heralded football players in the country. He attended Southern Methodist University, where he ran for 2,076 yards, passed for an additional 1,786 yards, and scored 303 points during his career. Sportswriter Grantland Rice called Walker "the most authentic player in football history." Walker won the Heisman Trophy as the outstanding collegiate player in the country in 1948, beating out North Carolina star Charlie "Choo Choo" Justice. Walker joined the Detroit Lions in 1950 and teamed with his high school friend, quarterback Bobby Layne, to lead the Lions to NFL titles in 1952 and 1953. Walker was named to the NFL Pro Bowl team in five of his six seasons as a professional. He died on September 27, 1998.

In 1948, Doak Walker exemplified the best of college football. Polite and personable off the field, Walker was an elusive open-field runner, a prolific passer, and an excellent punter. In winning the Heisman Trophy, Walker averaged 4.9 yards on 122 rushing attempts and passed for twelve touchdowns. He was named first-team All-American by the Associated Press and United Press International. In addition, *Collier's* magazine selected Walker for its coaches' All-America team. Then an influential weekly magazine, *Collier's* would poll college coaches to identify those players most deserving of All-American honors.

In 1949, Walker was plagued by a concussion and a severe thigh bruise. He missed two games due to injuries and played only a limited role in others. Still, he managed to rush for 449 yards and pass for 605 more. As a passer, it was Walker's best season ever, but his rushing yardage was the lowest since his freshman year. Nonetheless, Walker's accomplishments again put him in the running for All-American honors.

Walker learned that *Collier's* was considering naming him to its 1949 All-America team. He quickly wrote a letter to *Collier's* editor, Bill Fay. His letter read:

> I deeply appreciate the fact that the coaches are considering me for the All-America football team, even though illness and injuries have kept me out of

the lineup so much this season. However, I believe there are other All-America candidates who have seen more action and therefore are more deserving of consideration. Being selected on the coaches' team last year gave me one of the biggest thrills I've ever had in football. I know the players who are named to this year's All-America (squad) will be just as appreciative of the honor.

Walker never told his coaches, teammates, family, or even his fiancée that he had deliberately taken himself out of the running for the *Collier's* All-America team. His selflessness surfaced only after the editor sent a copy of Walker's letter to the publicist at Southern Methodist University.

For Walker, such modesty was typical. Harley Sewell, an All-American guard from the University of Texas and a member of the Detroit Lions in the early 1950s, said of Walker, "He's always been the most unselfish, kind, good-hearted person."

◆   ◆   ◆

Humility goes before honors.
—Proverbs 18, verse 12.

CHARLIE "CHOO CHOO" JUSTICE

As a child, Charlie Justice suffered from a leg ailment, thought to be a form of polio, that deprived him of two years of grammar school. By high school, his leg had healed and Justice developed into a triple threat in football. His passing, kicking, and running led his Asheville, North Carolina, high school team to undefeated seasons in 1941 and 1942. After high school, Justice joined the war-time Navy. Though slight of build at five feet ten inches tall and 155 pounds, he excelled as a member of the football team at the Bainbridge, Maryland Naval Training Station. He gained the nickname "Choo Choo" when a naval officer said that he ran "like a runaway choo choo." Discharged from the Navy in 1946, Justice enrolled at the University of North Carolina and led the Tarheels to a record of 32–8–2 in four years. He was a consensus first-team All-American in 1948 and 1949 and finished second in the Heisman Trophy balloting both years. Justice turned professional in 1950 and played four years with the Washington Redskins, retiring after the 1954 season. He died on October 17, 2003.

Charlie "Choo Choo" Justice's academic record at the University of North Carolina was unremarkable; classroom work was clearly not his forte. One of the university's professors once asked Justice how he could do so well on the football field in front of fifty thousand people and yet do such mediocre work in the classroom. With typical candor and modesty, Justice told the professor, "Out there I got ten guys helping me all the time, and in here I'm on my own."

On the football field, Justice needed less help than most. He was fast, capable of changing direction and speed instantly, and blessed with extraordinary field vision. His exploits during college made him a household name. A song, "All the Way Choo Choo," was written in his honor and became a national hit. Justice's jersey number, 22, became the most popular number in North Carolina. Fans frequently sent letters to Justice using only the address "22, Chapel Hill, N.C." The post office knew well that all mail addressed to Number 22 went to Choo Choo's four-room bungalow on Airport Road.

Through all the hype, Justice remained unaffected. According to biographer Bob Terrell, Justice never took credit for anything he did on the football field. He would tell people, "My grandmother could run behind those ten guys blocking for me." After a big game, people would ask how he did it. Justice would answer, "I don't have a clue. I owe it all to my teammates." In 1949, the Christian Athletes Foundation honored Justice for his "humility in the face of many honors."

Justice preferred to focus on his charitable work instead of his heroics. After he finished his career with the Washington Redskins in 1954, Justice became a businessman in North Carolina and used his influence to raise several million dollars for charitable causes. His popularity and fundraising efforts enabled the city of Charlotte to open the Charlie Justice Youth and Adult Center, a drug and alcohol rehabilitation center.

Justice's modesty and sense of commitment was a reflection of the influence of his brothers, especially his older brother Jack. Jack Justice once told Charlie, "If I ever hear of you refusing to sign a kid's autograph, I'll stomp the hell out of you!" Justice never forgot the lesson. From the time he first became a star at North Carolina until his death in 2003, he made sure to give his autograph to each child who asked for one.

◆   ◆   ◆

I will make your name renowned through all generations.
—Psalm 45, verse 18.

LEFTY O'DOUL

Francis Joseph "Lefty" O'Doul was born on March 4, 1897. He made it to the major leagues as a pitcher with the New York Yankees in 1919. Over the next five seasons, it became apparent that pitching was not Lefty's forte. He appeared in thirty-four games as a pitcher, walking forty-nine batters and striking out only nineteen. O'Doul gave up pitching, returned to the minor leagues, and recast himself as an outfielder. After compiling a batting average of .369 in four minor league seasons, he made it back to the majors in 1928. In 1929, playing for the Philadelphia Phillies, he enjoyed his finest season, batting .398, with thirty-two home runs. For his career, O'Doul hit .349 in eleven seasons, with 113 home runs. He died on December 7, 1969.

The inscription on Lefty O'Doul's tombstone reads, "He was here at a good time and had a good time while he was here." O'Doul's major league career was largely confined to the East Coast. He played six years in New York, two in Brooklyn, two in Philadelphia, and one in Boston.

When it came to "good times," however, there was no confining Lefty; his good times spanned oceans. O'Doul had been a frequent visitor to Japan during the 1930s. In the aftermath of World War II, when it was time to repair the relationship between the United States and Japan, Lefty was ready. In 1949, while managing the Pacific Coast League's San Francisco Seals, O'Doul brought his team to Japan for an eleven-game exhibition tour. The eleven games drew over five hundred thousand spectators and raised more than one hundred thousand dollars for Japanese charities. When the Seals arrived in Japan, O'Doul was shocked at the low esteem of citizens throughout the country. Accustomed to an era in which the Japanese routinely shouted "Banzai!" ("Long live!") as a term of greeting or congratulations, O'Doul found few Japanese who were willing to shout "Banzai." Within the span of six weeks, O'Doul almost single-handedly changed the mood of Japan. By the time he left, O'Doul said, "all of Japan was banzai-ing again." Douglas MacArthur, commander of U.S. occupation forces in Japan, called Lefty's presence in post-war Japan "the greatest piece of diplomacy ever."

In 1958, O'Doul opened a pub, "Lefty O'Doul's Restaurant and Piano Bar," near Union Square in the heart of San Francisco. The pub was open to the public every day of the year except for Thanksgiving and Christmas. On those two days, O'Doul admitted only vagabonds and street people to his restaurant. He treated each person in attendance to a festive holiday dinner. During the course of the meals, O'Doul and his staff read through the list of attendees, calling out each individual by name and handing her or him a special gift.

◆   ◆   ◆

East and west you make resound with joy.
—Psalm 65, verse 9.

References

Lou Costello

Leonard, Mike. *The Ride of Our Lives: Roadside Lessons of an American Family*. New York: Ballantine Books, 2006.

Eddie Rickenbacker

Lewis, W. David. *Eddie Rickenbacker: An American Hero in the Twentieth Century*. Baltimore: The Johns Hopkins University Press, 2005.

Nile Kinnick

Pennington, Bill. *The Heisman: Great American Stories of the Men Who Won*. New York: HarperCollins Publishers Inc., 2004.

Chris Rumburg

Jacquin Sanders, "The Tragedy of Troop Ship 'Leopoldville'," *St. Petersburg Times*, 10 June 1994, 1A.

Glenn Davis

Bill Dwyre, "Davis Remembered For More Than Athletic Achievements," *Los Angeles Times*, 15 March 2005, D7.

David Flores, "Other Half of Army Duo Offers Fitting Recollection," *San Antonio Express-News*, 11 March 2005, 3C.

Dave Kindred, "Once Army's Mr. Outside, Glenn Davis, Left Football; He Spent His Life On His Own Terms," *Pittsburgh Post-Gazette*, 18 March 2005, D2.

Richard Rothschild, "Davis A Gladiator in More Than One Arena," *Knight Ridder Tribune News Service*, 11 March 2005, 1.

Recollections of Yvonne Ameche Davis, December 2005 Heisman Awards Dinner.

Maddy English

Madden, W.C. *The Women of the All-American Girls Professional Baseball League.* Jefferson, NC: McFarland & Company, Inc., 1997.

Gloria Negri, "Madeline English, Pro Ball Player, Everett Teacher; At 79," *Boston Globe*, 24 August 2004, B5.

Byron Nelson

Davis, Martin. *Byron Nelson: The Story of Golf's Finest Gentleman and The Greatest Winning Streak in History.* New York: Broadway Books, 1997.

Brad Townsend and Bill Nichols, "Byron Nelson: Golf's Legend, Par Excellence," *The Dallas Morning News*, 27 September 2006, http://dallasnews.com/sharedcontent/dws/spt/golf/stories/092706nmetnelsonob.1b.

"Golf Legend Byron Nelson Dies At 94," CBS SportsLine.com, 26 September 2006, http://cbsnews.com/stories/2006/09/26/sportsline/main2041384.html.

Branch Rickey

Golenbock, Peter. *Bums: An Oral History of the Brooklyn Dodgers.* New York: G. P. Putnam's Sons, 1984.

Williams, Pat and Mike Sielski. *How to Be Like Jackie Robinson.* Deerfield Beach, FL: Health Communications, Inc., 2005.

Albert B. "Happy" Chandler

Golenbock, Peter. *Bums: An Oral History of the Brooklyn Dodgers.* New York: G. P. Putnam's Sons, 1984.

Williams, Pat and Mike Sielski. *How to Be Like Jackie Robinson.* Deerfield Beach, FL: Health Communications, Inc., 2005.

Jackie Robinson

Arthur Daley, "The Passing Baseball Scene," *The New York Times*, 13 May 1947, 32.

Eig, Jonathan. *Opening Day: The Story of Jackie Robinson's First Season*. New York: Simon & Schuster, 2007.

Golenbock, Peter. *Bums: An Oral History of the Brooklyn Dodgers*. New York: G. P. Putnam's Sons, 1984.

Golenbock, Peter. *Teammates*. New York: Harcourt Brace & Company, 1990.

Williams, Pat and Mike Sielski. *How to Be Like Jackie Robinson*. Deerfield Beach, FL: Health Communications, Inc., 2005.

Harold "Pee Wee" Reese

Golenbock, Peter. *Bums: An Oral History of the Brooklyn Dodgers*. New York: G. P. Putnam's Sons, 1984.

Golenbock, Peter. *Teammates*. New York: Harcourt Brace & Company, 1990.

Lonnie Wheeler, "Statue Captures Inspiring Moment," *Cincinnati Post*, 14 October 2005, C1.

Williams, Pat and Mike Sielski. *How to Be Like Jackie Robinson*. Deerfield Beach, FL: Health Communications, Inc., 2005.

Sam Lacy

Howard Bryant, "Story Not the Glory; Lacy's Legacy Illustrates How Sports Journalism Has Changed," *Boston Herald*, 19 May 2003, 111.

Elijah E. Cummings, "Samuel Harold Lacy: The Making of an American Hero," *Afro-American Red Star*, 30 May 2003, A7.

William Gildea, "Lacy's Legacy: Friend, Mentor, Inspiration," *The Washington Post*, 18 May 2003, E1.

Michael Wilbon, "Lacy Leaves Towering Legacy," *Los Angeles Times*, 18 May 2003, D2.

Doak Walker

Canning, Whit and Dan Jenkins, ed. *Doak Walker: More Than A Hero*. Indianapolis: Masters Press, 1997.

Charlie "Choo Choo" Justice

Terrell, Bob. *All Aboard! Charlie "Choo Choo" Justice*. Alexander, NC: Alexander Books, 1996.

Lefty O'Doul

Leutzinger, Richard. *Lefty O'Doul: The Legend That Baseball Nearly Forgot*. Carmel, CA: Carmel Bay Publishing Group, 1997.

Ritter, Lawrence S. *The Glory of Their Times: The Story of the Early Days of Baseball Told by the Men Who Played It*. New York: William Morrow, 1966.

1950–1959

1950–1959

In 1950, North Korea invaded South Korean territory. Shortly thereafter, United Nations combat forces mobilized under the direction of General Douglas MacArthur to defend South Korea. The Korean War was underway.

General Dwight D. Eisenhower led the Republican Party to victory in the presidential election of 1952. With casualties in the Korean War mounting, the U.S. Air Force conducted an extensive bombing campaign that destroyed critical irrigation and hydroelectric projects in North Korea. The widespread destruction caused North Korea to seek a cease-fire. The conflict ended on July 27, 1953.

In a unanimous decision issued on May 17, 1954 in the case of *Brown v. Board of Education*, the U.S. Supreme Court ruled that racial segregation in public schools was unconstitutional. "In the field of public education," Chief Justice Earl Warren wrote, "separate but equal has no place."

Notwithstanding the Supreme Court's decision, school districts throughout the country resisted integration. Central High School in Little Rock, Arkansas, emerged as a focal point in the contest of wills between entrenched segregationists and those supporting integration. On September 4, 1957, nine black students, who came to be known as the "Little Rock Nine," were set to enter previously all-white Central High. However, Governor Orval Faubus called in the state's National Guard troops to block the black students' path into the school. The students and other African Americans were spat on and threatened with violence and lynching. A degree of order was restored after the federal government intervened. Calling the rioting "disgraceful," President Eisenhower sent paratroopers from the Army's 101st Airborne Division to Little Rock to protect the black students. On what would be the school's third attempt to conduct a full day of classes, the Little Rock Nine finally entered Central High and began classes on September 25th, with each black student being escorted during the school day by an armed paratrooper.

Brown v. Board of Education would continue to have a disappointing legacy into the 1960s. By 1964, less than two percent of the school districts in the United States that were segregated in 1954 had experienced any desegregation.

On December 28, 1958, in what has been called the greatest football game ever played, the Baltimore Colts beat the New York Giants, twenty-three to seventeen, in "sudden death" overtime at Yankee Stadium. The Colts tied the game on a field goal with ninety seconds left in regulation after quarterback Johnny Unitas completed four straight passes. Baltimore won in overtime when fullback Alan Ameche scored a touchdown on a one-yard run.

TOM FEARS

Tom Fears joined the Los Angeles Rams as a wide receiver and tight end in 1948. He broke in with a splash, catching fifty-one passes for 698 yards in his rookie season. In each of his first three years, he led the National Football League in receptions. In 1950, during a game against the Green Bay Packers, Fears caught eighteen passes, setting an NFL record that remained unbroken for fifty years. For his career, he caught four hundred passes and gained an average of 13.5 yards per catch. After retiring as a player, Fears served as an assistant coach with the Rams and, later, the Green Bay Packers. He became the first head coach for the newly formed New Orleans Saints in 1967. Fears was elected to both the Pro Football and College Football Halls of Fame. He was diagnosed with Alzheimer's disease in 1994 and died on January 4, 2000.

As much as Tom Fears accomplished in football, perhaps his most heroic moments came as he was nearing death. As reported in *Sports Illustrated* magazine, Fears participated in a project in which all of the living members of the Pro Football Hall of Fame were asked to sign reproductions of specially commissioned portraits. The autographed pictures would then be sold. The sale would benefit the NFL Alumni Dire Needs Fund, a program established to help former pro football players who are indigent or disadvantaged.

Each day after Fears awoke, he would sit for an extended period and sign stacks of portraits depicting himself in uniform. At the time, Fears's memory had been ravaged by Alzheimer's. So, each day before beginning the autograph session, Fears would ask his wife, Luella, why he was signing the pictures. In response, Luella would tell her husband, day after day, that the autographed portraits were for the benefit of former players who needed help. Fears's response never varied. On each and every day, he made the same unequivocal commitment to help individuals in need.

Whatever the need, Fears responded. In 1949, fullback Paul "Tank" Younger joined the Los Angeles Rams as a rookie out of Grambling State University. Younger was the only African American on the team. Younger's presence raised the delicate question of whom the rookie would room with when the Rams traveled to away games. During a team meeting, the players were asked if anyone had a problem rooming with Younger. Before any other players could say anything, Fears shouted emphatically, "Hell no." His response left no opportunity for dissent. With the issue resolved, Fears became Younger's first roommate on the Rams.

◆   ◆   ◆

Yes, your wonders of old I will remember.
—Psalm 77, verse 12.

JUNIUS KELLOGG

Junius Kellogg was a six-foot-ten-inch basketball player from Portsmouth, Virginia. He was the youngest of eleven children in his family. In 1950, Kellogg became the first African American to play basketball at Manhattan College in New York. On January 11, 1951, as Manhattan was preparing to play DePaul University, a former teammate approached Kellogg and offered him one thousand dollars if he would make sure that Manhattan beat DePaul by less than the point spread. Kellogg immediately reported the bribe attempt to the Manhattan coach, who then informed the president of the college. In turn, the school reported the attempted bribe to the Manhattan district attorney. The incident prompted a police investigation, which uncovered a widespread conspiracy to fix the outcome of college basketball games, the so-called Scandals of 1951. Kellogg died on September 16, 1998.

Two factors caused the gamblers to pick Junius Kellogg as the focus of their efforts to fix the Manhattan–DePaul game. Kellogg was Manhattan's starting center and therefore was in a position to affect the outcome of the game by purposely missing a shot or failing to control a rebound. Equally important, Kellogg came from a poor family and could have used the money. Even so, the gamblers picked the wrong man. Kellogg would later tell reporters, "They said you could shave [points] and still win, but I knew it was dishonest."

Kellogg's honesty would come at a price. Police asked him to continue talks with the gamblers and secretly record the conversations. Kellogg was well aware that, by tipping off the police, he was going to hurt some people with whom he had been friends. As a result of Kellogg's cooperation, after the Manhattan-DePaul game, police arrested the former teammate who had made the bribe attempt. News of the arrest caused Kellogg to receive numerous death threats, both in the mail and over the phone. Ultimately, the investigation led to the arrest of thirteen more gamblers and twenty basketball players.

Kellogg gave credit to his father for guiding his actions. "My father would never have thought it was all right," he said. To celebrate Kellogg's integrity, the citizens of Portsmouth, Virginia, held a "Junius Kellogg Day" and presented

Kellogg with a check for one thousand dollars. Kellogg promptly gave the check to his mother.

After his college career, Kellogg played basketball with the Harlem Globetrotters. In April 1954, while touring with the Globetrotters, Kellogg was paralyzed from the waist down when a car in which he and other teammates were riding overturned. It took four years of therapy for Kellogg to recover the use of his hands. Undeterred by his paralysis, Kellogg became the player-coach for the Pan-Am Jets, a wheelchair basketball team that went on to win four international championships. Later, Kellogg worked for New York City as a deputy commissioner for community development. Kellogg used his position with the city to help handicapped individuals, especially children.

In 1992, Virginia Governor L. Douglas Wilder officially honored Kellogg as a Hero of the Commonwealth. When Kellogg died, his college roommate said of him, "Here's a guy who was dealt deuces and made aces out of them his whole life."

◆   ◆   ◆

Direct my heart toward your decrees and away from unjust gain.
—Psalm 119, verse 36.

JOHNNY BRIGHT

Johnny Bright, an African American, was born in the ghetto area of Fort Wayne, Indiana in 1930. He rose from poverty to become a celebrated running back and a community leader in Edmonton, Canada. An all-around athlete in high school, Bright attended Drake University on a basketball and track scholarship. His most prominent moments, however, occurred in football. As a junior, Bright set a collegiate record for total offense, gaining 1,232 yards running and 1,168 yards passing. Heading into his senior year, Bright was a preseason Heisman Trophy candidate. During a game between Drake and Oklahoma A&M on October 20, 1951, an opposing player viciously slugged Bright after an A&M coach had directed his players to "get that nigger." The punch broke Bright's jaw and caused him to miss most of three games. The so-called Johnny Bright incident was captured on film by a newspaper cameraman. The resulting sequence of pictures won the 1952 Pulitzer Prize for photography and appeared on the cover of Life *magazine. The Philadelphia Eagles selected Bright in the first round of the 1952 collegiate draft, but he chose to play in Canada. Bright starred for the Edmonton Eskimos for eleven seasons, during which he also earned a master's degree in education. After retiring from football, Bright embarked on a career as a public school coach and teacher. He died on December 14, 1983. At the time of his death, he was the principal of Hillcrest Junior High School in Edmonton.*

In 1980, nearly thirty years after the "Johnny Bright incident," Bright acknowledged that "the thing has been a great influence on my life." Ironically, over time, the incident prompted Bright to become more tolerant of others. "My total philosophy of life now is that, whatever a person's bias and limitation, they deserve respect. Everyone's entitled to their own beliefs."

The incident also influenced the way that Bright related to students, parents, and fellow teachers during his twenty-year career as an educator. Bright tried to learn from all of his experiences, good or bad. He encouraged his students to do the same. When speaking of his childhood dream of becoming a professional football player, he would tell others, "The things I've learned and experienced on the way to trying to achieve that dream would have been worthwhile by themselves."

When he taught at Bonnie Doon Composite High School in Edmonton, Bright also served as coach of the school's football, basketball, and baseball teams. At the end of each athletic season, Bright would send individual, handwritten letters to each athlete, whether first-string or bench warmer, who had played for him. It was Bright's way of thanking the students for the effort they had put in, and congratulating them on their accomplishments. Bright also used the letters to remind his athletes that their experiences in sports would help to prepare them for the challenges that would come later in life.

In one letter to a second-string end on the football team, Bright wrote,

> Lest I forget the thing that most impresses me about your achievements this year, let me get to them. Tom, in many ways an athletic event mirrors life—there are challenges, opportunities, tension, and small victories and losses.... The qualities you demonstrated this season will allow you to do well in school, accept the challenges of an honest life, and give you the perseverance to achieve your greatest dreams.

Reflecting on the significance of Bright's words, Tom Bledsoe, the recipient of the letter, once said, "The times in my life when I felt down or defeated, I turned to that letter and I remembered the qualities that Coach Bright saw in me. That helped me to … look forward to another day."

◆   ◆   ◆

You will shatter the jaws of all my foes; you will break the teeth of the wicked.
—Psalm 3, verse 8.

DAN TOWLER

From 1950 to 1955, "Deacon" Dan Towler was a hard-running 230-pound fullback for the Los Angeles Rams. Towler played his college football at Washington and Jefferson College in Pennsylvania. The Rams drafted him in the twenty-fifth round of the 1950 collegiate draft. He carried the ball sparingly for the Rams during the 1950 season, with most of the carries going to Dick Hoerner and former Army star Glenn Davis. The Rams installed Towler as the featured back in 1951. He responded by rushing for 854 yards and earning the first of his four Pro Bowl selections. For his career, Towler gained 3,943 yards on 672 rushing attempts. He died on August 1, 2001, at the age of seventy-three.

Fresh out of college, Daniel Lee Towler boarded a flight from Pennsylvania in the summer of 1950 to report to the Los Angeles Rams. If Towler didn't know what to expect, neither did the Rams. The team sent fullback Tank Younger to the airport to meet the rookie. When Towler's flight landed, Younger surveyed the incoming passengers, trying to identify the arriving football player. Minutes passed; Younger continued to search in vain. Finally, he found Towler, standing alone in the distance and carrying a Bible. Younger's world—a world in which football players did not carry Bibles—was about to change.

Towler and Younger teamed with veteran Dick Hoerner to form Los Angeles's famed "Bull Elephant" backfield. Before every game, Towler could be found absorbed in prayer. When asked about his routine, he explained, "I pray as if everything depends on God; then I go out and play as if everything depends upon me." Quietly, Towler also shared his faith with Younger and other teammates. He asked Joe Stydahar, the Rams' coach, if he could lead the team in a prayer before their games. Stydahar responded, "It sure wouldn't hurt anything and, who knows, it might help." With Deacon Dan leading the way, the Rams became the first National Football League team to pray before each game.

While playing for the Rams, Towler attended the University of Southern California's graduate school of religion and earned a master's degree in theology. He quit football after the 1955 season to become an ordained Methodist minister. For years, Towler ministered to the campus of the California State University, overseeing campus religious programs. He served as a member of the Los Angeles County Board of Education for twenty-six years. He was also a member of the Child Abuse Task Force of the California Senate and worked to promote child health and safety. He established a foundation that awarded thousands of dollars in scholarships to students.

On the day before his death, Towler went to visit a friend, long-time sportswriter Brad Pye, to see how Pye was doing and to bring him a health food supplement. The display of care and concern was vintage Towler. He was especially helpful to former teammates and to those who had lost their way, whether spiritually, financially, or emotionally. At his death, it was said that, wherever he found injustice, Towler tried to turn the situation into justice for all.

◆   ◆   ◆

The Lord secures justice for the oppressed, gives food to the hungry.
—Psalm 146, verse 7.

SAUL ROGOVIN

Saul Rogovin was a big league baseball player for eight years. Originally signed as an outfielder, Rogovin made it to the major leagues as a pitcher with the Detroit Tigers in 1949. After spending parts of three seasons with the Tigers, Rogovin signed with the Chicago White Sox in 1951. His best season came with the White Sox in 1952, when he won fourteen games and lost nine. He retired from baseball in 1957 with a career record of forty-eight wins and forty-eight losses. Rogovin died on January 23, 1995, at the age of seventy-one.

Saul Rogovin was thirty-three years old when he retired from baseball. He had lost his fastball but not his love for the game. For Rogovin, the adjustment to life after baseball was difficult. He was listless in his work, when he worked at all. For years, he was unable to watch baseball games in person. He yearned to visit his former clubs, to wear a uniform number on his back, to pitch a baseball, to once again be part of a team. Unable to keep company with teammates, he became a loner. For the better part of eighteen years, he struggled.

Not until he was in his fifties did Rogovin find a renewed purpose in life. At the age of fifty-one, he enrolled at Manhattan Community College. He studied. He grew. He even gained academic credit for being a former major-leaguer. When a dean at the college told him he would have to take a physical education course, Rogovin pulled out one of his Topps baseball cards. He persuaded the dean that his major-league career was an adequate substitute for the phys ed course. After two years, Rogovin transferred to the City College of New York, where he earned a bachelor's degree in English literature.

Rogovin went on to teach literature at an inner-city high school in Brooklyn. The experience filled a void. To the students, he imparted his knowledge of John Steinbeck and Ernest Hemingway. In return, the students infused Rogovin with their youthful enthusiasm. In helping to mold teenagers, Rogovin found the passion that had long eluded him.

◆   ◆   ◆

If you refuse to learn, you are hurting yourself.
—Proverbs 15, verse 32.

GIL HODGES

Gilbert Raymond Hodges spent seventeen years as a player in the major leagues, fifteen of them with the Dodgers. Before turning pro, he played third base at St. Joseph's College in Indiana, where he teamed with shortstop Frank Staucet to form one of the slickest fielding shortstop–third base combinations in college baseball. After military service with the Marines in World War II, Hodges joined the Dodgers as a catcher in 1947. The Dodgers shifted him to first base the next year. A key member of Brooklyn's "Boys of Summer" lineup, Hodges drove in more than one hundred runs every year from 1949 to 1955. He hit 370 home runs in his seventeen seasons, with a career best of forty homers in 1951. After his playing days, he managed both the Washington Senators and the New York Mets. Hodges led the 1969 "Miracle Mets" to victory over the Baltimore Orioles in the World Series. He died of a heart attack on April 2, 1972, at the age of forty-seven.

On the morning of Sunday, May 24, 1953, Father Herbert Redmond said the ten-o'clock Mass at Brooklyn's St. Francis Xavier Catholic Church. When Father Redmond finished the Gospel reading, he addressed the congregation. "It's too hot for a sermon today," he told his parishioners. "Go home, keep the commandments—and say a prayer for Gil Hodges."

Hodges was in a severe slump. He had gone to bat twenty-six times in the 1952 World Series without hitting the ball safely. The slump continued into 1953. Five weeks into the season, he was hitting .180. Puzzled and in distress, Hodges resorted to prayer. To his amazement, fans began to pray for him too. Just hours after Father Redmond's plea for prayers, Hodges hit two singles in five at bats against the Philadelphia Phillies. He hit over .400 in the week that followed, raising his batting average for the season to .254. By June 14, he reached the .300 mark.

Hodges was unique among players on the Dodgers. No matter how much he struggled and no matter how low his batting average fell, Brooklyn fans never booed him. They booed Duke Snider, they booed Carl Furillo. They never booed Gil Hodges. Teammate Roy Campanella explained, "They knew what kind of a man he was, so they never booed him."

Patient and understanding, Hodges was a mentor to other major-leaguers and a coach to small children. He sponsored Brooklyn's Gil Hodges Little League and appeared at hundreds of events for the benefit of children. He never accepted a fee for his time. When he became a manager, his primary concern was for the well-being of his players and their families. If a player's wife or children were ill, Hodges wanted the player to be at home, not at the ballpark.

Hodges lived every day with the thought that he was accountable for his actions. A devout Catholic, he adhered strictly to the requirement to abstain from eating meat on Fridays. After one road trip, the Dodgers flew home to Brooklyn on a Friday. The team was served steak on the plane. Hodges passed up the meal. A teammate suggested that Hodges was entitled to a dispensation because there was no other food available. Hodges could not be persuaded. "We're just a little bit too close to headquarters up here," he said.

◆   ◆   ◆

Lord, teach me the way of your laws; I shall observe them with care.
—Psalm 119, verse 33.

Brooklyn Dodgers Batting Records as of June 14, 1953

Player	AB	H	AVG.	Player	AB	H	AVG.
J. Robinson	189	66	.349	B. Morgan	52	14	.269
B. Cox	66	22	.333	J. Gilliam	217	57	.263
D. Snider	210	67	.319	G. Shuba	70	18	.257
C. Furillo	163	50	.307	D. Thompson	72	17	.236
G. Hodges	**170**	**51**	**.300**	R. Walker	21	4	.190
R. Campanella	188	55	.293	W. Belardi	16	3	.188
P. Reese	206	58	.282	B. Antonello	18	3	.167

ROY CAMPANELLA

There was a distinct pattern to the baseball career of Brooklyn Dodgers catcher Roy Campanella. Every other year, it seemed, he would win the National League's Most Valuable Player Award. He was MVP in 1951, 1953, and 1955. He enjoyed his finest season in 1953, when he batted .312 and hit forty-one home runs. He also drove in 142 runs, the highest in the league. "Campy" suffered a crushed vertebrae and broken neck on January 28, 1958, when he lost control of his car on an icy road. Doctors gave him virtually no chance of surviving. Though he never regained the use of his arms and legs, Campanella proved the doctors wrong and, in the process, became an inspiration to many. He died on June 26, 1993. He was seventy-one years old.

Fourteen months after Roy Campanella's accident, an elderly woman traveled from New York to Vero Beach, Florida, a trip of more than a thousand miles, to thank Roy Campanella for giving her hope. The woman had suffered a stroke shortly before Campanella's accident. She was recuperating at Glen Cove Community Hospital when the ambulance crew wheeled Campy in. The woman had lost the use of the limbs on her left side. She had also lost interest in living. When the woman saw Campanella's struggle to beat the odds, when she saw his determination to prove the doctors wrong, she decided to take up the fight also.

What the woman didn't know was that Campanella had experienced doubts of his own. In the days following his accident, he was feeling sorry for himself and questioning the value of spending the rest of his life in a wheelchair. One day, he gave a baseball to a little boy who was also hospitalized. Campanella apologized to the boy for not being able to autograph the ball, explaining that he could not move his arms. The boy told Campanella that he wouldn't be able to read the autograph anyway because he was blind.

Thankful for the gift of sight and thankful to be alive, Campanella stopped feeling sorry for himself, and began the process of transforming himself from baseball star to role model for the handicapped. As a ballplayer, Campanella was a hero to the borough of Brooklyn. As a quadriplegic with a near perpetual smile, he became a hero to individuals throughout the country. Campy also became an ambassador for baseball. He made frequent visits to schools to speak to children.

He talked to groups of handicapped individuals. He became an enthusiastic lecturer on the subject of Jackie Robinson's struggle to integrate the major leagues. He tutored young catchers in the Dodgers' farm system.

Campanella also spoke of his trust in God. He recalled that, in the days after his accident, he tried to move his legs, but there was no reaction. He tried to move his arms. Again, nothing happened. Then he turned to prayer. "I'm a good one for prayers," he said. "I prayed to the good Lord to let me accept whatever was happening."

Marty Adler, former assistant principal at the Jackie Robinson Intermediate School in Brooklyn, was one of many who formed a lasting friendship with Campanella. "He had a heart as big as his glove," Adler said.

◆   ◆   ◆

Lord, what future do I have?
—Psalm 39, verse 8.

JOE COLLINS

From 1950 to 1957, Joe Collins played first base for the New York Yankees in manager Casey Stengel's "platoon system." In the early years, Collins shared playing time with Johnny "The Big Cat" Mize. Mize, once a prolific National League slugger, was nearing the end of his playing career. From 1954 to 1957, Collins platooned with Bill "Moose" Skowron. Over the course of his career, in limited playing time, Collins put up creditable numbers. His best season came in 1952, when he played in 119 games at first base and batted .280, with eighteen home runs and fifty-nine runs batted in. Collins died on August 30, 1989.

By 1954 Johnny Mize was gone, his stellar fifteen-year major league career finished. In spring training of that year, the Yankees were looking at rookie Bill Skowron as their first baseman of the future. Skowron was no stranger to big-time athletics, having playing varsity football for Purdue University before signing with the Yankees. Nonetheless, Skowron was feeling considerable pressure. As usual, the Yankees had assembled an impressive array of talented ballplayers for spring training. Early on, it became clear to Skowron that, in order to secure a roster spot and earn any appreciable playing time, he would have to show well in the competition with Joe Collins.

Over the course of the previous four seasons, Collins had proven himself to be a dependable cog in the Yankees' lineup. Adding to the pressure facing Skowron was the fact that Casey Stengel was notoriously slow to make rookies feel welcome. Sensing Skowron's discomfort, Joe Collins took the rookie aside early in spring training and explained his approach in dealing with the awkward aspects of their competition for the first-base job. Collins told Skowron, "Bill, we'll work together. I'll pray for you when you're playing. And when I'm playing, I hope you'll pray for me."

The prayers proved fruitful. Both went on to enjoy productive seasons in 1954, with Collins playing 113 games at first base and Skowron playing sixty-one. In 215 at-bats that season, Skowron batted .340 with seven home runs. The Moose played thirteen more years in the big leagues, developing into a feared clutch hitter. In contrast, after the 1954 season, both Collins's prowess at bat and his playing time declined markedly, the end of his career hastened by Skowron's emergence. Collins retired after the 1957 season.

◆   ◆   ◆

In the morning, my prayer comes before you.
—Psalm 88, verse 14.

HANK BAUER

Henry Albert "Hank" Bauer played in the major leagues for fourteen years, twelve of them with the New York Yankees. Before beginning his baseball career, Bauer served with the Marines in World War II and was involved in the invasion of Okinawa. He joined the Yankees as an outfielder in 1948 at the age of twenty-six. The next year he became a regular member of manager Casey Stengel's rotation in right field, platooning with Gene Woodling. From 1949 to 1958, Bauer appeared in nine World Series with the Yankees, and was named to the American League all-star team three times. After his playing days, Bauer managed the Baltimore Orioles and led the team to a four-game sweep of the Los Angeles Dodgers in the 1966 World Series. He died on February 9, 2007, at the age of eighty-four.

Outfielder and catcher Elston Howard made the New York Yankees' roster out of spring training in 1955, becoming the first African American ever to play for the Yankees. As was the case with Jackie Robinson and other ballplayers who broke the color barrier, Howard was a frequent target of abuse from individuals in the stands. During one game at Yankee Stadium in Howard's rookie season, a fan sitting behind the Yankee dugout began yelling particularly hateful racial insults. When the fan showed no sign of stopping his crude comments, Hank Bauer crawled on top of the dugout and glared into the stands, trying to identify the source of the abuse. Bauer remained on top of the dugout for a long period, hoping the heckler would yell one more time.

Wisely, the heckler remained silent, and Bauer returned to the dugout. When the game was over, a reporter asked Bauer about his efforts to protect Howard. Bauer shrugged his shoulders and said simply, "Ellie's my friend."

◆　　　◆　　　◆

He who is a friend is always a friend.
—Proverbs 17, verse 17.

JIM WILLIAMS

During the 1930s through the 1950s, Jim Williams was a teacher and coach at prep schools in Pennsylvania and Delaware. He was the father of Pat Williams, a former professional baseball player and, more recently, the general manager of the Orlando Magic pro basketball team. Together with Bob Carpenter, one-time owner of the Philadelphia Phillies, Jim Williams founded Delaware's Annual Blue-Gold High School Football All-Star Game, pitting players from the northern half of Delaware against those from the south. Jim Williams died in 1962 in an automobile accident.

Bob Carpenter and Jim Williams were linked by a common bond. Both were the parents of children who were afflicted with cognitive disabilities. Williams's daughter, Mary Ellen, was born with Down syndrome. To promote awareness of mental retardation, Carpenter and Williams worked together to form the Delaware Foundation Reaching Citizens with Cognitive Disabilities, a non-profit organization that sponsors Delaware's annual Blue-Gold High School Football All-Star Game. The All-Star Game is dedicated to raising funds for citizens afflicted with cognitive disabilities. Since its inception, the game has raised millions of dollars for the mentally handicapped and has benefited thousands of children.

Under the direction of Williams and Carpenter, the first Blue-Gold All-Star Game was played on August 25, 1956. For two weeks preceding that game, players from high schools in the northern part of the state trained at Sanford Prep School, near the city of Wilmington. Two players on the North squad, Joe Peters and Alvin Hall, were African American. Concerned that some of Sanford's students might be prejudiced, the school's headmaster forbade the two players from staying with their white teammates in the Sanford dormitories. Peters and Hall were allowed on campus for the daily practice sessions but, with nightfall, had to leave the school grounds.

Jim Williams acted quickly to fill the void. "If they have to stay off campus," he told his son Pat, "let them stay at our house." For two weeks, Peters and Hall found sleeping accommodations, as well as warmth and understanding, in the Williams's household.

WILLIAMS 133

◆   ◆   ◆

Happy are those who dwell in your house!
—Psalm 84, verse 5.

MICKEY MANTLE

In the 1950s and 1960s, Mickey Charles Mantle, the son of an Oklahoma lead miner, was the most prominent athlete—if not the most prominent person—in all of New York City. Scores of New Yorkers looked upon Mantle as an icon, but all he wanted to be was a ballplayer. He played center field for the New York Yankees from 1951 to 1966, and then closed out his career as the Yankee first baseman for two seasons. Mantle hit .298 with 536 home runs in his eighteen seasons in the big leagues. His best year came in 1956, when he won the American League Triple Crown with a batting average of .353, fifty-two home runs, and 130 runs batted in. He died on August 13, 1995, at the age of sixty-three.

The day after Mickey Mantle died, the *Dallas Morning News* published a cartoon depicting Saint Peter escorting Mantle around heaven. The caption showed Saint Peter telling Mantle, "Kid, that was the most courageous ninth inning I've ever seen."

Mantle readily admitted that his first "eight innings" left a lot to be desired. "Don't be like me," he would say. His father, his uncles, and his grandfather all died before reaching the age of forty. Mantle expected the same fate. He often commented that if he knew he was going to live past forty, he would have taken better care of himself.

Yankee second baseman Bobby Richardson once threw a party at his house and invited all of his teammates. For Mantle, the party promised to be a rare evening without alcoholic beverages. Richardson had made it clear that he did not serve alcohol at his house. When the evening was over, Mantle told Richardson that he never knew a party without alcoholic beverages could be so much fun.

In June 1995, Mantle underwent a seven-hour liver transplant operation. A month later, doctors found evidence of cancer in Mantle's lungs. While Mantle was dealing with the effects of the liver transplant and the cancer, Richardson and other former teammates were a source of constant comfort. On one occasion, Mantle called Richardson and asked for prayers. It was one of the few times that Richardson had ever heard Mantle talk of prayer. Shortly thereafter, when Richardson visited the hospital, Mantle announced that he had become a Christian. "I want you to know that I've received Christ as my Savior," Mantle told Richardson. In response, Richardson asked Mantle why God should let him into heaven. Mantle answered, "For God so loved the world that He gave his only begotten son."

There was another reason to let Mantle into heaven—his "ninth inning." In the year before his death, Mantle made a concerted effort to help others. He worked with Bobby Murcer, a former teammate, to raise money for victims of the April 1995 bombing of the Alfred P. Murrah Federal Building in Oklahoma City. Mantle also ran charity golf tournaments in Oklahoma to benefit the Make-A-Wish Foundation. When he was in Dallas, he would spend entire days on a par three hole at the Preston Trail Golf Club in North Dallas and challenge other golfers to hit closer to the pin. Participants would pay a ten-dollar entry fee, which Mantle would then donate to charity. In the days following his liver transplant, Mantle formed the Mickey Mantle Foundation to raise money for organ and tissue donations. He explained, "I've got to give something back. I think God had a purpose for letting me have this extra time." In short order, the Mantle Foundation arranged to distribute organ donor cards to fans at all major league baseball parks throughout the country. More than eight million donor cards were distributed through the foundation. In the words of sportswriter Robert Lypsyte, "Just before he died, Mickey Mantle gave us a reason to love him."

◆   ◆   ◆

Remember no more the sins of my youth; remember me only in light of your love.
—Psalm 25, verse 7.

BYRON "MEX" JOHNSON

Byron Johnson was an all-star baseball player in the Negro Leagues, as well as a teacher, soldier, postal worker, and popular lecturer. Born in Little Rock, Arkansas, on September 16, 1911, Johnson was known as "Mex" because he wore a sombrero-like hat as a child. As a high school student, Johnson played quarterback for Little Rock's Dunbar High School and led his team to the state championship. From 1937 to 1940, he played shortstop for the Kansas City Monarchs of the Negro American League. Johnson possessed an exceptional arm and, as a fielder, was said to be the equal of St. Louis Cardinals Hall-of-Famer Ozzie Smith. Johnson retired from baseball after the 1940 season to teach biology at Dunbar and devote more time to his family. He was inducted into the Army in 1942 and participated in the Allied landing at Normandy in June 1944. Johnson died on September 25, 2005, at the age of ninety-four.

In September 1957, Carlotta Walls, the niece of Byron "Mex" Johnson, was poised to enter Central High School in Little Rock, Arkansas. From that period on, Carlotta would forever be known as one of the Little Rock Nine, the name given to the group of nine black students selected to integrate previously all-white Central High. With widespread rioting in Little Rock and with members of the Arkansas National Guard blocking the entrance to Central High, Carlotta and the other black students missed the first three weeks of the school year. On September 25th, the Little Rock Nine were allowed into the school, but only because President Dwight D. Eisenhower had sent the Army's 101st Airborne Division to displace the National Guard troops and restore a measure of calm.

While Carlotta was at school, individual soldiers walked with her to ensure her safety. However, the task of protecting Carlotta on the way to and from school fell to Mex Johnson. The drive between Carlotta's home and Central High took Johnson and his niece through packs of angry white rioters. The rioters would routinely stand in the way of Johnson's automobile, blocking his path, and then start rocking the car back and forth. In the words of Johnson's daughter, who would sometimes ride in the car with Carlotta, "It was terrifying."

Throughout the terror, Johnson never gave up—and he didn't let Carlotta give up either. When Carlotta missed classes, Johnson would tutor her and help her with her homework. As a result of the guidance of Johnson and others, Carlotta was one of only two students from the original Little Rock Nine to graduate from Central High.

Johnson's influence extended far beyond his niece. He volunteered his time for church youth activities and coached youths of all ages in baseball and other sports. Johnson also donated sports equipment for youth leagues, making it possible for many children to participate in organized sports.

Late in life, Johnson became instrumental in helping to educate college students and others about the history of the Negro Leagues. He delivered lectures as part of a curriculum at Metropolitan State College in Denver. Speaking of Johnson's lectures, a Metropolitan State professor said, "My students were captivated. Negro League baseball was ... well, invisible. Byron brought it to life, they loved him." Johnson's energy and engaging style played a key role in establishing what became known as "The Byron and Christine Johnson Lecture Series."

According to Don Baylor, former manager of the Colorado Rockies, Johnson believed to his core in giving back. Said Baylor, "Byron rarely shunned an opportunity to transfer his knowledge to the persons most in need of a role model: our youth."

Acknowledging the role that Mex Johnson played in and out of baseball, former President William Clinton called Johnson "a pioneer, paving the way for African Americans to enjoy equal rights and equal opportunities."

◆   ◆   ◆

Even with thousands of people arrayed against me on every side, I do not fear.
—Psalm 3, verse 7.

MAURICE STOKES

Standing six feet seven inches tall, Maurice "Mo" Stokes was an outstanding basketball player at every level. As a high school player in Pittsburgh, he helped his Westinghouse High School team win consecutive city championships in 1950 and 1951. He then played four years at Pennsylvania's St. Francis College and earned second-team All-American honors in his senior season. Stokes joined the Rochester Royals of the National Basketball Association in the fall of 1955 and was an immediate sensation, scoring thirty-two points and collecting twenty rebounds in his first game. He was named the NBA's Rookie-of-the-Year for the 1955–56 season, and was selected for the NBA's all-star team in each of his first three years. In the last regular season game of the 1957–58 season, while playing for the Cincinnati Royals, the twenty-four-year-old Stokes fell to the court, hit his head, and was knocked unconscious. Three days later, he fell into a coma. He regained consciousness after several weeks, but was left permanently paralyzed. Stokes died on April 6, 1970. He was thirty-six years old.

The last twelve years of Maurice Stokes's life presented a profound test of his faith, courage, and fortitude. Stokes had suffered post-traumatic encephalopathy, an injury that damaged his motor control center and left him a quadriplegic.

In the first years after his injury, Stokes had no use of his hands, arms, and legs. His only means of communicating was by blinking his eyes. There was ample reason for Stokes to give up, but he refused to quit. From the time he regained consciousness until the day he died, he fought to overcome his paralysis. Confined to Cincinnati's Good Samaritan Hospital, he endured painful physical therapy sessions in the hope of again being able to use his limbs. In a painstaking process, he communicated with his court-appointed guardian, former teammate Jack Twyman, by blinking his eyes. Twyman would slowly recite the letters of the alphabet. When Twyman pronounced a letter that Stokes needed to form a word, Stokes would blink his eyes. Character after character, word after word, Stokes expressed his thoughts, concerns, and appreciation to Twyman.

While Twyman's help was indispensable to Stokes, Twyman himself gained immeasurably from the relationship. "To see the way he conducted himself, I just stood in awe of him," Twyman said. "It got so bad, when I would be having a bad day myself, I would go to see Maurice, selfishly, to say, I want to get pumped up. And he never failed to pump me up." Twyman saw up close what others saw from a distance—Stokes never let his paralysis dull his zest for life or his spirit.

Through incremental and incredibly small advances in his condition, Stokes reached a stage where he was able to move, minimally, his limbs and joints. Sweating profusely, Stokes endured hours of therapy and was eventually able to take small steps in the hospital hallway using braces, with nurses supporting his torso. Although it was difficult to control the movement of his fingers, Stokes learned to type, paint, and even make pottery. It was his intense effort that made a lasting impression on those who knew him.

After Stokes died, *New York Post* columnist Milton Gross wrote, "Stokes lived as a symbol of the best that a man is, despite the terrible things which can happen to him. He was a beautiful man who believed that surrender was not the way, even though he couldn't walk, couldn't talk, except agonizingly." Those who spent time with Stokes found their visits to be both inspiring and therapeutic. "I'd go and spend thirty minutes with Maurice and leave feeling like a million bucks," Twyman said.

Despite his physical limitations, Stokes was able to clearly convey his sense of humor. In the words of Milton Gross, "Stokes laughed when he should have cried."

◆   ◆   ◆

Those who trust in the Lord are unshakable, forever enduring.
—Psalm 125, verse 1.

MEL OTT

Melvin Thomas Ott joined the New York Giants as a seventeen-year-old in 1926. Standing five feet nine inches tall and weighing 170 pounds, Ott was small of stature but a gifted baseball player nonetheless. He played for the Giants for twenty-two years, without ever spending a day in the minor leagues. Ott hit 511 home runs during his career. When he retired, he held the National League records for total home runs, runs batted in, runs scored, total bases, and extra base hits. He died on November 21, 1958.

Noted author and baseball authority Arnold Hano described Ott as "a little man with a bashful smile and a silken swing, baseball's legendary nice guy." The "silken swing" produced a total of 1,071 extra base hits during Ott's career. Baseball Hall-of-Famer Stan Musial, who would end his career with 1,377 extra base hits, remembers that when he had passed one thousand extra base hits and was closing in on Ott's record, Ott encouraged Musial to keep going. For Ott, displaying good sportsmanship was more important than preserving individual records. At his 1969 induction into the Hall of Fame, Musial said, "When my records fall, I hope I am as gracious as Ottie was." Hall of Fame manager Casey Stengel said of Ott, "He never had an enemy, and I never heard him speak bad about anyone."

In 1951, when it was announced that Ott had been elected to the baseball Hall of Fame, he was not immediately available to give his reaction because he was visiting patients at a Louisiana leprosarium. He spent his time visiting veterans' hospitals as well. "These fellows need to see a friendly face to tide them over the bad days," Ott would say to his wife. He was also fond of visiting children in hospitals in the New Orleans area and would often take young patients outside to play catch with them. According to fellow Giant Lefty O'Doul, Ott was "one of the finest men I have ever met."

◆   ◆   ◆

He who refreshes others will himself be refreshed.
—Proverbs 11, verse 25.

PRENTICE GAUTT

Prentice Gautt was an honor student and outstanding halfback at Oklahoma City's Douglass High School in the mid-1950s. During Gautt's senior year of high school, Oklahoma University football coach Bud Wilkinson paid particular attention to Gautt's exploits in football and his conduct off the field. Wilkinson had been Oklahoma's head coach since 1947. Under his leadership, the Sooners won national championships in 1950 and 1955. However, Oklahoma had never had an African American football player. In Wilkinson's view, Gautt possessed the strength, character, and intellect necessary to successfully integrate Oklahoma's team. Gautt enrolled at the university in the fall of 1956. He played varsity football from 1957 to 1959. In the 1959 Orange Bowl, he averaged 15.7 yards per carry, the highest average ever by an Oklahoma player in any bowl game. After completing his college career, Gautt played in the National Football League from 1960 to 1967, primarily as an all-purpose running back for the St. Louis Cardinals. He gained 2,466 yards in eight pro seasons, averaging 3.9 yards per attempt. Gautt died suddenly on March 17, 2005, after being hospitalized for flu-like symptoms. He was sixty-seven years old.

As the first black player for Oklahoma University's storied football team, Prentice Gautt carried a heavy burden. Entering the 1957 season, the Sooners had won forty straight games, the longest winning streak in the history of major college football. The team proceeded to win its first seven games of 1957, extending the record to forty-seven games. On November 16th, Oklahoma put its winning streak on the line in a game against Notre Dame. The Fighting Irish were led by fullback Nick Pietrosante, halfback Dick Lynch, and other future NFL stars. Lynch scored the only touchdown of the game, leading Notre Dame to a 7–0 victory. Oklahoma fans pinned blame for the defeat on Gautt. When Bud Wilkinson announced that he was awarding Gautt a football scholarship, several veteran Sooners had quit the team in protest. The common perception among fans was that the defections had left the team ill-equipped to beat a powerhouse such as Notre Dame. Gautt became a convenient scapegoat, both for the loss to Notre Dame and for the end of the team's forty-seven-game winning streak.

Off the football field, Gautt's life was not significantly easier. The threat of physical violence was ever-present. As Gautt began his sophomore year at Oklahoma, African American high school students in the neighboring state of Arkansas were forcibly prevented from attending classes at Little Rock's Central High School. To Gautt, the violence in Little Rock was one of many constant reminders that he was different from other students. When he traveled to away games, he was subjected to threats and was routinely denied admission to restaurants and hotels. On campus, his social life was non-existent. He had to avoid walking to and from classes with white female classmates, for fear of creating controversy. If he even attempted to talk to a white coed, he risked hateful comments or worse. "I felt like half a person," he would say, years later.

In spite of the ordeal, Gautt flourished. He was named All-Big Eight Conference running back two years in a row and selected as the Most Valuable Player of the 1959 Orange Bowl. He also excelled in the classroom and was named to the collegiate academic All-American team. Teammate Jakie Sandefer, who roomed with Gautt on road trips, once commented on the reasons for Gautt's success. "He had more class than the rest of us, and he was smarter than the rest of us," Sandefer said. "None of the rest of us could even spell biology, and he was majoring in it." Oklahoma University athletic director Joe Castiglione offered a different perspective. "This guy oozed leadership qualities," Castiglione said, "and yet he was the most humble person."

After retiring from professional football, Gautt became an assistant coach at the University of Missouri and simultaneously pursued postgraduate studies. He eventually earned a doctorate in counseling psychology. In 1979, Gautt joined the staff of the Big Eight Conference as an assistant commissioner. In that position, he developed a model Life Skills program aimed at improving the academic performance of athletes and helping former players adjust to life after sports.

Prentice Gautt was a pioneer. His graceful response to hostility paved the way for a steady influx of black students at Oklahoma University. His pioneering work in developing a Life Skills program for student-athletes led to a more widespread commitment among colleges and universities to making sure that student-athletes were prepared for life away from the playing fields.

◆   ◆   ◆

The just shall flourish like the palm tree.
—Psalm 92, verse 13.

JOHNNY UNITAS

John Unitas rose from obscurity to become the best National Football League quarter-back of his era. In 1956, one year removed from playing semi-pro for the Bloomfield Rams at six dollars a game, Unitas became a starter for the Baltimore Colts. He was at quarterback when the Colts came from behind to defeat the New York Giants in sudden-death overtime in the 1958 NFL championship game at Yankee Stadium. In front of a TV audience of more than forty million people, Unitas led the Colts to a field goal late in the fourth quarter to tie the game. On the Colts' first possession in overtime, Unitas directed a scoring drive that culminated in a one-yard game-win-ning touchdown run by Alan Ameche. The game is commonly recognized as the great-est game in the history of pro football. Unitas died on September 11, 2002, at the age of sixty-nine.

According to Baltimore sportswriter John Steadman, Johnny Unitas never met a cause he didn't want to help. He went to visit U.S. troops in Germany and Vietnam, took the lead in the effort to locate soldiers who were missing in action, and spearheaded campaigns against cystic fibrosis, prostate cancer, and child abuse.

Cardinal William Keeler, archbishop of Baltimore, officiated at the funeral service for Unitas. Cardinal Keeler spoke of the Hall-of-Fame quarterback as a "man who would shake the hand of a homeless person and say that it was an honor for him to shake that man's hand."

When he played for the Colts, Unitas would stay at Baltimore's Memorial Sta-dium long after the games were over to sign autographs for fans. On one occa-sion, his young daughter, Paige, watched silently as her father signed every football, autograph book, and scrap of paper handed to him. Paige grew increas-ingly impatient with all the autograph seekers. Finally, her patience exhausted, she let her father know that she wanted to go home. Unitas took hold of his daughter's hands and told her, "It takes so little to make someone smile."

◆   ◆   ◆

Happy those who do what is right, whose deeds are always just.
—Psalm 106, verse 3.

ALAN AMECHE

Alan "the Horse" Ameche was a hard-running fullback from the University of Wisconsin. In 1954, he had an outstanding senior season at Wisconsin and won college football's Heisman Trophy. He was a first-round draft pick of the Baltimore Colts in 1955. Until his career was cut short by injuries, Ameche was one of the toughest and most versatile running backs in the National Football League. He was rookie-of-the-year in 1955 and was named All-Pro for four consecutive years, from 1955 to 1958. In his five-year career, he ran for 4,045 yards and scored forty touchdowns, including the dramatic sudden-death touchdown that won the 1958 NFL championship game for Baltimore. Ameche died on August 8, 1988. He was fifty-five.

Upon entering the chapel at the Loyola Retreat House in Faulkner, Maryland, a Jesuit priest saw a lone man kneeling in the dim light cast by a single flickering candle. The priest moved about quietly, so as not to disturb the individual. As the priest drew closer, he recognized the prayerful man as Alan Ameche, football player, successful businessman, and man of charity.

It was not unusual for people to find Ameche in unexpected places. When the Horse ended his senior season at the University of Wisconsin as the all-time leading runner in the history of college football, fans in his hometown of Kenosha, Wisconsin scheduled a banquet in his honor. As the festivities started, the banquet chairman directed the attendees to take their seats. When the assembly came to order, the chairman noticed that Ameche's seat at the head table was vacant. In a mild panic, the chairman asked some assistants to track down Wisconsin's most famous citizen. They found him elsewhere in the banquet hall, playing cards with an elderly shoemaker.

After his playing days, Ameche entered the fast-food business with former Colts teammate Gino Marchetti. The two launched a chain of Gino's Restaurants. At its height, the company owned 365 outlets. The venture earned Ameche a profit of twenty million dollars and enabled him to retire at the age of thirty-six. As Ameche stood on the brink of retirement, a friend asked what he was going to do with his free time. Ameche answered, "If I could help just one individual in the rest of my life, I would consider that I accomplished something significant."

Working in his typically quiet manner, Ameche found a way to help scores of individuals. Once a former Colts teammate, Jim Mutscheller, asked Ameche for help in raising money for a local community center. Ameche met with Mutscheller to review the plans for the center. At the end of the meeting, Ameche said he would be willing to help out. Mutscheller asked, "What amount?" Ameche replied, "Put me down for fifty thousand dollars."

Ameche bought a row of slum properties in Philadelphia, bulldozed all the buildings, built a park, and donated the land to the city. He started a program to arrange educational grants for inner-city children in Philadelphia and Baltimore. The park and the educational grants represented Ameche's most visible efforts. The Horse's other charitable activities were unknown to all but a few confidants. Art Donovan, teammate and friend, remarked, "The things he would do for people, out of the goodness of his heart, were amazing."

◆   ◆   ◆

Majestic and glorious is your work, your wise design endures forever.
—Psalm 111, verse 3.

References

Tom Fears

Steve Bisheff, "Tom Fears, 1922–2000, Catch Became Fears' Legacy," *Orange County Register*, 6 January 2000, D1.

Frank Litsky, "Obituary: Tom Fears," *Pittsburgh Post-Gazette*, 9 January 2000, E5.

"Saints' First Coach Was Hall-of-Famer, Dies at 77," (New Orleans) *Times-Picayune*, 6 January 2000, D3.

"Funeral for Tom Fears Wednesday," *Orange County Register*, 11 January 2000, D9.

Junius Kellogg

Filip Bondy, "New York Loses True Sports Hero," *New York Daily News*, 18 September 1998, 100.

Jay Lidington, "'Portsmouth Family' Remembers the Moral Giant, Junius Kellogg," (Norfolk) *Virginian-Pilot*, 27 September 1998, 10.

"Junius Kellogg; Character Wins," (Norfolk) *Virginian-Pilot*, 27 September 1998, J4.

"Kellogg's Moment, Life Defined Integrity," *Richmond Times-Dispatch*, 29 September 1998, E1.

"Statement by Mayor Giuliani on the Death of Junius Kellogg," Press Office for the Mayor of the City of New York, 17 September 1998, http://nyc.gov/html/om/html/98b/pr438-98.html.

Johnny Bright

Barrett, Warrick Lee, M.D. *Johnny Bright, Champion*. Lincoln, NE: iUniverse, 2000.

Dan Towler

Earl Gustkey, "'Deacon' Dan Towler, 73, Dies; Rams All-Pro Back, Minister," 4 August 2001, B6.

Brad Pye, Jr., "Remembering Deacon Dan Towler," *Los Angeles Sentinel*, 15 August 2001, B1.

Saul Rogovin

Ralph Berger, "Saul Rogovin," *The Baseball Biography Project*, The Society of American Baseball Research (SABR), http://bioproj.sabr.org.

Gil Hodges

Amoruso, Marino. *Gil Hodges, The Quiet Man.* Middlebury, VT: Paul S. Ericksson Publisher, 1991.

Ed Fitzgerald. *Champions in Sport and Spirit.* New York: Vision Books, 1956.

Roy Campanella

Campanella, Roy. *It's Good to Be Alive.* Boston: Little, Brown and Company, 1959.

Joe Gergen, "Campy Always Had Spirit," *Newsday*, 29 June 1993, 135.

Dick Heller, "Crash Ruined Campy's Body But Not Spirit," *The Washington Times*, 24 January 2005, C9.

"Campanella's Heroic Life," *Orange County Register*, 29 June 1993, B6.

"Dodgers' Campanella Remembered As 'Man Who Set Great Example'," *Seattle Times*, 1 July 1993, C7.

"Friends Say So Long to Campy," *Chicago Sun-Times*, 1 July 1993, 90.

"Campanella's Personality, Grace Inspired Millions," *Austin American Statesman*, 1 July 1993, C5.

Joe Collins

Golenbock, Peter. *Dynasty: The New York Yankees, 1949–1964.* Englewood Cliffs, NJ: Prentice-Hall, Inc., 1975.

Hank Bauer

> Golenbock, Peter. *Dynasty: The New York Yankees, 1949–1964.* Englewood Cliffs, NJ: Prentice-Hall, Inc., 1975.

Jim Williams

> Williams, Pat and James D. Denny. *Ahead of the Game: The Pat Williams Story.* Grand Rapids, MI: Fleming H. Revell, 1999.

Mickey Mantle

> Castro, Tony. *Mickey Mantle: America's Prodigal Son.* Washington, D.C.: Potomac Books, Inc., 2002.

> Jeffrey Weiss, "Mantle Foundation To Aid Awareness of Organ Donation," *Dallas Morning News*, 23 January 2006.

Byron "Mex" Johnson

> Sumner, Jan. *Legacy of a Monarch: An American Journey.* Denver: Jadan Publishing, 2005.

Maurice Stokes

> Bob Carter, "Stokes' Life a Tale of Tragedy and Friendship," *Sports Century Biography*, http://espn.go.com./classic/biography/s/stokes_maurice.html, 2006.

> Chuck Finder, "Labor of Love Assures Memory of Stokes Lives On," *Pittsburgh Post-Gazette*, 11 April 2004, http://post-gazette.com/pg/04102/298980.stm.

> Chuck Finder, "At Long Last, Stokes in Hall of Fame," *Pittsburgh Post-Gazette*, 11 September 2004, B1.

> Dave Mackall, "Stokes Lauded As Hall of Fame Induction Nears," *Pittsburgh Tribune-Review*, 8 April 2004.

> Jon Paul Morosi, "He Touched the Stars, and Now He Joins Them," (Albany, NY) *Times Union*, September 11, 2004, C1.

> Lonnie Wheeler, "Stokes Was Special," *Cincinnati Post*, 19 February 2004, B1.

Mel Ott

Hano, Arnold. *Greatest Giant of Them All.* New York: G.P. Putnam's Sons, 1967.

Stein, Fred. *Mel Ott: The Little Giant of Baseball.* Jefferson, NC: McFarland & Co., Inc., 1999.

Prentice Gautt

John E. Hoover, "Former Sooner Standout Gautt Dies," *Tulsa World,* 18 March 2005, B1.

"Prentice Gautt," *Tulsa World,* 19 March 2005, A20.

"Prentice Gautt, Ushered in Oklahoma Football Era," *Newsday,* 18 March 2005, A66.

"Sad Day for Sooners," *Tulsa World,* 17 March 2005, MM.

"Prentice Gautt Just Wanted to Play Football and Get An Education—Then Fate Took Him By the Hand," http://oufoundation. org/sm/spring2005/prologue.asp?ID=156.

Johnny Unitas

William Gildea, "In Baltimore, No. 19 Receives A No. 1 Salute," *The Washington Post,* 18 September 2002, D1.

Sean Kirst, "Unitas Never Lost Common Touch," *The (Syracuse) Post-Standard,* 14 October 2002, B1.

Mike Klingaman, "The Mix That Made Him Great; To Get the Most Out of His Golden Arm, Unitas Combined Intelligence, Poise, Leadership, Confidence and Sheer Will to Create A Legend," *The (Baltimore) Sun,* 20 October 2002, 6U.

John Steadman, "Unitases Take Anti-Abuse Fight Personally," *The (Baltimore) Sun,* 19 March 2000, 4E.

Alan Ameche

Mark Hyman, "Teammates Say That Ameche's Greatness Went Beyond Football," *Los Angeles Times,* 14 August 1988, 2.

Thomas Rogers, "Alan Ameche, 55, Football Star Who Helped Colts Win '58 Title," *The New York Times*, 10 August 1988, B8.

"Obituary: Alan Ameche, Football Star Known for Big TD," *The (Toronto) Globe and Mail*, 11 August 1988, C8.

"Old Pal Braatz Testifies to Ameche's Fine Spirit," *Chicago Sun-Times*, 14 August 1988, 92.

1960–1969

1960–1969

In 1960, Democratic nominee John F. Kennedy narrowly defeated incumbent Republican vice president Richard Nixon in the Presidential election. In his inaugural address, Kennedy told Americans to "ask not what your country can do for you, but what you can do for your country."

Five months into Kennedy's administration, the South faced a growing crisis. State and local police in Alabama refused to stop Ku Klux Klan-inspired violence against groups of black and white "Freedom Riders," who were challenging state-ordered segregation on buses. In May 1961, Kennedy sent four hundred U.S. marshals to Alabama, under the leadership of Deputy Attorney General Byron R. White, to protect against violence. The federal marshals entered Montgomery, Alabama, the site of the most violent Klan activity, and restored peace.

New York Yankee outfielder Roger Maris hit his sixty-first home run on the last day of the regular season in 1961, breaking the previous mark of sixty homers set in 1927 by Babe Ruth. Also in 1961, Syracuse University running back Ernie Davis won college football's prestigious Heisman Trophy, becoming the first African American ever to win the award. In March 1963, Dr. Martin Luther King, Jr. and an estimated two hundred and fifty thousand others participated in the March on Washington in support of the civil rights movement. The march featured King's legendary "I Have a Dream" speech. On November 22, 1963, President Kennedy was assassinated during a motorcade procession in Dallas, Texas. Vice President Lyndon B. Johnson was sworn in as president.

In 1964, the St. Louis Cardinals defeated the New York Yankees, four games to three, to win the World Series. St. Louis third baseman Ken Boyer hit two home runs during the Series, one a grand slam, and made several key defensive plays to lead the Cardinals to victory.

President Johnson authorized the first bombing raids in the war against insurgents in South Vietnam in 1965. The bombing signaled an increased presence by the United States in Vietnam, and coincided with a dramatic increase in the level of American soldiers stationed in Southeast Asia.

In June 1968, Democratic presidential candidate Robert Kennedy, brother of the former president, was assassinated in Los Angeles during a campaign stop, leaving the Democratic nomination to Hubert H. Humphrey. In September

1968, Arthur Ashe won the U.S. Open tennis championship at Forest Hills. Richard Nixon narrowly defeated Humphrey in the presidential election later that year, to become the country's thirty-seventh president.

FLOYD PATTERSON

Born on January 4, 1935, Floyd Patterson was raised in Brooklyn, New York, in a family of eleven children. He took up boxing at the Wiltwyck School for Boys during his teenage years. By the time he was seventeen, Patterson was a five-foot-eleven-inch 180-pounder with exceptionally quick feet and a powerful punch. He won the middleweight gold medal at the 1952 Helsinki Olympics and turned pro shortly after. On November 30, 1956, the twenty-one-year-old Patterson defeated Archie Moore in a heavyweight title fight to become the youngest heavyweight champ in history. Patterson lost the crown to Sweden's Ingemar Johansson in 1959. The fight was stopped after Johansson knocked Patterson down seven times in the third round. Based largely on the Johansson fight, it was said that Patterson was knocked down more times over the course of his career than any other fighter. Patterson did not disagree. "But I also got up the most," he would say. Patterson won fifty-eight of his professional bouts and lost eight, with one match ending in a draw. He died of cancer on May 11, 2006, at the age of seventy-one.

On June 20, 1960, Floyd Patterson faced Ingemar Johansson in a rematch of their 1959 title fight. The fight turned out to be one of the defining moments in Patterson's life. Propelled by a desire to avenge his earlier loss, Patterson struck Johansson with a crushing left hook in the fifth round. The punch knocked Johansson to the floor. When Johansson dared to get up, Patterson unleashed another thunderous left hook that knocked Johansson out cold. Johansson lay motionless on his back for several minutes, blood trickling from his mouth. Shaken by the sight, Patterson rushed over to Johansson, knelt down, and cradled his arms around the head of the fallen fighter. When Johansson regained consciousness, Patterson kissed him on the cheek and helped him to his feet. After the fight, Patterson told reporters, "I was filled with hate when I entered the ring. I never want that to happen again." Patterson learned from the experience. "I do not believe God put us here to hate one another," he would say.

Patterson approached every fight thereafter with compassion for his opponent. When he fought Eddie Machen in 1964, Patterson deliberately eased up on Machen in the later rounds. "I looked in his face and all I could see was the look of hurt and defeat," he told *Sports Illustrated*. "He was tiring and wasn't hurting me, so what was the point in hurting him more? ... I'm glad I didn't knock him out. It wasn't necessary."

In retirement, Patterson became renowned for the help and guidance he gave to youths. He worked with amateur boxers in a gym that he had built near his home. He provided a small dormitory on top of the gym for fighters who needed a place to live. He also served as a counselor for a New York State program to help troubled children. According to long-time friend Father Dan O'Hare, a Catholic priest who worked with Patterson in ministering to youths, Patterson had a special talent for reaching kids.

Patterson also had a special gift for reaching out to individuals who were confined to their homes by illness or other circumstances. A devout Catholic and Eucharistic minister at his local church, Patterson spent many hours on Sundays bringing Holy Communion to those who were homebound. "He always loved God," Father O'Hare said.

◆   ◆   ◆

For the just man falls seven times and rises again.
—Proverbs 24, verse 16.

BYRON R. WHITE

Byron "Whizzer" White was a three-sport star at the University of Colorado in the 1930s. As a halfback on Colorado's football team, he finished first in the country in scoring, rushing yards, and total offense during his senior year, and earned All-American honors. White was also an All-Conference selection in basketball and baseball. After graduation, he played professional football for the Pittsburgh Pirates, later to be renamed the Steelers. In 1938, his rookie season, he led the league in rushing and was named rookie-of-the-year. White then spent a year at Oxford University as a Rhodes Scholar. After serving in the Navy during World War II, he graduated from Yale University Law School. During the Kennedy administration, he was the deputy to attorney general Robert F. Kennedy. President John Kennedy appointed White to the Supreme Court in 1962, a position he held for thirty-one years. White died on April 15, 2002.

In 1961, Byron White, then the deputy to Robert Kennedy in the Department of Justice, found himself in hostile territory in Alabama. The South was ablaze with confrontations over racial issues. It was a time when, in the words of Gene Patterson, editor of the *Atlanta Constitution*, "it took guts to have guts." Change was coming in the United States, sometimes accompanied by forcible resistance. Alabama, Arkansas, and Louisiana, among other Southern states, clung tenaciously to the politics of segregation. Civil rights marchers were met with violent opposition.

Five months into John F. Kennedy's administration, the President ordered four hundred federal marshals to Alabama to protect biracial groups that were protesting segregated seating on municipal buses. The Ku Klux Klan had been attacking the so-called Freedom Riders with ax handles and chains, while local police stood and watched. White led the marshals into Alabama's capital, Montgomery, which had been the site of much of the Ku Klux Klan activity. Tensions were at a feverish pitch. Alabama's governor, John M. Patterson, threatened to arrest the federal marshals. With White in the lead, the marshals never flinched. They restored peace and preserved civil order.

Coming out of college, White was intent on going to England to begin his studies as a Rhodes Scholar. Art Rooney, owner of the Pittsburgh Pirates football team, was equally intent on convincing White to play football. Rooney offered a fifteen-thousand-dollar contract for the 1938 season. White signed. Midway through the season, while leading the league in rushing yards, White stopped accepting paychecks. The team was losing and White felt he was not earning his money. Rooney strenuously disagreed, but to no avail. White would not accept the paychecks. Later, Rooney would say, "Byron came closer to giving one hundred percent every day than any human being I know. We didn't have a very good team and he took some terrific beatings, but he never let down."

In and out of football, White gave one hundred percent. One November day, long after White had established himself as a fixture on the Supreme Court, Washington, D.C. awoke to a near-record snowfall. White left his house early in the morning to go to work. With noon approaching, White still had not arrived at the Court. His staff became concerned. White's clerks made frantic phone calls trying to find the Justice. In early afternoon, White finally arrived at the Court. He had spent the morning trying to help stranded drivers dig their cars out of the snowdrifts. When grateful drivers would ask his name, he would simply identify himself as "a government worker."

White's humility and compassion for others was unmistakable. Once, before the Court was to release a ruling on a case in which a police officer had inadvertently performed an illegal search during an arrest, White called in the law clerk who was drafting portions of the decision. The Justice instructed the clerk not to identify the officer by name in the opinion. "No sense embarrassing that fellow before his fellow cops," White explained.

When White died, former NFL place-kicker Nick Lowery, a friend and neighbor for more than forty years, commented that, as both athlete and government worker, the former Justice had "cut a path through life that helped make this country more just, more proud, and more strong."

◆   ◆   ◆

The Lord brings justice to all the oppressed.
—Psalm 103, verse 6.

ART ROONEY

In his youth, Arthur J. Rooney, Sr., the long-time owner of the Pittsburgh Steelers, was one of the best athletes in the city of Pittsburgh. As a scholastic football player, Rooney was good enough to receive a scholarship offer from the University of Notre Dame. In baseball, he drew offers from the Boston Red Sox and the Chicago Cubs. Rooney went to college at Pittsburgh's Duquesne University, where he excelled in boxing. He was selected for the 1920 U.S. Olympic boxing team, but did not participate. During his playing days, Rooney competed against Jim Thorpe in football and Satchel Paige in baseball. In 1933, he bought the Steelers, then known as the Pittsburgh Pirates, for two thousand and five hundred dollars. He continued as the team's owner until his death on August 25, 1988.

People never had to look hard to find Art Rooney. In 1931, shortly after he and his wife married, Rooney bought a Victorian house on the North Side of Pittsburgh, near downtown. For the next fifty-seven years of his life, he stayed in the same house. Over the years, the character of Rooney's neighborhood changed dramatically. The area deteriorated and became crime-infested. Despite the changes, the Rooneys stayed put. Rooney's wife died in 1982. Rooney stayed put. He lived in the house until his death, never altering his routine. He loved to go for walks in the neighborhood and talk to people. Before going out, he would fill his pockets with dollar bills. Every time he saw a child who looked like he or she might be in need of an ice cream cone, he would pull out a dollar and give it to the child.

One time, well after Rooney had made his millions and become an icon in Pittsburgh, he was walking on the street when a nun from a local college was driving around with a friend. The nun saw Rooney and said to her friend, "Come meet Mr. Rooney." The friend said, "We can't do that." The nun replied, "Yes, we can." They stopped and talked to Rooney. A few days later, the nun received a note from Rooney thanking her for introducing her friend to him.

Rooney donated money for charitable causes as readily as he handed out ice cream money. Over the years, he gave away millions. Once, a former Steelers coach went to Los Angeles to talk to influential sportswriter Jim Murray. The coach wanted to see if he and Murray could drum up support to nominate Whizzer White for president. Murray and the coach started talking about Art Rooney. The more stories Murray heard about Rooney, the more intrigued he became. Finally, Murray said to the coach, "I think you got the wrong guy. Why don't we make Art Rooney president?" The coach shook his head and told Murray, "Art would probably give Texas to some country that needed it."

◆   ◆   ◆

He shows pity to the needy and the poor.
—Psalm 72, verse 13.

EDDIE SADOWSKI

Edward Roman Sadowski was a major league catcher for five seasons. He was one of three brothers to play in the majors. Sadowski struggled offensively but was an excellent defensive backstop. He spent his rookie season, 1960, with the Boston Red Sox. After the season, the expansion Los Angeles Angels drafted Sadowski, and he spent the next four years in the Angels' organization. His best day in the major leagues came on June 4, 1961, when he hit two doubles and a home run in a Sunday doubleheader. He closed out his career in 1966 with the Atlanta Braves. Sadowski died of Lou Gehrig's disease, amyotrophic lateral sclerosis, on November 6, 1993. He was sixty-one.

After his playing days, Eddie Sadowski was the physical education teacher at St. Columban Catholic School in Garden Grove, California. For Sadowski, it was the perfect job; he loved exercise and he loved children. On school days, he would cheerfully lead his students in calisthenics. Teachers would look out the school windows, see Coach Sadowski and his students going through their exercise routines, and marvel at Sadowski's boyish enthusiasm. His gentle manner made him a favorite of both students and teachers.

When Sadowski died, the pastor of St. Columban's Church spoke glowingly of the former Angel:

> He gave new meaning to the word "coach." He gave new meaning to the word "friend" and, especially, new meaning to the term "California Angel." That is truly what Ed Sadowski was to this community. We need to feel sorry for those who have never known Ed Sadowski.

◆　　　◆　　　◆

Bless the Lord, all you angels.
—Psalm 103, verse 20.

ERNIE DAVIS

Ernie Davis, the "Elmira Express," grew up in Uniontown, Pennsylvania. When he was twelve years old, Davis moved to Elmira, New York, where he earned high school All-American honors in both football and basketball. He attended Syracuse University and became the most celebrated running back in Syracuse history, winning the Heisman Trophy in his senior season. In December 1961, Davis signed a lucrative contract to play for the Cleveland Browns. Before he could start his pro career, however, he contracted leukemia. The disease was first diagnosed in July 1962. After two months of treatment, the leukemia went into remission but came back in February 1963. Davis died on May 18, 1963, at the age of twenty-three.

John Brown, one of Ernie Davis's teammates at Syracuse University, shared an apartment with Davis in Cleveland after their college days. Someone once asked Brown what it was like to watch a young man die. Brown replied, "I don't know. I watched a young man live."

Football Hall-of-Famer Jim Brown expressed the same thought in a different way. Speaking of Davis, Brown said, "He took his illness on his own shoulders, carried it, lived normally, simply. It was a tremendous thing to watch."

Once, while Davis was riding in a taxi with his lawyer in Cleveland, a book fell from Davis's coat pocket. The book was titled *Burial Masses*. The incident was one of the few times that friends ever got the feeling that Davis knew his days were numbered.

Though it was common knowledge that he had leukemia, Davis steadfastly refused to disclose the extent of his condition to family members and friends. A few weeks before his death, Davis was eating at a restaurant in his hometown of Elmira. Upon recognizing Davis, the young waitress who was taking his order began to cry. The waitress had read in the newspapers that Davis was dying. When Davis noticed her tears, he patted her on the hand and said, "I know they have me dead and buried, but don't worry, I've got this thing licked. I feel great. I'm looking forward to playing football this season." Upon hearing Davis's reassuring words, a big smile came over the waitress's face.

Davis's stoicism in the face of his illness presented a problem for doctors. Trying to shield others from worry and not wanting to be a bother, Davis rarely complained. He was forever greeting doctors with a smile on his face. He would tell the doctors, "I feel fine. I feel strong." Out of necessity, his physicians had to base their evaluations on analyses of Davis's blood work because he provided little insight into the symptoms he was experiencing.

On May 16, 1963, Davis checked himself into the hospital for the last time. He died two days later. Before going to the hospital, he left a note for John Brown. The note read, "Going to the hospital for a few days. Don't tell anybody. I'll see you around." He also paid a final visit to Cleveland Browns' owner Art Modell. Davis told Modell that he had to go into the hospital again, but that it was nothing serious. The cost of medical care weighed heavily on Davis because the Browns were paying for his treatments. As he had many times previously, Davis used his last visit to thank Modell for paying his expenses and apologize for being a financial burden.

Davis didn't want others to mourn for him. Even on his last visit with his mother, he refrained from talking about himself, instead focusing on relatives and friends. According to his mother, "he wanted to know how everybody back home was doing." The humility with which Davis approached death was typical of the way he lived his life. "Ernie was the same kid at the end as he was at the start," said Jim Flynn, his high school basketball coach.

Once, when Davis was in high school, a fellow student, trying out for football for the first time, inadvertently put his shoulder pads on backwards. Other players began to tease the boy and make fun of him. Davis, a junior and already a star, hurried across the room, lifted the shoulder pads from the boy and said: "Let me help you. These things can be confusing. Don't be embarrassed. I did the same thing on my first day here." Davis then put the shoulder pads in their proper place and laced them up.

Davis's humility and compassion were always in evidence, causing Ben Schwartzwalder, his football coach at Syracuse, to say, "I never met another human being as good as Ernie."

◆   ◆   ◆

Lord, let me know my end, the number of my days.
—Psalm 39, verse 5.

KEN HUBBS

As a twelve-year-old, Ken Hubbs led his Colton, California, Little League baseball team to the finals of the 1954 Little League World Series in Williamsport, Pennsylvania. In the championship game, Hubbs played shortstop with a broken toe and hit a home run in a 7–5 loss to a team from Schenectady, New York. A straight-A student in high school and president of the student body, Hubbs received scholarship offers to play football at Notre Dame and basketball at the University of California, Los Angeles. Preferring to join the pro ranks immediately, Hubbs turned down the scholarships and signed with the Chicago Cubs for fifty thousand dollars. He made his major league debut in September 1961, at the age of nineteen. The next season, he took over as the Cubs' regular second baseman, set a major league record by handling 418 consecutive chances in the field without an error, and was named National League rookie-of-the-year. Hubbs would play only one more season with the Cubs. He died on February 13, 1964, when the Cessna airplane he was piloting crashed in a heavy snowstorm shortly after takeoff from Provo, Utah. He was twenty-two years old.

On February 3, 1964, Ken Hubbs sat at home in Colton, California, and wrote out his goals for the upcoming baseball season. First and foremost, Hubbs aspired to help the Cubs win the National League pennant. Each succeeding goal hinted at Hubbs's passion for baseball and his determination to excel. Ten days after setting down his goals, Hubbs died, the victim of a violent snowstorm that blew through Utah's Wasatch Mountains.

After Hubbs's funeral, his family received a letter postmarked from Chicago. The letter was from Hubbs's landlady. The woman wrote that, as a result of bad experiences in the past, she had been reluctant to rent an apartment to a ballplayer. Some ballplayers, she said, were too rowdy. The landlady wrote that, in contrast, Hubbs was a gentleman. She told of how he would come home after playing nine innings at Chicago's Wrigley Field, and then join in football and baseball games with the neighborhood kids. She also said that she enjoyed having Hubbs as a tenant so much that she wasn't planning to charge him any rent if he had continued to stay at her place the next year.

Hubbs learned modesty and concern for others early in life. During his years at Colton High School, he starred in baseball, basketball, and football. He was named to the prep school All-American teams in both football and basketball. The more publicity Hubbs received, the more humble he became. He would complain to his parents that the local newspapers paid too much attention to his individual accomplishments. "There are other kids on the team," he would say. "Why don't they write about them?" Eventually, embarrassed by the attention paid to him, Hubbs stopped reading the sports pages.

Hubbs also learned the value of small acts of kindness. While playing for the Cubs, Hubbs would frequently stay at the ballpark for an hour or more after games to accommodate fans seeking his autograph.

Though both his father and brother tried to discourage him, Hubbs started taking flight lessons in 1963. His decision to become a pilot stemmed, in part, from the fact that he was apprehensive about being in an airplane. He hoped that the flying lessons would help him overcome his fear. In the end, he found an unanticipated benefit in being at the controls of his own plane. He told teammate Ron Santo that flying made him feel closer to God.

◆   ◆   ◆

I would soon find a shelter from the raging wind and storm.
—Psalm 55, verse 9.

KEN BOYER

Ken Boyer played major league baseball for fifteen seasons, eleven as a third baseman and sometime center fielder for the St. Louis Cardinals. He was a powerful hitter and an accomplished, often spectacular, fielder. During the course of his major league career, he batted over .300 five times. For four consecutive years, 1961 through 1964, he finished the season with exactly twenty-four home runs. In 1964, he compiled a .295 batting average, with 119 runs batted in, to lead the Cardinals to the National League championship. Boyer clubbed two home runs against the New York Yankees in the 1964 World Series, helping St. Louis defeat the Yankees for the World Championship. Overall, he batted .287 with 282 homers during his major league career. Boyer was a rare combination of athletic talent, grace on the playing field, humility, and unselfishness. He died on September 7, 1982, at the age of fifty-one.

Author David Halberstam told of a time in which Ken Boyer, playing third base, moved almost all the way to the shortstop position to field a hard-hit ground ball. After Boyer had completed the play, home plate umpire Dusty Boggess said to St. Louis catcher Tim McCarver, "Take a good look, son, because you're not going to see anyone like him again." When the game ended, McCarver related Boggess's comment to Boyer. "Never get caught up in stuff like that," Boyer replied.

Late in Boyer's career, he became an occasional first baseman for the Los Angeles Dodgers. He was at first base for a contest between the Dodgers and the Cardinals in 1968 when Ted Simmons, a young Cardinals catcher, singled for his first hit in the major leagues. With Simmons perched on first base, Boyer asked him, "Is that your first big-league hit?" Simmons said it was. Boyer then told him, "That's great—I hope it's the first of twenty-five hundred."

Such incidents led Halberstam to describe Boyer as a great role model and "consummate professional who played hard every day, and never lost sight of his essential purpose."

◆   ◆   ◆

Distant peoples stand in awe of your marvels.
—Psalm 65, verse 9.

DON STEINBRUNNER

Donald Thomas Steinbrunner played football and basketball for Washington State University from 1950 to 1952. A punishing blocker and occasional receiver for the Cougars' football team, Steinbrunner was named first-team All-Conference in his junior year. After graduation, he spent the 1953 season with the Cleveland Browns as an offensive lineman. The next year, Steinbrunner went on active duty with the Air Force to fulfill his Reserve Officer Training Corps obligation. He spent the next thirteen years in the Air Force, including four years as a member of the Air Force Academy coaching staff. In December 1966, Steinbrunner was assigned to Vietnam, where he served as the navigator for a C-123 aircraft. Steinbrunner and the other four members of his crew died on July 20, 1967, when their plane was shot down over Kontum, Vietnam. Steinbrunner was thirty-five years old.

Long after Don Steinbrunner had passed away, Steinbrunner's son, David, met a man who had played football against Washington State in the 1950s. The man told David that playing opposite Don Steinbrunner was a brutal assignment. "He beat the crap out of me for four years," the man told David. "I couldn't wait to finish those games. But every time he knocked me down, he was there to pick me up."

In football as well as in life, Don Steinbrunner played tough but fair. After Steinbrunner had logged several missions in Vietnam as a flight navigator, he was shot in the knee when his plane was hit by small arms fire. When Steinbrunner returned to duty, the Air Force offered him the opportunity to take a less dangerous assignment. Steinbrunner turned down the offer, choosing instead to return to his air commando squadron. Steinbrunner told the Air Force that it would be better for him to continue flying because he was a seasoned veteran. He didn't want a younger and less experienced officer flying in his place. Steinbrunner reasoned that if a less experienced man were to take over as navigator, it could endanger the lives of everyone on board the C-123. With that decision, Steinbrunner rejoined his crew and returned to flight status.

On July 20, 1967, Steinbrunner's plane was hit by enemy fire, plummeted to the earth, and burned. There were no survivors.

◆   ◆   ◆

We do not fear, though earth be shaken.
—Psalm 46, verse 3.

ARTHUR ASHE

Arthur Robert Ashe, Jr. was born on July 10, 1943, in Richmond, Virginia. At an early age, he demonstrated an aptitude for tennis. While still in high school, Ashe left Richmond and moved to St. Louis in order to gain access to better facilities and exposure to stronger competition. After a highly successful collegiate career at the University of California, Los Angeles, he was commissioned as a lieutenant in the Army. He spent two years on active duty, during which he coached the varsity tennis team at West Point. In 1968, he won the U.S. Open title and, shortly after, was ranked number one in the world. In 1975, he won the men's singles title at Wimbledon. Ashe was named captain of the U.S. Davis Cup team in 1980. He was elected to the International Tennis Hall of Fame in 1985. He died on February 6, 1993, of complications from AIDS, which he had contracted after a tainted blood transfusion.

As a teenager, Johnnie Ashe, the younger brother of Arthur, would sarcastically ask his brother, "If the world breaks down, are you going to fix it with a tennis racket?" Johnnie's question was a not-so-subtle reference to Arthur's well-established ineptness in the use of screwdrivers and wrenches. Ultimately, however, the joke was on Johnnie—Arthur indeed found a way to use his tennis racket to fix the world.

In 1985, while Arthur Ashe was the captain of the U.S. Davis Cup team, he was arrested at the South African Embassy in Washington, D.C. for protesting the apartheid policy of the South African government. In 1992, less than a year before he would die, Ashe was arrested for protesting U.S. policies toward refugees from Haiti.

The arrests aside, Ashe did not relish public attention, preferring to do his work quietly. In May 1992, he was invited to attend a sports night at the National Center for Disability Services. Ashe ignored the many celebrities in attendance and spent the entire evening visiting with the disabled students who were being honored. He bent down to talk to those who were on crutches and knelt next to teenagers in wheelchairs, talking intently with each of the disabled. When talking to students, Ashe would invariably emphasize three themes that he believed were essential to success in school and in life. "Sit in the front row," he would tell the students. "Get the maximum benefit from your professors; be proactive."

On January 20, 1993, Ashe spent much of the day writing a farewell letter to his six-year-old daughter, Camera. The farewell was inevitable. Having been infected with the HIV virus after a 1983 blood transfusion, Ashe was diagnosed with AIDS in 1988. He wrote to Camera in the hope that it would help, in later years, to prompt some memory of him. In his letter, titled "My Dear Camera," Ashe provided guidance on a wide range of subjects, including family relationships, sports, religion, racial matters, and life. His guidance to Camera serves as useful instruction to all.

With respect to developing a relationship with God, Ashe had a simple message for his daughter. He advised her to ask God for two things: (1) the wisdom to know what is right and what God wants, and (2) the will to do it. Read the psalms and the Sermon on the Mount, Ashe told Camera. In the Bible, he assured her, she would find consolation in her darkest hours, the meaning of life, and the way she should live.

Long before, Ashe had figured out for himself the way he should live. He sought to live with a humane purpose and to try to help the poor and unfortunate. He said, "The purest joy in life comes with trying to help others." Toward that end, Ashe established several charitable foundations during his life. Together with tennis guru Nick Bollettieri, he formed the Ashe–Bollettieri Cities program, which brought tennis and mentoring to children in some of the poorest neighborhoods in the country. He founded Athletes' Career Connection to improve the low graduation rate among African American college athletes. With a third program, the Safe Passage Foundation, Ashe sought to help children, especially black children, escape the effects of poverty and crime.

◆   ◆   ◆

Happy the man who finds wisdom.
—Proverbs 3, verse 13.

References

Floyd Patterson

Wally Carew, "Floyd Patterson: A Knight Whose Reach Went Beyond the Ring," *Columbia*, November 2006, 23.

Bill Gallo, "Floyd Was a True People's Champ," *New York Daily News*, 21 May 2006, 79.

Singular, Stephen and Carl A. Anderson. *By Their Works: Profiles of Men of Faith Who Made a Difference*. New York: HarperCollins Publishers Inc., 2006.

"Tribute to a Humble Heavyweight," (Albany) *Times Union*, 28 May 2006, C2.

Byron R. White

Ira Berkow, "Justice Byron White: A Friend and a Mentor," *New York Times*, 21 April 2002, 8.7.

Ray Didinger, "White Left Mark On and Off the Field," *Boulder Daily Camera*, 4 July 1993.

Laura Kalman, "John Kennedy's Nonconformist," *The New York Times*, 23 August 1998, http://nytimes.com/books/98/23/reviews/980823.23 kalmant.html.

Nick Lowery, "Byron White Balanced Brains, Sports, Character," *USA Today*, 17 April 2002, C8.

Lisa Levitt Ryckman, "Justice Byron White Laid to Rest; Colorado's Superman Led Life of Effortless Excellence," *Rocky Mountain News*, 20 April 2002, 1A.

"Byron Raymond White, An Incredible Athlete," U.S. Court of Appeals for the Tenth Circuit, http://ck10.uscourts.gov/edu.cfm?part=12.

Art Rooney

> Will McDonough, "Rooney Man of People," *Boston Globe*, 26 August 1988, 59.

> Jim Murray, "Art Rooney: Gentle Man, Gentleman," *Los Angeles Times*, 1 September 1988, 1.

> "Rooney Mourned by Thousands," *New York Times*, 27 August 1988, 1.46.

Eddie Sadowski

> Comments of Rev. Don Romito, Officiating at Funeral Service for Edward R. Sadowski, 10 November 1993, St. Columban Catholic Church, Garden Grove, CA.

Ernie Davis

> Gallagher, Robert C. *Ernie Davis: The Elmira Express*. Silver Spring, MD: Bartleby Press, 1999.

> Pennington, Bill. *The Heisman: Great American Stories of the Men Who Won*. New York: HarperCollins Publishers Inc., 2004.

Ken Hubbs

> Fred Claire, "Lidle Tragedy Stirs Memories of Hubbs," http://chicago.cubs.mlb.com/ NASApp/mlb/news/article_perspectives. jsp?ymd, 2006.

> Earl Gustkey, "Memories of Ken Hubbs Live On; Nearly 30 Years Later, the Town of Colton Still is Recovering From His Death At 22," *Los Angeles Times*, 5 July 1993, 8.

> Dick Rosetta, "Hubbs Remembered For What He Did and What He Could Have Done," *The Salt Lake Tribune*, 14 February 1994, B1.

Ken Boyer

> Halberstam, David. *October 1964*. New York: Villard Books, 1994.

Don Steinbrunner

> Steve Doerschuk, "Don Steinbrunner Went to War and Left Quite A Legacy," http://sports.group.yahoo.com, 12 November 2004.

> John C. Witter, "Veterans Day Special: Real Crimson Soldiers," 10 November 2005, http://washingtonstate.scout.com/2/100714.html.

Arthur Ashe

> Ashe, Arthur and Arnold Rampersad, *Days of Grace: A Memoir*. New York: Ballantine Books, 1993.

1970–1979

1970–1979

The seventies began in turmoil in the United States. Across the country, colleges and universities closed their doors in the spring of 1970 in response to widespread student and faculty protests against expansion of the war in Vietnam. On May 4, 1970, Ohio National Guard troops killed four students at Kent State University who were protesting the U.S. invasion of Cambodia. In 1971, the U.S. Supreme Court, ruling in the case of *Swann v. Charlotte-Mecklenburg Board of Education*, approved the compulsory busing of students as an appropriate means for ending segregation in public schools.

In September 1972, ten members of Israel's Olympic team and one Israeli wrestling referee were killed after Arab terrorists overran the Olympic compound that housed Israeli athletes in Munich, Germany. On December 31, 1972, the world lost baseball player and humanitarian Roberto Clemente, who died when a plane carrying relief supplies to earthquake victims in Nicaragua crashed after takeoff from San Juan, Puerto Rico.

During the Supreme Court's 1972 term, the Court issued its decision in *Flood v. Kuhn*. Long-time major-leaguer Curt Flood had sought to have the Court declare baseball's reserve clause to be an unreasonable restraint of trade and in violation of federal antitrust laws. Relying on Justice Holmes's 1922 decision in the *Federal Baseball Club of Baltimore* case, however, the Court ruled that federal antitrust laws did not apply to baseball.

In January 1973, the governments of the United States, South Vietnam, North Vietnam, and the North Vietnamese-backed National Liberation Front signed a peace agreement ending U.S. involvement in Vietnam. The last American troops departed South Vietnam on March 29, 1973. Newspapers throughout the world carried photographs of Army Master Sergeant Max Beilke, the last U.S. combat soldier in all of Vietnam, boarding a C-130 transport plane at Tan Son Nhut airport for the flight home. In 1974, Richard Nixon resigned as U.S. president after it became clear that he had been involved in obstructing the investigation of the Watergate burglary. Vice President Gerald R. Ford succeeded Nixon as president. The government of South Vietnam collapsed after North Vietnamese troops invaded the South in 1975. North Vietnam consolidated the two countries under Communist rule.

In a storybook ending to a twenty-year career in coaching, Al McGuire led the Marquette University basketball team to a 67–59 victory over the University of North Carolina in the finals of the 1977 NCAA championship tournament. On December 25, 1979, the Soviet Union began sending armed troops to Afghanistan to counteract the threat posed by insurgents, who were fighting to overthrow the incumbent government of the Marxist People's Democratic Party of Afghanistan.

BRIAN PICCOLO

Louis Brian Piccolo was a running back for the Chicago Bears for five seasons, 1965 through 1969. As a senior at Wake Forest University in 1964, Piccolo finished first in the nation in yards gained, with 1,044, and in points scored, with 111. Though named second team All-American by both the Associated Press and United Press International, Piccolo was not drafted by either the American Football League or the National Football League. He signed with the Bears as a free agent and spent his rookie season on the taxi squad. Piccolo made the Bears' active roster in 1966 and developed into an excellent blocking back and a reliable ball carrier. In the ninth game of the Bears' 1969 season, Piccolo took himself out of the game after having trouble breathing. Doctors conducted tests and found a malignant tumor. He died on June 16, 1970, at the age of twenty-six.

Between November 1969 and June 1970, Brian Piccolo shuttled in and out of Memorial Sloan-Kettering Cancer Center in Manhattan for testing and treatment. Early in 1970, two of Piccolo's friends from Chicago stopped at Sloan-Kettering to visit. Upon seeing his friends, Piccolo said, "Hey, let's get out of here. This place is full of sick people."

In fact, Piccolo never shied away from "sick people." In the nine months before his death, he encountered many people who were suffering from illness and injury, both at Sloan-Kettering and at Illinois Masonic Hospital in Chicago. Whether visiting cancer victims at Sloan-Kettering or young children at Illinois Masonic who had suffered spinal injuries, Piccolo was quick to embrace his fellow patients, offering them an autograph, a friendly smile, and unending encouragement.

When Freddie Steinmark, a Chicago Bears fan and starting safety for the 1969 University of Texan Longhorns, had to undergo an emergency amputation of his left leg in December 1969, Piccolo sent a long letter to Steinmark. Piccolo's letter provided solace and comfort during some of Steinmark's most difficult days. In his letter, Piccolo reminded Steinmark that "our lives are in God's hands." Piccolo told Steinmark of his firm belief in the power of prayer. "I shall never stop praying to God for the strength to carry out the plans he has laid out for me," Piccolo wrote.

◆   ◆   ◆

Escape from death is in the Lord God's hands.
—Psalm 68, verse 21.

FREDDIE STEINMARK

Freddie Joe Steinmark was the starting safety for the University of Texas football team for two years, 1968 and 1969. Before joining the Longhorns, he had been an all-state halfback in high school at Wheat Ridge High in Colorado. Steinmark was an all-around athlete, who also excelled in baseball and basketball in high school. During fourteen years of organized football, from the second grade through his junior year at the University of Texas, he played in only seven losing games. Steinmark helped Texas defeat the University of Arkansas, 15–14, on December 6, 1969, to claim the national championship. Less than a week later, doctors were forced to amputate his left leg after discovering a malignant tumor. Steinmark later wrote an autobiography, titled I Play to Win, *detailing his experiences leading up to and following his illness. He died of cancer on June 6, 1971, at the age of twenty-two.*

In his autobiography, Freddie Steinmark used a line from an old poem to illustrate his outlook on life. The poem read,

> Two men looked out from prison bars;
> one saw mud, the other saw stars.

Through all his medical challenges, Steinmark remained focused on the "stars." He found abundant blessings, even after his leg was amputated. Steinmark found that the experience of his illness had helped him to become more understanding, more patient with people, and more interested in the problems of others. Forced to give up football, he found he had more time to enjoy other activities. He picked up a golf club for the first time in eight years. For each shot, he would lay down his crutches, balance himself on his one leg, and swing away. His first time on the course after his surgery, he shot a fifty-three for nine holes. He eventually lowered his score to forty-six.

Steinmark was quietly religious. He prayed the rosary before each of his football games. When he needed consolation, he would retreat to the dimly lit chapel in the Catholic Student Center at the University of Texas, sit in the first pew, and pray. Both before and after his surgery, Steinmark felt the tangible presence of

God. In his autobiography, Steinmark attempted to explain his faith in God and the benefit he derived from prayer. Quoting an old Chinese proverb, Steinmark asked, "Do you need proof of God? Does one light a torch to see the sun?"

As a boy, Steinmark's ambition was to become a professional athlete and make enough money to buy his mother a Cadillac. After his surgery, Steinmark's goals changed. He wanted to inspire others and to demonstrate that the human spirit could triumph over doubt and misfortune. Above all, he wanted to find ways to help others.

Steinmark lived less than eighteen months after doctors discovered his tumor. In that time, however, he became an inspiration to others. He never gave up. If he couldn't play safety for the Longhorns, he hoped to become the team's kicking specialist. He resumed attending classes and made plans to go to law school. He found humor in his handicap. Texas quarterback James Street, when speaking to Longhorn fans, would ask, "Have you ever noticed how Steinmark walks, like he's on his last leg?" Steinmark laughed as loud as anyone. He recited his favorite prayer, the *Memorare*, with fervor. He appeared at fund-raising events for the American Cancer Crusade. He made a special effort to learn of children who had undergone amputations and called them on the telephone or wrote letters to them.

In the words of his friend and frequent companion, Father Fred Bomar, a Catholic priest, Steinmark was everything that "a young Christian in the twentieth century should be."

◆   ◆   ◆

My steps have kept to your paths; my feet have not faltered.
—Psalm 17, verse 5.

GERRY BERTIER

Gerry Bertier was born on August 20, 1953. He grew up in Alexandria, Virginia. As a youth, he was an active participant in several sports. His long-term goal was to compete for the United States in the Olympics. After graduating from middle school, Bertier attended Francis Hammond High School in Alexandria. In response to the April 1971 Supreme Court ruling that busing was a valid means of achieving school desegregation, the city of Alexandria mandated that all of the city's students would attend T.C. Williams High School for their junior and senior years. With that ruling, Bertier enrolled at T.C. Williams and joined the Titans' 1971 football team. He excelled as a linebacker, sacking opposing quarterbacks forty-two times and recording 142 individual tackles. Bertier led T.C. Williams to an undefeated season and the Virginia state championship. He was named one of the top one hundred high school players in the country and received football scholarship offers from Notre Dame and other major colleges. Later in the school year, hours after he had received the T.C. Williams Defensive Award in Football, Bertier was involved in an automobile accident that left his legs permanently paralyzed. He became an accomplished wheelchair athlete and won a gold medal in the shot-put at the 1980 National Wheelchair Games competition. He also played on the U.S. Wheelchair Olympics basketball team. His storied high school football career became the focal point of the movie, Remember the Titans. *Bertier died on March 20, 1981.*

Confined to a wheelchair, Gerry Bertier found that he was unable to navigate many of the sidewalks and streets in his hometown of Alexandria, Virginia. Similarly, the entrances to most public and commercial buildings proved to be impassable. Capitalizing on the attention he had gained through football, Bertier became a tireless advocate for the rights of the disabled. Seeking to improve access for the handicapped, he enlisted the help of Virginia State Representative David Speck. Bertier led Speck on tours of streets and facilities in Alexandria, demonstrating the range of physical barriers confronting disabled individuals. Bertier exerted pressure on Alexandria's restaurants and office buildings to install wheelchair ramps. His efforts resulted in wholesale changes in Alexandria and elsewhere in Virginia. In the span of a few years, the city of Alexandria reconfigured all of its sidewalks to accommodate the handicapped.

Bertier's work drew widespread recognition. The Virginia General Assembly adopted a resolution in his honor. In 1981, the Presidential Committee on Employment of the Handicapped awarded him its national Volunteer of the Year Award. Bertier's legacy lives on through the Gerry Bertier Scholarships, which are awarded each year to graduating high school students from the city of Alexandria who are afflicted with physical or learning disabilities.

◆   ◆   ◆

Your word is a lamp for my feet, a light for my path.
—Psalm 119, verse 105.

TOM LANDRY

At the age of nineteen, Thomas Wade Landry was intent on playing football for the University of Texas. World War II intervened, however, and Landry found himself piloting a B-17 bomber over Nazi-occupied Europe. Before the war ended, he had flown thirty combat missions. Once back home, Landry returned to the University of Texas, where he excelled on the gridiron. After graduating, Landry spent 1949 playing football for the New York Yankees in the old All-America Football Conference. From 1950 to 1955, he was a defensive back, punter, and sometime quarterback for the NFL's New York Giants. In each of three seasons, 1951, 1952, and 1954, Landry intercepted eight passes from his defensive back position. After retiring as a player, he served as an assistant coach for the Giants. He was named head coach of the Dallas Cowboys before the team's inaugural season of 1960. Landry served as the Cowboys' head coach for the next twenty-nine years, retiring after the 1988 season. For twenty consecutive seasons, 1966 to 1985, Landry's teams finished with winning records, a mark that no other NFL coach has ever equaled. On January 16, 1972, Landry led the Cowboys to the team's first ever Super Bowl victory, a 24–3 drubbing of the Miami Dolphins. It was one of five Super Bowl appearances for Dallas under Landry. Overall, the Cowboys won 270 games and lost 178 during his tenure. Landry died on February 12, 2000, at the age of seventy-five.

In 1989, after the Dallas Cowboys had struggled through three straight losing seasons, the team's new owner, Jerry Jones, fired coach Tom Landry. The news sent shock waves throughout Dallas, where Landry was regarded as an institution. The city quickly made plans to honor the coach with a "Tom Landry Day." When city officials informed Landry of their plans, Landry was skeptical. He didn't think many people would show up. On the day of the event, however, upwards of one hundred thousand people came out to bid the coach farewell.

Landry, a humble man, expected little for himself. In his twenty-nine seasons as coach of the Cowboys, he never demanded a pay raise. He was also painfully honest. In 1965, after the Cowboys started the season with only two wins in the first seven games, Landry announced to his players that he had let them down. He praised the players' efforts, but said that the flex defense that he had designed and his multiple-shift offense were ineffective. The next twenty years would prove Landry wrong, as the flex defense and multiple-shift offense produced one winning season after another.

Landry would tell his players that he had three priorities in life—God, family, and football—in that order. Landry didn't identify service to others among his three priorities, but it was abundantly clear that he made a special effort to treat everyone with respect and to share his love of God. He regularly made visits to cheer children in hospitals. He met with prison inmates to talk about football and life. When the Cowboys suffered a bitterly disappointing last-minute, one-point loss to the San Francisco 49ers in the 1981 National Football Conference title game, Landry abruptly terminated a postgame press conference. Reporters speculated that Landry's anger over the loss may have caused him to leave the press conference prematurely. In fact, Landry had to catch an early flight back to Texas in order to honor a commitment to attend a benefit for crippled children in Houston. In true Landry fashion, he did not disclose his reason for leaving the press conference.

Landry's reserved demeanor sometimes led those who did not know him to conclude that he was a distant, if not cold, individual. To the contrary, however, he was gracious and caring. During his twenty-nine years with the Cowboys, he would meet with his secretary every Friday to send out personal responses to the hundreds of people who would write him letters each month. When he left the Cowboys in 1989, after he had packed up his office, he took the time to meet with every secretary and staff member in the organization, as well as every player on the team, to thank them for their help.

Former Cowboys general manager Tex Schramm, who worked directly with Landry during the first three decades of the team's existence, said that Landry was the finest man he had ever known. Roger Staubach, the Cowboys' quarterback during many of the team's most successful years, developed a special bond with Landry. Staubach said, "He had a decency about him that was unsurpassed. He was our rock, our hope, our inspiration."

◆   ◆   ◆

Blessed be my rock!
—Psalm 18, verse 47.

SHIRLEY POVICH

Shirley Povich, sportswriter and columnist for The Washington Post, *was an institution in Washington, D.C. Povich began covering sports for the* Post *in 1924. He worked for the* Post *continuously for the next seventy-four years. Povich was a leader in the fight to integrate the sporting world. His columns decried the Washington Redskins' policy of refusing to employ black players, a policy that continued well into the 1960s. The Redskins' colors, Povich wrote in December 1960, "are inflexibly burgundy, gold, and Caucasian." He died on June 4, 1998, at the age of ninety-two. He wrote his last column for the* Post—*a commentary on Babe Ruth's rightful place in baseball history, the glory of Don Larsen's perfect game, and the ingenuity of baseball veteran Paul Richards—the day before his death.*

Early in the morning of September 5, 1972, Shirley Povich found himself with a decision to make. Povich was in Munich, Germany to cover the 1972 summer Olympics. At 4:30 AM, Arab terrorists, armed with high-velocity machine guns and wearing Olympic warm-up suits, had invaded the compound at the Olympic Village that housed the Israeli Olympic team. The terrorists quickly killed two Israeli team members and then took nine other Israelis as hostages. Povich was riding in a taxi to the Olympic Village when he heard news of the attack over the car radio. He could either return to the safety of the Munich Hilton or continue to the Village. Without hesitation, Povich said to his German driver, "My God, faster to the Olympischen. Mach schnell."

Upon arriving at the Village gates, Povich slipped past the security guards, donned a sweatsuit, and posed as a member of the Puerto Rican contingent. He then found a vantage point less than forty yards from the Israeli compound. He was one of only a handful of reporters inside the Village. Equipped with binoculars and a telephone, Povich dictated dispatches to the *Post-Newsweek* station in Paris. For the better part of two days, his reports provided readers throughout the world with eyewitness accounts of the tragic events.

Using the same resolve that he displayed at the Olympic Village, Povich tackled issues in the world of sports with compassion and conviction. At a time when Washington, D.C. was very much a segregated society, Povich took the lead in

193

integrating the press box at D.C.'s Griffith Stadium, home to the Senators and Redskins. At a 1942 boxing match held at the Stadium, Povich noticed that African American sportswriter Sam Lacy had been relegated to the standing room area in the back of the press section. Povich went up to where Lacy was standing and asked, "What are you doing here, Sam?" Lacy replied, "They don't have a seat for me." Povich led Lacy down to a seat in the third row, right next to Povich's own seat. With that simple act, black sportswriters gained admission to seats that were previously "whites only." Lacy would later explain, "When somebody like Shirley would support you, all of them started to accept you."

When the Professional Golf Association prohibited golfer Casey Martin, who suffered from a degenerative circulatory condition in his legs, from using a golf cart on the pro tour, Povich took up Martin's cause in his column. The PGA argued that use of a golf cart would give Martin an unfair advantage. Povich elevated the discussion to a higher level. "Whatever happened to compassion and understanding and human concern and plain old sympathy?" he wrote.

If Povich expected compassion and understanding in others, it was undoubtedly because those traits were so deeply ingrained in his own character. In the early 1970s, acclaimed sportswriter and author Tom Boswell, then a copy boy at *The Washington Post*, was considering whether to pursue a career in sportswriting. While enthusiastic about sports, Boswell was disturbed by what he perceived as a tendency for aging sportswriters to turn bitter, nasty, even deceitful. He sought reassurance that not everyone in the profession ended up that way. As Boswell recalled, "I wanted to see just One Exception—one person who proved that you could age with dignity, have a face still capable of a sincere smile and, in general, have a full life and family while still keeping your integrity as a journalist."

Shirley Povich proved to be Boswell's "one exception." "There he was, day after day," Boswell would write, "in what seemed to be an elegant suit, treating everyone in a gentle, friendly manner.... He laughed. He still enjoyed the people he talked to."

◆   ◆   ◆

Though I walk in the midst of dangers, you guard my life when my enemies rage.
—Psalm 138, verse 7.

ROBERTO CLEMENTE

In eighteen seasons as an outfielder for the Pittsburgh Pirates, Roberto Clemente had exactly three thousand base hits. He compiled a career batting average of .317, led the National League in batting four times, and played in twelve All-Star games. His final hit in the major leagues, the three thousandth of his career, came on September 30, 1972. Leading off for Pittsburgh in the fourth inning against the New York Mets, Clemente doubled off the wall in left-center field. With that hit, he became only the eleventh player in major league history to reach the three-thousand-hit milestone. He died three months later, on December 31, 1972. Less than four months after his death, Clemente was voted into baseball's Hall of Fame.

On December 23, 1972, an earthquake devastated the city of Managua in Nicaragua, killing six thousand people, injuring twenty thousand more, and leaving three thousand homeless. Less than twenty-four hours later, Roberto Clemente, a native of Puerto Rico, was organizing a massive effort in San Juan to send supplies to Nicaragua. The day after the earthquake, Clemente appeared on television in Puerto Rico to appeal for donations of money, medicine, food, and clothing. He spent Christmas Day at Hiram Bithorn Stadium in San Juan organizing and packing the supplies.

A month before the disaster, Clemente had visited Nicaragua as the manager of a team of Puerto Rican ballplayers who were participating in the Annual World Series of Amateur Baseball. When the earthquake hit, he felt compelled to help. In the span of a week, Clemente and other relief workers collected more than 110,000 pounds of supplies. The supplies were transported to Nicaragua by cargo ship and airplane. In Nicaragua, however, an unanticipated problem arose. Members of the Nicaraguan national guard were siphoning off some of the supplies.

Clemente arranged for a DC-7 cargo plane to fly out of Puerto Rico on December 31 with medical supplies. Against the wishes of his family, Clemente decided to go along on the DC-7, so that he could oversee the distribution of the supplies. Before the plane departed, Roberto's wife, Vera, made one last appeal, urging her husband to remain in Puerto Rico for New Year's Eve. Clemente was

195

determined. "Babies are dying over there," he told Vera. The plane left San Juan shortly after 9:00 PM, with Clemente, two pilots, a flight engineer, and one of Clemente's friends on board. Within minutes after takeoff, a fire developed in the plane's left wing. The DC-7 lost power and plummeted into the sea. Clemente and the four others on board died.

When explaining why, in all his years of baseball, he had never held out of spring training in an effort to obtain a more lucrative contract, Clemente told reporters, "I will never let money come between me and this game." Similarly, he never let money come between him and his love of people. He donated large sums of money to the Children's Hospital in Pittsburgh. He would routinely spend afternoons at the hospital visiting young patients. "Anything for kids," he would say. Before one of Pittsburgh's games, a Pirates' announcer took Clemente over to the stands to meet a fourteen-year-old boy who was deaf. Roberto met the boy and returned to the Pirates' dugout. He then grabbed one of his bats, autographed it, climbed into the stands, and walked fifteen rows up into the reserved seats to hand the bat to the teenager.

On another occasion, a television company asked Clemente to record a film urging teenagers to avoid using drugs. When Clemente arrived to record the video, he expressed dismay that the company planned to record the film in English only. Clemente remarked that there were many Spanish-speaking children who were also at risk. The producer told Clemente that the script was only in English and there was no one to translate it. Clemente then sat down with pen and paper and spent an hour translating the script into Spanish.

Once, while playing right field at Pittsburgh's Forbes Field, Clemente watched an older fan in the stands wrestle a foul ball away from a young boy. The incident left the boy crying. The next inning, when Clemente returned to his right-field position, he gave the boy a ball from the dugout and told him, "Here's a ball for the one they took away from you."

Clemente dreamed of building a "Sports City" in Puerto Rico where children could stay for weeks at a time. He envisioned a complex that would have baseball fields, basketball and tennis courts, a swimming pool, and other recreational sites to help children pursue their dreams. After Clemente's death, contributions flowed in for Sports City. The Roberto Clemente Sports City opened in Puerto Rico in 1974. It was the legacy of an individual who would tell his children, "Anytime you have an opportunity to make a difference in this world and you don't, then you are wasting your time on Earth."

◆   ◆   ◆

May your compassion come quickly, for we have been brought very low.
—Psalm 79, verse 8.

MAX BEILKE

In 1972, Max J. Beilke, a master sergeant in the U.S. Army, was assigned to duty at Camp Alpha, located at Tan Son Nhut Airbase on the outskirts of Saigon, Vietnam. At forty years of age, Beilke was on the downside of his athletic career. Nonetheless, at six feet four inches tall, he could still be a force in pickup basketball games. Every day during the hours preceding dusk, Beilke would lace up his Converse low-cut sneakers and take to the court. Lacking a reliable outside shot, he positioned himself near the hoop and battled for rebounds. He scored his points by gathering in wayward shots and kissing the ball off the backboard. In January 1973, the United States signed the Paris Peace Accord, ending the Vietnam conflict. On March 29, 1973, Beilke boarded an Air Force C-130 "freedom bird" at Tan Son Nhut, his tour of duty finished. He was the last member of the U.S. combat forces to leave Vietnamese soil. After retiring from active military duty, Beilke became an advocate for military retirees, serving as the Army's Deputy Chief of Retirement Services. He was killed in the terrorist attack at the Pentagon on September 11, 2001. In March 2007, the U.S. Army established the Max J. Beilke Human Resource Center at Fort Meade, Maryland in his memory.

When the United States and North Vietnam signed the Paris Peace Accord in January 1973, it set in motion an elaborate process for the withdrawal of the 23,500 U.S. combat forces still remaining in Vietnam. All U.S. combat troops were to leave Vietnamese soil by March 29, 1973. Similarly, by that same date, Hanoi was to release all of the 587 Americans being held as prisoners of war.

With the signing of the peace accord, U.S. military personnel stationed throughout South Vietnam began filtering into one of two Army camps used as processing centers, Camp Horn, which was located near the city of Danang, and Camp Alpha. For every prisoner of war who boarded an evacuation plane in Hanoi, forty American combat troops were to depart from South Vietnam. Departing U.S. troop transports were not permitted to take off until an Air Force plane carrying a corresponding number of POWs had safely lifted off from Hanoi.

At all three departure points, Hanoi, Danang, and Tan Son Nhut, there were officials on hand from both the United States and North Vietnam to supervise the process. The North Vietnamese observer team at Tan Son Nhut Airbase was headed by an army colonel named Bui Tin.

On March 29, Colonel Tin watched as U.S. soldiers boarded the final troop transport out of Vietnam. Tin attempted to shake hands with the departing troops. Most rebuffed his gesture. One uttered an obscenity. Then Max Beilke, the last American combat soldier in all of Vietnam, approached the plane's ramp. "Peace," Tin said to Beilke.

Tenacious on the basketball court but ever gracious off it, Beilke reacted with quiet dignity. He looked Tin in the eye, accepted the colonel's gift of a small painting of a pagoda, and said, "Thank you."

◆   ◆   ◆

Blessed are the peacemakers.
—Matthew 5, verse 9.

JIM and GLORIA SMITH

Jim and Gloria Smith, husband and wife, teamed together to establish the Franklin Field Tennis Center, a not-for-profit mecca for tennis located in the middle of Boston's ghetto area. Gloria Smith was an accomplished tennis player in the 1950s and the first African American woman to gain a U.S. Tennis Association ranking in New England. She would later win the New England women's tennis championship. Much more portly and far less nimble than his wife, Jim Smith was noted more for his enthusiasm for tennis than for competence on the court. In 1969, the Smiths had only a blueprint for a tennis facility, twenty-eight dollars in assets, and the dream of building a center for street kids. The Smiths parlayed those modest assets into a warehouse-size tennis complex that opened in 1973. Gloria Smith died on April 25, 1997, at the age of sixty-four. Jim Smith died on November 21, 1997. He was eighty-three years old.

In 1969 Australian tennis legend Rod Laver came to Boston to play in a professional tournament. During a lull in his schedule, Laver gave a tennis clinic at the Carter Playground in Dorchester, a Boston subdivision. The Carter tennis courts were cracked and in terrible condition. Laver was shocked. "How can a major city in this wealthy country have such awful courts?" he asked.

Laver wasn't the only one to ask the question. Jim Smith had posed the same question on countless occasions to Boston city officials. By Smith's count, there were only seven public tennis courts in Boston that were playable. Smith would tell anyone who would listen that "if we keep kids on a court, they will stay out of a judge's court."

Rebuffed with regularity at City Hall, Smith decided on a different tactic. He worked to raise private funds to build a tennis center. Smith talked Arthur Ashe into coming to Boston for a fund-raising dinner. He drew up blueprints for a complex that would have both indoor and outdoor courts. He appealed to the Gillette Company, Polaroid, and other prominent corporations for financial support. He persuaded the *Boston Globe* to lend editorial support. He worked with Ashe to organize fund-raising matches at Harvard featuring Davis Cup veterans.

He lobbied members of the City Council, ultimately obtaining Council approval to use a block of land in Dorchester.

Armed with a dream that wouldn't die and the assistance of his tennis-playing wife, Smith labored tirelessly to achieve his goal. "Spit in one hand and wish in the other," he would say, "and see which one fills up faster." His efforts proved fruitful. By 1973, the Smiths opened the Franklin Field Tennis Center on Dorchester's Blue Hill Avenue, with seven indoor and five outdoor courts. The facility was the first tennis club in the country owned by African Americans.

Since the Tennis Center opened, its instructors have combined tennis lessons for children with guidance on the importance of staying in school. The Center has helped more than thirty thousand inner-city children, at least three hundred of whom have won college tennis scholarships. An average of thirteen hundred children receive instruction at the center each year.

In the words of a former Tennis Center student, "to play for Mister Smith was to learn how to deal with strategy, human nature, pressure, and the white, white world. He brought this beautiful game to us." Gloria Smith walked with her husband every step of the way, encouraging his dreams, finding hope in children, and serving as the housemother of the Tennis Center.

◆   ◆   ◆

Train a boy in the way he should go; even when he is old, he will not swerve from it.
—Proverbs 22, verse 6.

JOEY CAPPELLETTI

Joey Cappelletti was the youngest of five children born to Anne and John Cappelletti. During the 1970s, Joey's older brother, John, Jr., was a highly acclaimed running back, first as an All-American at Penn State University and, later, as an all-purpose back for the NFL's Los Angeles Rams. Joey was diagnosed with leukemia when he was five years old. In 1971, he lapsed into a coma that lasted for several months. He came out of the coma, learned to walk and talk again, and lived to see his brother John win the Heisman Trophy in 1973. Joey died on April 8, 1976, at the age of thirteen.

On Monday afternoon, December 13, 1973, as John Cappelletti performed a final review of his notes for his Heisman Trophy acceptance speech, he scribbled the words "something special" at the bottom of the page. A few hours earlier, Jean Cappelletti, sister of the Heisman Trophy winner, had addressed her younger brother Joey in one of the guest rooms at Manhattan's Downtown Athletic Club. "Hey, Joey," she said, "I'll bet the bellman doesn't know you're a celebrity." "I'm not a celebrity," Joey responded. "John's a celebrity. I'm not anything at all."

Celebrity status would come quickly to Joey Cappelletti. That evening, after Vice President Gerald R. Ford had presented the Heisman to John Cappelletti, the All-American launched into his acceptance speech. He thanked his college teammates and the Penn State coach, Joe Paterno. He spoke of his father and of his brothers, Martin and Michael, and sister Jean. Then John Cappelletti got to the "something special" portion of his speech. Bereft of notes, Cappelletti turned his attention to Joey:

> The youngest member of our family, my brother Joseph, is ill. He has leukemia. If I could dedicate this trophy to him, if it could give him one day of happiness, it would all be worthwhile. They say I've shown courage on the football field, but for me it's only on the field, and only in the fall. Joey lives with pain all the time. His courage is round the clock. I want him to have this trophy. It's more his than mine, because he's been such an inspiration to me.

At the end of the festivities, photographers rushed to the Cappelletti's table. "How do you feel, Joey?" a newsman asked. "I feel great!" Joey answered.

◆   ◆   ◆

The Lord sustains them on their sickbed, allays the malady when they are ill.
—Psalm 41, verse 4.

GERALD R. FORD

On August 9, 1974, Vice President Gerald Ford was sworn in as the thirty-eighth President of the United States. Earlier that day, Ford's predecessor, Richard M. Nixon, had left the White House in disgrace. The country was in turmoil. Day after day, new evidence was surfacing that confirmed Nixon's involvement in covering up the White House-inspired burglary of the Democratic National Committee's head-quarters at the Watergate building. On August 9, with an impeachment vote looming in the House of Representatives, Nixon resigned and Ford assumed the Presidency. Ford came to the White House with a well-stacked resume. An excellent high school and collegiate athlete, he was a member of two national championship football teams while playing for the University of Michigan. In his senior year at Michigan, he was voted the team's Most Valuable Player. Following graduation, Ford earned his law degree from Yale University. During World War II, he was an officer in the U.S. Navy, with eighteen months of service as an antiaircraft officer aboard the USS Monterey. After returning to civilian life, Ford campaigned for and won a seat in the U.S. House of Representatives, beginning a period of twenty-five years in Congress. From 1965 to 1973, he served as the Republican Minority Leader of the House. Ford died on December 26, 2006, at the age of ninety-three.

In his teenage years, Gerald Ford displayed a quick temper. To teach Ford to control his childish outbursts, his mother insisted that he memorize and be able to recite, word for word, Rudyard Kipling's poem, *If.* In the years that followed, the lessons ingrained in Ford through recitation of the poem served him well.

By 1934, Ford's senior year at the University of Michigan, he was already a prominent athlete, having played center on the 1932 and 1933 national championship teams. Nonetheless, Ford was ready to sacrifice his position on the football team for the sake of friendship. Michigan's schedule for the 1934 season included a game against Georgia Tech. Well before the start of the season, the Georgia Tech athletic director had made it known that Tech would not take the field against Michigan if African American Willis Ward, one of the Wolverines' best players and Ford's roommate for road games, would be playing. On the day of the game, even as kickoff approached, Michigan steadfastly refused to disclose

204

whether Ward would play. However, when the Michigan team took the field, Ward was not in uniform. The University's refusal to support Ward angered Ford. He decided not to play against Georgia Tech and considered quitting for the season. Ultimately, Ford did take the field against Georgia Tech—but only because Ward urged him to play.

In later life, Ford used the lessons learned from the Georgia Tech episode when minority admission policies came under attack at colleges and universities. In August 1999, Ford composed an op-ed essay for the *New York Times* in which he strongly supported affirmative action programs. "Tolerance, breadth of mind, and appreciation for the world beyond our neighborhoods," Ford wrote, "can be learned on the football field and in the science lab, as well as in the lecture hall. But only if students are exposed to America in all her variety." Ford concluded his essay with the question, "Do we really want to risk turning back the clock to an era when the Willis Wards were isolated and penalized for the color of their skin, their economic standing, or national ancestry?"

As president, no issue weighed more heavily on Ford than the question of whether to pardon his predecessor, Richard Nixon, for Nixon's role in covering up the burglary of the Democratic National Committee headquarters. On September 8, 1974, a month after he was sworn in as president, Ford announced to the country that he had granted a "full, free, and absolute" pardon to Nixon for "all offenses against the United States which he ... [had] committed or may have committed" during his time in the White House. Ford was well aware that the decision would provoke a storm of criticism throughout the country. He was also convinced, however, that the country would remain needlessly mired in the Watergate scandal unless it could put the issue of Nixon's criminal conduct to rest. "It is not the ultimate fate of Richard Nixon that most concerns me," Ford stated, "but the immediate future of this great country." There were two simultaneous, almost immediate effects, of the pardon: (1) as Ford had hoped, the country was able to move past Watergate and focus on more pressing economic and social issues; and (2) Ford's political future was all but doomed. Predictably, in the presidential election of 1976, Democratic challenger Jimmy Carter prevailed, ending Ford's tenure in the White House after 895 days.

In the three decades that have passed since Ford vacated the Oval Office, his decision to pardon Nixon—at the cost of his own political future—has come to be viewed as an act of extraordinary political courage. In 2001, the John F. Kennedy Library Foundation honored Ford's decision by awarding him its Profile in Courage Award.

◆   ◆   ◆

You forgave the guilt of your people, pardoned all their sins.
—Psalm 85, verse 3.

If

by Rudyard Kipling (1865–1936)

If you can keep your head when all about you
Are losing theirs and blaming it on you;
If you can trust yourself when all men doubt you,
But make allowance for their doubting too;
If you can wait and not be tired by waiting,
Or, being lied about, don't deal in lies,
Or, being hated, don't give way to hating,
And yet don't look too good, nor talk too wise;

If you can dream—and not make dreams your master;
If you can think—and not make thoughts your aim;
If you can meet with triumph and disaster
And treat those two imposters just the same;
If you can bear to hear the truth you've spoken
Twisted by knaves to make a trap for fools,
or watch the things you gave your life to broken,
And stoop and build 'em up with wornout tools;

If you can make one heap of all your winnings
And risk it on one turn of pitch-and-toss,
And lose, and start again at your beginnings
And never breathe a word about your loss;
If you can force your heart and nerve and sinew
To serve your turn long after they are gone,
And so hold on when there is nothing in you
Except the Will which says to them: "Hold on!";

If you can talk with crowds and keep your virtue,
Or walk with kings—nor lose the common touch;
If neither foes nor loving friends can hurt you;
If all men count with you, but none too much;
If you can fill the unforgiving minute

With sixty seconds' worth of distance run—
Yours is the Earth and everything that's in it,
And—which is more—you'll be a Man my son!

AL McGUIRE

Alfred "Al" McGuire spent four years as a pro basketball player, twenty years as a col-
lege coach, twenty-three years as a broadcaster, and an entire lifetime as an eccentric.
He was thus able to view both life and basketball from a variety of different perspec-
tives. McGuire starred in basketball at St. John's University, and then went on to play
professionally for both the New York Knicks and the Baltimore Bullets. He began his
coaching career at Belmont Abbey in North Carolina in 1957 and moved to
Marquette University in 1964. In 1977, he led underdog Marquette to victory over
the University of North Carolina in the finals of the NCAA Tournament, the first
and only time that Marquette has won the NCAA Championship. During his two
decades as a college coach, McGuire recorded 405 wins and 143 losses. He died of
acute leukemia on January 26, 2001, at the age of seventy-two.

Al McGuire used to say that "the size of the funeral was dependent on the
weather." On Monday, January 29, 2001, the weather in Milwaukee—cold and
rainy—provided ample excuse for people to stay home. Even so, a crowd of fifteen hundred packed the Gesu Church in downtown Milwaukee for McGuire's
funeral. One man who stayed home, a McGuire fan from Kentucky, wrote a letter to express his sentiments. Years earlier, the man had spoken to McGuire in an
airport for two minutes. Those two minutes with McGuire, the man said, had
"touched him forever."

McGuire possessed a unique personality, a fact of which he was keenly aware.
"When I'm losing, they call me 'nuts'," he once said. "When I'm winning, they
call me 'eccentric.'"

If people called McGuire eccentric, it was not without reason. In one of Marquette's games, McGuire strode onto the court during a lull in the action to protest a foul called on one of his players. As the Marquette opponent who had been
fouled prepared to shoot the free throw, McGuire sidled up to the referee. "That
was a lousy call," McGuire said. "You can't be here," the referee responded.
"Yeah, but it was a lousy call," McGuire repeated. Losing patience, the referee
told McGuire, "I'm going to give you a technical foul for each step it takes you to
get back to the bench." Loath to pick up unnecessary technical fouls, McGuire

motioned to two of his players to come pick him up and carry him back to the Marquette bench. Safely ensconced on the bench—without having taken a step—McGuire yelled to the referee, "Now what are you going to do?"

In 1978, McGuire and fellow NBC announcer Billy Packer were in St. Louis on Easter Sunday to broadcast the NCAA men's Final Four championship basketball game. On Easter morning, Packer attended church services at a Catholic chapel. From the back of the chapel, Packer noticed a row of worshipers in the front who, judging by their ragged clothes, appeared to be homeless. Packer said a quick prayer for those less fortunate than he. After moving up closer to the front, Packer saw that his esteemed broadcasting partner, dressed in the clothes of a pauper, was seated in the midst of the homeless individuals. "A damn nut," Packer concluded. Much later, after Packer and McGuire had become close friends, Packer learned that McGuire usually dressed in "homeless garb" when not working. Or, as McGuire once explained, "Whenever I put on my sincere suit—the three-piece job—I feel I should be getting paid."

McGuire stood out as much for his unconventional observations as for his attire. In 1972, when Marquette fans learned that McGuire had encouraged sophomore All-American center Jim Chones to pass up his final two years of college and turn pro, McGuire felt compelled to explain. "I looked at my fridge and it was full. I looked at Jim's and it was empty. Case closed," McGuire said. "There was no way I could tell Jim not to take the money." McGuire retired from coaching in May 1977, months after leading Marquette to the NCAA championship. There's more to life, he had concluded, than "coaching guys in short pants."

"Dream big," McGuire encouraged Chones and the rest of his players. "Don't be just another guy going down the street and going nowhere." To others, he said, "Help one kid at a time. He'll maybe go back and help a few more. In a generation, you'll have something." For McGuire, the secret to both good basketball and a good life was simple: "It all gets down to love," he said. "If we have love, we'll be good. If we don't, we'll be bad."

McGuire was one of the first coaches to recruit players from poverty-stricken areas like the Robert Taylor Homes in Chicago or Bedford-Stuyvesant in New York. "My rule was that I wouldn't recruit a kid if he had grass in front of his house," McGuire said.

In 1978, McGuire founded Al's Run, an annual five-mile charity run and walk event that, even after McGuire's death, attracts twenty-five thousand participants annually. Since its inception, Al's Run has raised millions of dollars for the Milwaukee Children's Hospital. An avid motorcycle rider, McGuire also started McGuire's Run, which has grown into the third largest motorcycle ride in the country. McGuire's Run draws more than twenty-six thousand riders each year. The proceeds also go to benefit the Children's Hospital.

McGuire was an impassioned fan of *The Little Prince*, Antoine de Saint-Exupéry's fairy-tale novel of love and compassion. McGuire often gave copies of the novel to friends and colleagues. It was his distinctive way of spreading smiles.

During the last few months before McGuire died, there was a steady stream of visitors to see him at the hospice where he stayed. Each guest was limited to fifteen minutes. Just before it was time for a visitor to leave, McGuire would say, "Give me a hug." Then, with great effort, McGuire would get out of his bed and stand up to receive the hug. After observing the same sequence, visitor after visitor, McGuire's son, Allie, told his father, "You don't always have to get up." McGuire replied, "Son, I have to get up. They have to remember me as strong."

◆　　◆　　◆

The mouths of the just utter wisdom; their tongues speak what is right.
—Psalm 37, verse 30.

MAURA O'DONNELL

When Maura O'Donnell was three weeks old, doctors diagnosed her as having cystic fibrosis. The disease continued to afflict her throughout her life, but she rarely let it slow her down. O'Donnell graduated with honors from Bishop O'Connell High School in Arlington, Virginia, in 1976. During her four years at O'Connell, she earned nine varsity letters in field hockey, softball, basketball, and diving. She was a Virginia State High School diving champion. O'Donnell died on May 11, 1978, at the age of twenty.

For the better part of her life, Maura O'Donnell had to undergo aerosol inhalation therapy three times each day. The therapy involved putting on a face mask and breathing in a medical agent that would liquefy the mucus in her lungs. O'Donnell never seemed to dwell on her affliction. Her concern for others was paramount. In the words of one high school friend, "No matter how sick she was, she always asked first about you." Another friend observed that O'Donnell "gave everybody something to live for."

After her younger sister died at the age of sixteen, O'Donnell helped to organize the first Bishop O'Connell cystic fibrosis Super Dance in memory of her sister. O'Donnell danced for twelve hours at that event, helping to raise thirty-one thousand dollars for the Cystic Fibrosis Foundation. Upon graduating from high school, O'Donnell enrolled in the nursing program at Marymount College. She aspired to help children suffering from chronic diseases. O'Donnell was hospitalized in March of her sophomore year at Marymount, but left her hospital bed to attend the third annual Bishop O'Connell Super Dance. She died two months later. At her death, Marymount's director of health services said, "She was full of energy, never bitter. She thought she had lived a full life."

◆　　◆　　◆

Remember how brief is my life, how frail the race you created!
—Psalm 89, verse 48.

DARRYL STINGLEY

Darryl Stingley spent five years, from 1973 to 1977, with the New England Patriots as a wide receiver. A first-round draft choice out of Purdue University, Stingley caught 110 passes during his pro career and scored fourteen touchdowns. His best year came in 1977, when he had thirty-nine receptions for 657 yards and five touchdowns. Stingley's football career ended abruptly on August 12, 1978, when Oakland Raiders safety Jack Tatum hit him while Stingley was diving to catch a pass during an exhibition game. The collision severed Stingley's fourth and fifth vertebrae, paralyzing him from the neck down. Stingley was confined to a wheelchair for the rest of his life and required round-the-clock assistance. He died on April 5, 2007, at the age of fifty-five.

"Star patient, my ass," Darryl Stingley yelled from his bed in a Chicago hospital. "Get out of here right now. I'm not on exhibit for anyone." The outburst came when a doctor attempted to introduce Stingley to a group of visitors. Someone in the group had made the mistake of referring to Stingley as a "star patient."

In the weeks following his injury, Stingley was far from a star patient. He was a football player who had been deprived of both his identity and his career.

At first, Stingley questioned why God would allow him to suffer such a devastating injury. It wasn't until he stopped asking "why" that he began to live again. He came to see the injury as a test of his faith—and, in time, as a blessing. "I've been touched by God in a special way, allowing him to work through me to inspire people," Stingley said.

For a long time after his injury, Stingley refused to give interviews. Gradually, however, he began to discuss his situation with others, and he began to live again. He completed his bachelor's degree at Purdue. He served on the Big Ten advisory commission on affirmative action and was a member of a Chicago advisory committee on the disabled. He attended Chicago White Sox and Chicago Bulls games. With assistance from others, he published an inspirational autobiography in 1983 titled *Happy to Be Alive*. He also established a nonprofit organization, the Darryl Stingley Youth Foundation, to encourage self-esteem and growth among inner-city children.

Stingley became a popular motivational speaker, one blessed with a special appeal to youngsters. When preparing to give a speech, he never put his words on paper. Instead, he would say a prayer before the speech, asking God to give him the right words. Stingley found that prayer gave him "a boldness, like King David must have felt in facing Goliath."

When others, particularly children, suffered paralyzing injuries, Stingley was often the first individual whom people consulted for help. He was a mentor and best friend to Kenneth Jennings, a Chicago high school student who was paralyzed during a football game in 1988. Jennings found that many people treated him as if his life was over. With Stingley's guidance, Jennings came to realize that his "second life" had just begun.

Stingley consciously rejected any inclination to be bitter about his condition. "You've got to let it go," he said, "and be happy with yourself, happy to be alive." He also admitted, however, that "it took me time to exorcise all the demons." He gratefully acknowledged the role that God played in helping him to accept his physical limitations. "Human nature teaches us to hate," he would say, but "God teaches us to love."

For Stingley, being thankful was the key. "When I started thanking God that I was still alive," he told others, "that's when I really started living again."

◆   ◆   ◆

This is my comfort in affliction, your promise that gives me life.
—Proverbs 119, verse 50.

LYMAN BOSTOCK

Lyman Wesley Bostock broke into the major leagues with the Minnesota Twins in 1975 and quickly established himself as a bona fide baseball star. In his rookie season, he hit .282. He followed up his rookie year by hitting .323 in 1976. The next year, playing in 153 games for the Twins, Bostock batted .336 and hit fourteen home runs. In November 1977, he signed a five-year, $2.3 million contract to play for the California Angels. A deranged gunman in Gary, Indiana shot and killed Bostock on September 23, 1978. At his death, Bostock was twenty-seven years old.

One of the first things that Lyman Bostock did after signing his $2.3 million contract with the Angels was to donate ten thousand dollars to help rebuild a church in Birmingham, Alabama, that had been destroyed by fire. It would not be the last time that Bostock made a sizeable donation for a charitable cause. Weighted down by the expectations that accompanied his new million dollar contract, Bostock hit below .200 during the first month of the 1978 season. Deeply disappointed, Bostock told Angels owner Gene Autry that he wanted to give back his pay for the first month. Autry refused to accept the money. Sensing Bostock's resolve, however, Autry helped him donate his paychecks for the month to charity.

On Sunday, September 10, 1978, the Angels played the Kansas City Royals in a twilight game at Anaheim Stadium. It would be the last game that Bostock would ever play at the Angels' home park. After the game, Bostock was the last California player to leave the team's dressing room. As he exited the gate near the clubhouse, he encountered two young teenagers in search of autographs. Bostock chatted with the boys and expressed concern that they were out too late by themselves. He learned that the father of one of the boys would be coming later to pick them up. Not wanting to leave the boys all alone, Bostock took them across the street to a restaurant and stayed with them until their ride arrived.

The next day, the Angels embarked on a twelve-game road trip that would take them to Texas, Kansas City, Minnesota, and Chicago. On Saturday, September 23, the Angels played an afternoon game against the White Sox in Chicago. After the game, Bostock traveled to nearby Gary, Indiana, to sign autographs for children in the Gary ghetto and visit his uncle. Bostock was killed that same evening while riding in the back seat of his uncle's car.

◆   ◆   ◆

For God commands the angels to guard you in all your ways.
—Psalm 91, verse 11.

WILLIE STARGELL

Outfielder and first baseman Wilver "Willie" Stargell began his major league baseball career in 1962 at the age of twenty-two. He spent the next twenty seasons in the major leagues, all as a member of the Pittsburgh Pirates. Stargell twice led the National League in home runs. For his career, he hit 475 regular season homers with a lifetime batting average of .282. Led by Stargell's forty-eight home runs and teammate Roberto Clemente's .341 batting average, the Pirates won the 1971 National League pennant and went on to defeat the Baltimore Orioles in the World Series. In 1979, Stargell clubbed thirty-two home runs, leading the Pirates to the World Series and a repeat engagement with Baltimore. The Pirates again beat Baltimore in the Series, with Stargell hitting three home runs and collecting twelve hits in thirty at bats. That year, he became the first and only major league player ever to win the Most Valuable Player awards for the regular season, the league playoff series, and the World Series in the same season. Stargell died of a kidney disorder on April 9, 2001, at the age of sixty-one.

"When Clemente died," former Pittsburgh Pirates pitcher Steve Blass said, "I went to Willie's house. When Willie died, I didn't know where to go."

Blass was not alone. From the day of Roberto Clemente's death in 1972, Willie Stargell was the undisputed leader of the Pirates, both on and off the field. He was affectionately called "Pops" by nearly everyone in the Pittsburgh organization. His passing left a huge void.

Early in his career, Stargell learned a lesson that helped to forge his leadership skills. He had traveled with his minor league team to play a game in Plainview, Texas. He was nineteen years old, a pro ballplayer for less than a year. Stargell arrived at the Plainview ballpark early. As he was entering the stadium, two men approached him. One of them put a shotgun to Stargell's head and said, "Nigger, if you play today, we're going to blow your brains out."

Stargell played that day in Plainview—and played well. No shots were fired. Stargell never again saw the men who had threatened him. From that day on, he decided never to let anyone interfere with what he was trying to accomplish.

Stargell was a leader in the Pirate clubhouse, in the community, and in his neighborhood. During heavy snowfalls, when the snowplows would leave mounds of snow blocking the driveways in his neighborhood, Stargell would roust his neighbors from their homes and organize shoveling crews. Later, after the shoveling had been completed, Stargell would start a bonfire in the middle of the street and stage a neighborhood party.

Stargell loved to spend time with children. He could often be found at Pittsburgh's Mellon Park, playing basketball with local teenagers. One year at Christmas, Stargell encountered two women in a grocery store. He overheard one of the women comment that, if she spent too much on food, she might not have enough money for Christmas presents. When the women were checking out, Stargell approached them and said, "Ladies, will you do me a favor? Will you let me buy your groceries?" Initially, the women resisted, telling Stargell that he didn't have to pay. Stargell insisted. "It would make my Christmas," he told the women.

For Stargell, such acts of charity were commonplace. He also devoted much of his spare time to raising money for research on sickle cell anemia. "He taught us about love," former teammate Al Oliver said. "He proved that people of different races and backgrounds can come together for one common purpose."

◆   ◆   ◆

Be not afraid of sudden terror.
—Proverbs 3, verse 25.

References

Brian Piccolo

Morris, Jeannie. *Brian Piccolo: A Short Season*. New York: Dell Publishing Company, Inc., 1971.

Freddie Steinmark

Steinmark, Freddie. *I Play to Win*. Boston: Little, Brown and Company, 1971.

Gerry Bertier

Sullivan, Steve. *Remember This Titan: Lessons Learned From a Celebrated Coach's Journey*. Boulder, CO: Taylor Trade Publishing, 2005.

Recollections of Becky Britt, sister of Gerry Bertier, http://71Original Titans.com.

Tom Landry

Kirk Bohls, "Tom Landry, 1924–2000: Recalling 'A Holy Man' Who Coached," *Austin American Statesman*, 18 February 2000, C1.

Rick Cantu, "Landry's Stars, Fans Recall A Life Well Lived," *Austin American Statesman*, 18 February 2000, A1.

Mickey Herskowitz, "Coach's Legacy Will Remain Strong," *Houston Chronicle*, 18 February 2000, 1.

Richard Justice, "'God, Family and Football'; Landry's Priorities Recalled at Memorial," 18 February 2000, D1.

Terry Mattingly, "Tom Landry Realized There Was More to Life Than Football," *Knoxville News-Sentinel*, 19 February 2000, B2.

"Cowboys Tom Landry Was A True Role Model," (Bloomington, IL) *Pantagraph*, 2 March 2000, A10.

Shirley Povich

> Povich, Shirley. *All Those Mornings ... At the Post*. New York: Public Affairs, 2005.

Roberto Clemente

> Joseph Durso, "A Man of Two Worlds," *The New York Times*, 2 January 1973, 48.

> Leonard Koppett, "Clemente A Player Involved On and Off the Diamond," *The New York Times*, 2 January 1973, 48.

> Wagenheim, Kal. *Clemente!* Chicago: Olmstead Press, 2001.

> "Clemente, Pirates' Star, Dies in Crash Of Plane Carrying Aid to Nicaragua," *The New York Times*, 2 January 1973, 73.

Max Beilke

> Jo Colvin, "A Brother to All," *Alexandria Echo Press*, 20 June 2007.

> Steve Vogel, "From War Veterans to Pentagon Victims; Battle Survivors Became Casualties of New War," *The Washington Post*, 27 May 2002, B1.

Jim and Gloria Smith

> Touré, "The Last of the Great Dreamers," in *Coach: 25 Writers Reflect On People Who Made A Difference*, Andrew Blauner, ed. New York: Warner Books, 2005.

Joey Cappelletti

> McNeely, Jerry. *Something for Joey*. New York: Random House Children's Books, 2001.

Gerald R. Ford

> Bob Ford, "Everyone Could Learn A Little From Gerald Ford," *Knight Ridder Tribune News Service*, 3 January 2007, 1.

> Gerald R. Ford, "Inclusive America, Under Attack," *The New York Times*, 8 August 1999, Sec. 4, 15.

William Gildea, "Ford Always Managed to Be a Good Sport," *The Washington Post*, 28 December 2006, E1.

John Pomfret, "A Regular Guy Who Showed a Devotion to Local Causes," *The Washington Post*, 29 December 2006, A18.

Richard Sisk, "He Tackled Racism At U of Michigan," *Daily News World & National Report*, http://nydailynews.com/news/wn_report/story/485231p-408535c.html.

Al McGuire

Jimmy Breslin, "Al McGuire: A Coach That Everyone Loved," *Seattle Times*, 30 January 2001, C1.

Bill Dwyre, "Milwaukee Was Touched By A Warrior: Former Coach and Broadcaster McGuire Inspires Tears and Laughter at Funeral," *Los Angeles Times*, 30 January 2001, D1.

Gary D. Howard, "Coach Was A True Pioneer in Bringing Races Together," *Milwaukee Journal Sentinel*, 30 January 2001, 1C.

Don Walker, "Holding Court One Last Time," *Milwaukee Journal Sentinel*, 30 January 2001, 1C.

Dick Weiss, "Farewell To A True Warrior; Basketball World Honors McGuire," *New York Daily News*, 30 January 2001, 59.

Judd Zulgad, "Al McGuire: A Tribute, 1928–2001," (Minneapolis) *Star Tribune*, 30 March 2001, 34N.

Maura O'Donnell

Jean R. Halley, "Sister of 3 Other Victims Dies From Cystic Fibrosis," *The Washington Post*, 13 May 1978, B4.

Darryl Stingley

John Altavilla, "Despite Paralysis, An Inspiration to the End; Darryl Stingley: 1951–2007," *Hartford Courant*, 6 April 2007, C1.

Joe Fitzgerald, "Through Faith, Stingley Never Stopped Giving," *Boston Herald*, 6 April 2007, 82.

Dave Goldberg, "Receiver Was Paralyzed by Tatum's Hit," (Torrance, CA) *Daily Breeze*, 6 April 2007, D4.

Neil Hayes, "Symbol of Hope, Triumph; Paralyzed by Tatum Hit at 26, Ex-Marshall Star Thrived by Looking to Future, Not Past," *Chicago Sun-Times*, 6 April 2007, 122.

Bob Ryan, "Hit Never Led to Hate," *Boston Globe*, 6 April 2007, E1.

Clyde Travis, "Jennings: 'Everything I Am … Was Because of Him'," *Chicago Sun-Times*, 6 April 2007, 123.

"For the Record: Darryl Stingley, 1951–2007," *Sports Illustrated*, 16 April 2007, 18.

Lyman Bostock

Daniel Michael, "A Very Good Ballplayer But An Even Better Man," The Lyman Bostock Tribute Page, http://angelfire.com/journal2/davismi/lymanbostock.html.

"Angel Star Bostock Dies In Shooting," *The Washington Post*, 25 September 1978, D1.

Willie Stargell

Ron Cook, "Stargell Touches 'Em All Again," *Pittsburgh Post-Gazette*, 15 April 2001, A1.

Terence Moore, "'Pops' Did It His Way," *Milwaukee Journal Sentinel*, 15 April 2001, 4C.

Jack O'Connell, "Stargell Always Had the Model Stance," *Hartford Courant*, 15 April 2001, E6.

1980–1989

1980–1989

As the eighties began, the Soviet Union continued its buildup of military forces in Afghanistan. The Soviet occupation of Afghanistan drew widespread opposition from the United States, England, China, Saudi Arabia, Egypt, and many other countries. In response to the Soviet aggression, the United States and sixty-five other countries agreed to boycott the 1980 summer Olympics that were to be held in Moscow.

In 1980, Republican Ronald Reagan and running mate George H. W. Bush easily defeated the incumbent tandem of Jimmy Carter and Walter Mondale in the presidential election. That same year, a deranged fan shot and killed former Beatle John Lennon outside Lennon's New York City apartment. In 1981, Iran released fifty-two Americans who had been taken as hostages. The Americans had spent 444 days in captivity.

Seventy-eight people died in 1982 when an Air Florida jet crashed into the Potomac River in Washington, D.C., during a winter blizzard. In 1983, a suicide bombing attack in Beirut killed a total of 241 personnel from the U.S. Navy and Marines. The year 1983 also saw U.S. forces invade Grenada to guard the evacuation of American citizens after a Marxist takeover. That same year, Sally Ride became America's first woman in space as a crew member of the space shuttle *Challenger*.

In 1985, an all-star cast of performers created the musical video *We Are the World*, raising millions of dollars for starving children in Africa. Domestically, the Reagan administration continued to reduce federal housing expenditures for the poor. Overall, as part of its plan to trickle down economic benefits to the most impoverished segments of society, the Reagan administration would trim more than thirty-five billion dollars from the federal housing budget between 1981 and 1988.

The space shuttle *Challenger* disintegrated shortly after takeoff in 1986. Elementary school teacher Christa McAuliffe, a member of the *Challenger* crew, died in the blast as her students watched television coverage from their Concord, New Hampshire classroom. In 1987, Chicago Bears running back Walter Payton retired. At the time, Payton was the National Football League's career rushing leader with 16,726 yards.

In 1989, baseball superstar Pete Rose, then manager of the Cincinnati Reds, was banned for life from involvement with Major League Baseball for betting on big league games, including games involving Cincinnati.

HAROLD McLINTON

The Washington Redskins drafted linebacker Harold McLinton in the sixth round of the 1969 NFL draft. A graduate of Southern University, McLinton played for the Redskins for ten seasons, from 1969 to 1978. He starred as the Redskins' middle linebacker on the 1972 team, which won the National Football Conference championship. McLinton and his teammates went on to play in Super Bowl VII but lost to the Miami Dolphins. McLinton died on October 31, 1980, when a motorist struck him as he stood on the shoulder of a Virginia interstate highway. McLinton had gotten out of his car to thank an acquaintance for leading him to the interstate. He was thirty-three years old.

Upon learning of Harold McLinton's death, former teammate Mike Bass said, "There are givers and there are takers. Harold was a giver." When McLinton died, he was returning from a trip to Lorton, Virginia where he had spent time talking to prison inmates.

Whether working with children or speaking to groups of at-risk adults, McLinton's generosity, with both his time and money, was endless. During his years in professional football, the Redskins held their summer training camps in Carlisle, Pennsylvania. In the evenings, after practices had ended, McLinton would invite some of the poorer children from the Carlisle area to sit down at the team's training table and eat dinner with himself and other players. McLinton routinely volunteered his time on weekends at the Hillcrest Children's Center in the District of Columbia to work with inner-city children.

Working with Washington running back Larry Brown, McLinton filmed a public service clip for television at the Children's Center. The TV spot showed the two players instructing a group of children in water safety measures. It was the first NFL community involvement commercial ever to appear on national TV, and became the model for hundreds of similar announcements that would follow.

◆   ◆   ◆

All ate a meal fit for heroes; food he sent in abundance.
—Psalm 78, verse 25.

MICHAEL HALBERSTAM

Michael Halberstam, a Washington, D.C. cardiologist and the brother of author David Halberstam, was an avid fisherman, rower, and sports fan. In his adult years, he played tennis as well as playground baseball and basketball. On the night of December 5, 1980, Halberstam and his wife returned home to find that a burglar had broken into their house. The burglar fired a pistol at Halberstam, wounding him in the chest. Halberstam died hours later after undergoing emergency surgery. He was forty-eight years old.

Well into his late forties, Michael Halberstam continued to harbor the dream of playing in the National Basketball Association. Toward that goal, he played pickup basketball at every opportunity.

Halberstam would bemoan the fact that many of the outdoor basketball hoops in the District of Columbia lacked nylon nets. He believed that basketball players should all enjoy the privilege of shooting at hoops that had nylon nets attached. He especially wanted children to experience the thrill of sinking a shot and seeing the ball tickle the net as it descended.

Equipped with a supply of nylon nets and a ladder, Halberstam spent his spare hours driving around to the playgrounds in Washington and stringing nets on the hoops that were lacking nylon.

◆　　　◆　　　◆

God has shattered my strength in mid-course, has cut short my days.
—Psalm 102, verse 24.

WALTER "RED" SMITH

Walter "Red" Smith was a sports writer and columnist in New York for thirty-five years. He was widely regarded as the best sportswriter of his era, a man whose writings were of literary quality. Smith studied journalism at the University of Notre Dame and began his journalism career with the Milwaukee Sentinel *in 1927. He joined* The Philadelphia Record *in 1936 and moved to* The New York Herald Tribune *in 1945. He became a sports columnist at* The New York Times *in 1971, writing for* The Times *until his death on January 15, 1982. Smith won the Pulitzer Prize for distinguished commentary in 1976.*

On January 4, 1980, Red Smith used his column in *The New York Times* to argue that the United States should boycott the summer Olympic games to be held that year in Moscow. Smith questioned how the United States could go to the Soviet Union when that country was committing "a naked act of aggression" against Afghanistan. Smith was the first sportswriter to propose a boycott of the Moscow Olympics. "I was thinking in terms of common decency," he would later explain. The day after Smith's column appeared, U.S. President Jimmy Carter began to talk of the possibility of a boycott. Two weeks later, Carter formally proposed a boycott. With the United States at the forefront, sixty-six countries decided against sending athletes to Moscow.

"Common decency" was the hallmark of Smith's career in journalism. His columns in the 1950s brought widespread attention to the discrimination experienced by black athletes. In the words of the Reverend John Quinn, who officiated at Smith's funeral, "Blacks had a very sensitive, thoughtful, and prophetic friend in Red Smith."

Smith was both modest and self-deprecating. He was fond of talking about his rocky transition from journalism student to professional newspaperman. Armed with his degree from Notre Dame, Smith had mailed out job applications to one hundred newspapers. "I got back one reply," he would say, "from *The New York Times*—and it said 'no'."

Warm and generous, Smith took a sincere interest in others and was always willing to help young writers in any way that he could. Smith regarded sportswriting as a noble calling. "The people we're writing about in professional sports, they're suffering and living and dying and loving and trying to make their way through life, just as the bricklayers and politicians are," he said.

At the height of his career, Smith would produce up to seven columns a week. The pressure of a daily deadline posed little concern to Smith; he typically waited until the day a column was due before deciding upon a topic. "God is good," he would say. "God will provide."

◆   ◆   ◆

Happy is he who trusts in the Lord!
—Proverbs 16, verse 20.

JIM VALVANO

Throughout his high school and collegiate basketball career, Jim Valvano was a steady, if unspectacular, point guard and an aggressive defensive player. In his three years playing for Rutgers University, he scored 1,122 points. As a senior, he teamed with All-American Bob Lloyd to lead Rutgers to a berth in the National Invitation Tournament, and was honored as the University's Senior Athlete of the Year. After graduation, Valvano became an assistant basketball coach at Rutgers and gradually worked his way up the coaching ranks. In March 1983, Valvano coached North Carolina State University to the NCAA Division I championship. Valvano died of cancer on April 28, 1993, at the age of forty-seven.

The 1966–67 Rutgers basketball team could hold its own against almost any team in the country. Led by the high-scoring backcourt duo of Valvano and Bob Lloyd, Rutgers played its way into the National Invitation Tournament at Madison Square Garden. In the opening round, the team defeated Utah State. It was Rutgers' biggest win in years. When the team bus arrived back at the school after the game, the cheerleaders and students gave the players a rousing reception. One by one, the players climbed down the steps of the bus and the school's cheerleaders gathered round, kissing each player in succession. Like the players in front of him, Valvano got off the bus, passed through the line formed by the cheerleaders, and received kisses from each and every cheerleader. After passing through the huddle of cheerleaders, the players moved into the crowd and mingled with the other students—with the singular exception of Valvano. Not content with one pass through the cheerleaders, Valvano crawled back onto the bus and got in line behind the players still waiting to exit. He then climbed down the steps of the bus a second time, receiving another round of kisses.

Whether conniving to get extra kisses from the cheerleading corps or trying to inspire a bunch of college basketball players, Valvano dreamed big. From his first day as a college coach, he talked of someday winning the NCAA championship. Valvano would methodically write down his goals and dreams on three-inch by five-inch index cards, often leaving them in the pockets of his shirts and slacks. Before his wife, Pam, would drop off Valvano's clothes for dry cleaning, she would dutifully check his pockets for index cards. On a trip to the dry cleaners in 1993, shortly before her husband died, Pam found an index card in one of his pockets that read, "To find a cure for cancer." It was Valvano's last dream card.

As with others who worked with Valvano, Pat Kennedy, an assistant for "Coach V" at Iona College, found Valvano's enthusiasm for life to be contagious. Every day, Kennedy said, Valvano left him with a smile on his face and the belief that Kennedy could do more with his life than he ever before thought possible.

When cancer struck, Valvano reacted in typical fashion—he fought back. He spent idle moments in hospitals trying to cheer up other cancer patients who were waiting for treatment. He also created the V Foundation to raise money for cancer research and awareness.

On March 4, 1993, less than two months before his death, Valvano was honored at the ESPY Awards as the recipient of the Arthur Ashe Courage Award. In spite of fierce pain and debilitating weakness, Valvano delivered an acceptance speech that was unforgettable. He urged his audience to do three things every day: laugh, spend time in thought, and have your emotions moved to tears. "You do that seven days a week," Valvano told the crowd, "you're going to have something special."

Above all, it was Valvano's hope that, whatever their troubles, people would strive to keep their dreams alive. "Don't give up," he urged the audience. "Don't ever give up."

◆   ◆   ◆

A man's spirit sustains him in infirmity.
—Proverbs 18, verse 14.

JOE DELANEY

Joe Delaney came out of Northwestern State University in Natchitoches, Louisiana, to become an All-Pro running back with the Kansas City Chiefs. He was small, five feet nine inches tall and 180 pounds, but ran with explosive speed. In his first season as a professional, Delaney gained 1,121 yards in 234 attempts, an average of 4.8 yards per carry. He also caught twenty-two passes for 246 yards. He was named the American Football Conference rookie-of-the-year and played in the 1981 Pro Bowl. Delaney died on June 29, 1983, as he was preparing to begin his third season with the Chiefs. He was twenty-four years old.

Joe Delaney had plans for Sunday, July 3, 1983. He was going to spend the day recording a song with his older sister Lucille and his uncle Frankie Joe. Delaney played the guitar, his sister sang, and his uncle played the piano. The trio had previously recorded a couple of songs. On that Sunday, they planned to record "Save the Last Dance For Me."

The recording session never happened. On Wednesday, June 29, Delaney was attending a Kids' Day in Monroe, Louisiana. He was playing softball when he heard the screams of three young boys. The boys were frolicking in a pit that had filled with rain water. The pit, excavated for construction of a water slide, dropped off abruptly. Unaware, the boys had wandered into deep water. Delaney ran to help. Someone asked him if he could swim. Delaney answered, "I can't swim good, but I've got to save those kids. If I don't come up, go get somebody." With that, Joe Delaney, fully clothed, jumped into the water. He took hold of one boy, LeMarkits Holland, who was sinking toward the bottom of the pit, and threw him into shallow water.

Holland survived. Delaney and the two other boys drowned. Delaney left a wife and three young children. After his death, Lucille Delaney said of her brother's efforts, "Joe was always like that. He just seemed to care about people." Delaney's college coach, A. L. Williams, echoed Lucille Delaney's thoughts. "That's Joe, always trying to help someone else," Williams said. "It cost him his life, but he'd do it a hundred times. He was so unselfish. He always tried to help."

◆   ◆   ◆

To safe waters you lead me.
—Psalm 23, verse 2.

PETE MARAVICH

With a basketball in his hand, "Pistol Pete" Maravich was a genius. Playing for his father, Press Maravich, at Louisiana State University from 1967 to 1970, Maravich averaged 44.2 points per game. He stood six feet five inches tall and possessed an uncanny ability to shoot from anywhere inside the half-court line. The Atlanta Hawks selected Maravich as the third overall pick in the 1970 National Basketball Association draft. He went on to play ten seasons in the NBA. Labeled "the best ball handler I ever saw" by long-time player and coach Pat Riley, Maravich thrilled audiences throughout the country with his wizardry. For his pro career, he averaged 24.2 points per game. On January 5, 1988, Maravich toppled over and died while playing a series of friendly half-court games at a church gym in Pasadena, California. The cause of death was determined to be a congenital heart defect. Maravich was forty years old.

In September 1980, at the age of thirty-three, Pete Maravich quit the Boston Celtics and walked away from his professional basketball career. Unable to crack the Celtics' starting lineup and unwilling to spend the year as a backup, he went home to Metairie, Louisiana. That season, the Celtics, minus Maravich, won the NBA championship. It was, Maravich figured, just another instance of the black cloud that seemed to follow him for much of his life.

For Maravich, missing out on the opportunity to join in the Celtics' championship run was a severe disappointment, but it was far from the low point of his retirement. That came in the spring and summer of 1982 as Maravich battled thoughts of suicide. Away from pro basketball, he had no identity. He also had plenty of time to think about the ways in which his life had gone wrong. He thought about the times that he had said or done things that hurt people. He thought about all the letters he had received from basketball fans who said they were praying for him—and how he had nonchalantly thrown those letters in the trash. One night in November 1982, unable to sleep and drenched in sweat, Maravich heard an inner voice say to him, "Be strong. Lift thine own heart." He began to pray.

The inner voice and the prayers brought peace. Tonya Crevier, a former star for the University of South Dakota women's basketball team, worked with

Maravich at basketball camps that he organized for youths. Crevier noticed the change. "He just had such a fun, energetic, caring attitude toward the kids after he became a Christian," she said. "All he wanted to talk about was the Lord. He now had a purpose."

Maravich found that the Bible and basketball formed a unique combination. He traveled the country playing basketball with Meadowlark Lemon's Shooting Stars, a Christian version of the Harlem Globetrotters. He used the opportunity to talk to others about his faith. When people would ask why he continued to play, he would tell them, "When I'm out here playing basketball, because of this ball in my hand, we could have a press conference and anywhere from five to twenty-five reporters will show up. And you know what? They'll listen to what I've got to say. If I want to talk about Jesus, I can…. You take the ball and you use it—as a tool to help people."

When the Shooting Stars stopped at restaurants to eat, Maravich would consistently pay the bills of the other players. When the players tried to pay their own way, Maravich would tell them, "You know how you guys can repay me? When you're on this team five years from now and you're the star, you can take the rookies to breakfast and lunch and pick up the check."

When not playing basketball, Maravich often spoke to groups about his life and his relationship with God. He opened a special checking account that he used solely for depositing the money he earned from his speaking engagements. At the end of each year, he would withdraw all of the money in the checking account and donate it to charity.

In October 1985, Maravich traveled to Phoenix to speak at an outreach party for inner-city youths. He headlined a show that also included singer Glen Campbell and former Phoenix Suns guard Paul Westphal. It was the first time Westphal had seen Maravich in more than five years. Westphal was astounded at the transformation. In Westphal's words, "Pete went from this guy who was chasing everything to having an inner calm. You looked at him and he had a different look in his eye." When Maravich addressed the Phoenix youths, he told them, "I don't have much time left, and the time I have left, I'm giving to the Lord Jesus Christ."

His words proved prophetic. Maravich would have less than three years left. Three months before he died, he was scheduled to travel to a speaking engagement in Illinois. Awaking early in the morning, he prepared to leave the home he shared with his wife, Jackie, and their two sons. Before leaving, he penned a note for Jackie. "Please kiss the boys for me," he wrote. "I love them so much also. Oh, how I love them. They are both going to be super athletes, but with a Christly heart."

◆   ◆   ◆

The Lord is close to the brokenhearted.
—Psalm 34, verse 19.

TRAVIS WILLIAMS

There was a time when Travis "The Roadrunner" Williams could run with the fastest players in the National Football League. Blessed with the speed to cover one hundred yards in 9.3 seconds, Williams was once the most feared kickoff returner in the NFL. He spent four seasons with the Green Bay Packers as a kick returner and running back. In 1967, his rookie year, he averaged 41.1 yards on kickoff returns, and set a league record by returning four kickoffs for touchdowns. Traded to the Los Angeles Rams in 1971, Williams played one year in Los Angeles, once running back a kickoff 105 yards. In 1972, injuries ended his career. In the years immediately following football, Williams worked at a variety of different jobs but was unable to find stable employment. He endured several years of sleeping on the streets of Richmond, California. His experiences as a homeless person helped to transform him into a nationally recognized advocate for the poor. He died on February 17, 1991, at the age of forty-five.

When Travis Williams died, his friend and colleague, Susan Prather, commented that, in his days as an NFL star, "Travis lived in a world that people only dream about." Prather added that, when Williams passed away, "he died in a world nobody wants to acknowledge."

During the late 1960s, a visit by Williams to the halls of the United States Senate would have been cause for celebration. By 1988, however, Williams had lost both the dazzling speed that had made him famous and the luster that accompanied his stellar five-year pro career. So, in July 1988, when Williams and Prather made their way to the Washington, D.C. office of Senator Alan Cranston, it was as intruders and not as guests. The pair vowed to stage a sit-in until Cranston met to discuss their concerns over federal housing policy. The Senator was unavailable. Police arrested Williams and Prather and hauled them away.

For Williams, it was a long and tortuous road to a different sort of celebrity. In 1977, out of work and fighting alcohol addiction, he lost his home in Richmond, California, when he was unable to make the mortgage payments. Over time, with Prather as his inspiration, Williams turned his experiences as a homeless person into an asset, becoming a relentless advocate for the poor. The story of Williams's progression from football star to street person to social activist captivated the nation, and brought unparalleled attention to the devastating effects of massive cuts in federal housing funds. Capitalizing on his status as a former football player, Williams eagerly gave speeches and granted interviews to publicize the plight of the homeless. He appeared on national television news shows and led a Home Box Office film crew on a tour of the homeless shelter where he worked as kitchen manager. His post-football experiences formed the subject of a 1989 news feature that was broadcast nationwide as part of the Super Bowl XXIII coverage.

Relying on both his compelling story and deeply felt personal convictions, Williams gained as much acclaim for his work on behalf of America's homeless as he did for his touchdown runs during his storied years with the Green Bay Packers.

◆   ◆   ◆

Within you is my true home.
—Psalm 87, verse 7.

References

Harold McLinton

Ken Denlinger, "McLinton's Special Talent Must Not Be Forgotten," *The Washington Post*, 2 November 1980, D1.

Jane Leavy, "McLinton: Critical but Stable," *The Washington Post*, 4 October 1980, D1.

Jane Leavy, "McLinton, 33, Dies of Accident Injuries," *The Washington Post*, 1 November 1980, A1.

Jane Leavy, "A Sad Farewell To McLinton," *The Washington Post*, 4 November 1980, D1.

Michael Halberstam

J. Y. Smith, "Michael J. Halberstam; Physician, Author and Sportsman," *The Washington Post*, 7 December 1980, C6.

Martin Weil and Sean Kelly, "Intruder Kills Dr. Halberstam," *The Washington Post*, 6 December 1980, A1.

Walter "Red" Smith

Dave Anderson, "Columnist 'The Best'," (Toronto) *Globe and Mail*, 16 January 1982, S5.

Dave Anderson, "'Living is the Trick,' But Without the Lime, Thank You," *The New York Times*, 17 January 1982, A3.

Ira Berkow, "Red Smith, Sports Columnist Who Won Pulitzer, Dies At 76," *The New York Times*, 16 January 1982, 1.

David Bird, "Rites For Smith Are Held 'With Tears, With Laughter'," *The New York Times*, 21 January 1982, D23.

Jim Valvano

Towle, Mike. *I Remember Jim Valvano*. Nashville, TN: Cumberland House, 2001.

Jim Valvano, "Arthur Ashe Courage Award Address," 4 March 1993, http://americanrhetoric.com/speeches/jimvalvanoespyaward.htm.

Joe Delaney

Mike Bianchi, "Hero, Redefined," *Orlando Sentinel*, 23 August 2002, H2.

Pete Maravich

Federman, Wayne and Marshall Terrill, *Maravich*. Toronto: Sport Classic Books, 2006.

Travis Williams

Dave Anderson, "He Thought Football Was Forever," *The New York Times*, 5 March 1991, B9.

Mike Penner, "The Roadrunner Had No One To Run To," *Los Angeles Times*, 1 March 1991, 1.

"Sad Trail of Former Packer Ends," *Chicago Tribune*, 19 February 1991, 3.

"Travis Williams, 45, Green Bay Packers Star," *The New York Times*, 20 February 1991, D23.

1990–1999

1990–1999

In 1990, the United States military engaged in Operation Desert Shield, sending 527,000 American military personnel to Saudi Arabia and the Persian Gulf. Desert Shield was the response to Iraq's August 1990 invasion of oil-rich Kuwait. In January 1991, with United States and other coalition troops poised to strike, Iraq ignored a United Nations deadline for withdrawing troops from Kuwait. Less than forty-eight hours later, the United States and coalition forces attacked Baghdad. The high-tech assault, dubbed Operation Desert Storm, ended forty-one days later with an announcement that Kuwait had been liberated.

In July 1992, President George H. W. Bush designated Kansas City Chiefs All-Pro linebacker Derrick Thomas as the 832nd Daily Point of Light in the Administration's Thousand Points of Light Campaign. The President honored Thomas for his efforts in establishing the Third and Long Foundation, an inner-city reading program for children.

Former Arkansas Governor William Clinton was inaugurated in 1993 as the forty-second president of the United States, with former Senator Al Gore as vice president.

South Africa's white government voted itself out of existence and African National Congress leader Nelson Mandela assumed the presidency in 1994. In Rwanda, more than one hundred thousand people died in a bloody civil war. Also in 1994, Republicans gained control of the House and Senate under the leadership of Representative Newt Gingrich and Senator Robert Dole. That same year, major league baseball players went on strike to express their dissatisfaction with plans by team owners to implement a cap on player salaries. The strike caused cancellation of the 1994 World Series.

On April 19, 1995, in the worst terrorist attack in U.S. history up to that time, the front half of the Alfred P. Murrah Federal Building in Oklahoma City was blown up, killing 168 people and injuring hundreds more. Former U.S. Army soldiers Timothy McVeigh and Terry Nichols were arrested and charged with plotting and carrying out the bombing. In August 1995, Hall-of-Fame baseball player Mickey Mantle died of cancer.

In 1997, on the fiftieth anniversary of Jackie Robinson's debut as the first African American baseball player in the major leagues, Major League Baseball retired his uniform number, 42.

SHELBY STROTHER

After serving with the Air Force in Vietnam as an intelligence officer, Shelby Strother embarked upon a career as a sportswriter and columnist. He began his career with Florida Today *in Cocoa Beach, Florida, and later worked for the* St. Petersburg Times, Denver Post, *and* Detroit News. *Colleagues would say that good stories had a way of finding Strother, but what they meant was that he had a talent for getting people to reveal things to him that they would never disclose to others. According to one writer, "you'd wind up telling him things you would not confide in confession." After uncovering a good story, Strother would write about it with compassion. He died of cancer on March 3, 1991, at the age of forty-four.*

Colleagues used to say that Shelby Strother saw beauty where others didn't, and listened when others did not hear.

One of the places where Strother found beauty was in a leper community in Louisiana. One year, Strother went to New Orleans to cover a Super Bowl. While other writers focused on football, Strother traveled to the leper community to visit a former boxer who was suffering from the disease. Strother spent hours with the boxer, exchanging stories about Muhammad Ali and other fighters. After leaving Louisiana, Strother kept in touch with the former boxer, sending him fight magazines and messages from other fighters.

On another occasion, a gentleman in his nineties, who was near death in a Detroit hospital, contacted Strother to complain about the way the Detroit Tigers had forced their long-time baseball announcer, Ernie Harwell, into retirement. After learning how fond the man was of Harwell, Strother brought the legendary announcer to the hospital to meet the gentleman. With Harwell by his side, Strother spent all day with the elderly patient, singing songs and telling stories. The gentleman died the next day. According to the deceased man's family, the visit from Strother and Harwell had made his life complete.

When Strother died, every Detroit Pistons basketball player wore a black patch on his uniform jersey for the rest of the season. Strother is the only sportswriter ever honored in this way. "Shelby was a unique person, loved by all facets of the Detroit community," Pistons coach Chuck Daly explained.

◆   ◆   ◆

Sing praise, play music; proclaim all his wondrous deeds!
—Psalm 105, verse 2.

JEROME BROWN

For five seasons, from 1987 to 1991, Jerome Brown played defensive tackle for the Philadelphia Eagles. A product of the University of Miami, Brown was six feet two inches tall and weighed 288 pounds. He was a key member of the Miami Hurricanes' 1983 national championship team. The Eagles selected Brown as the ninth overall pick in the 1987 collegiate draft. His best season came in 1989 when he was credited with ten and a half sacks of opposing quarterbacks. In 1990 and 1991, he was named to the National Football Conference Pro Bowl squad. Brown died on June 25, 1992, as a result of an automobile accident in his hometown of Brooksville, Florida.

When told of Jerome Brown's death, George Maura, one of Brown's Brooksville neighbors and a lifelong friend, had difficulty putting his thoughts into words. Finally, he said, "It feels not too good." Maura, who is mentally handicapped, was the same age as Brown. The two grew up together. Despite Maura's limitations, Brown spent hours tossing a football with him when they were children. Even after Brown became an NFL star, he always made time for Maura. When the Eagles traveled to Florida to play the Tampa Bay Buccaneers in 1991, Brown made arrangements for Maura and forty other individuals from the Key Training Center for the Handicapped to go to the game. Brown chartered a bus to drive Maura and his friends to the game, gave every person on the bus an Eagles hat, and bought them dinner.

It was not the only time that Brown rented buses to help others. In January 1991, the local Brooksville school district agreed to provide buses to transport seventy students to a football clinic being held in Tampa, before the New York Giants and Buffalo Bills squared off in Super Bowl XXV. When the school district backed out of its commitment, Brown rented two Greyhound buses for the forty-five-mile trip to Tampa.

Brown was an enthusiastic fundraiser. He was heavily involved in raising money to install a weight room at his former high school, Hernando High. In the year before he died, he organized a fundraising drive to assist a young girl who had terminal cancer. Before that, he spearheaded a fundraiser for an eleven-year-old girl who was critically injured in a car accident.

A disruptive force on the football field, Brown could be disruptive off the field as well. The Ku Klux Klan once tried to conduct a rally in Brooksville. Klan members had hooked up a sound system to transmit speeches to those gathered for the event. In the middle of the rally, Brown pulled his Bronco sport utility vehicle up next to the Klan's site and began pumping rap music out of the Bronco's twelve-speaker, one thousand-watt stereo system. The Klan's loud-speakers were no match for Brown and his Bronco. When Brown ignored requests to turn down the rap music, the Klansmen called off the rally.

Brown's devotion to the residents of his hometown knew no bounds. At night during the off-season, he would frequently drive his Bronco through stretches of neglected housing along Brooksville's Martin Luther King Boulevard, and pick up teens who were standing idly on street corners. When the Bronco was filled to capacity, Brown would drive his passengers to see a movie at a local theater, thereby ensuring that the youths stayed out of trouble. He attended high school graduations in Brooksville and, if prompted, would sing karaoke at the ceremonies. He visited schools to give pep talks to students and anonymously paid off bills for residents of Brooksville who were experiencing financial troubles.

◆   ◆   ◆

My foes turn back when I call on you.
—Psalm 56, verse 10.

DERRICK THOMAS

Derrick Thomas was an outstanding linebacker for the University of Alabama and, later, the Kansas City Chiefs. Born on January 1, 1967, Thomas was raised by his mother after his father, an Air Force pilot, perished when his plane was shot down during a combat mission in Vietnam. Thomas enjoyed a superb season for Alabama in 1988, winning the Butkus Award as the best collegiate linebacker in the country. The Kansas City Chiefs selected him with the fourth overall pick in the 1989 draft, and Thomas quickly established himself as a fixture in the NFL. In his first season, he was named Defensive Rookie-of-the-Year by the Sporting News *and was selected to play in the Pro Bowl. During his career, Thomas was named to the Pro Bowl nine times. President George H. W. Bush selected Thomas as a Point of Light in July 1992 in recognition of Thomas's work in encouraging inner-city children to devote more time to reading. Thomas died on February 8, 2000, due to complications from injuries suffered when his vehicle went out of control on an icy highway in Missouri and overturned. Thomas was thirty-three years old.*

"I'm no saint," Derrick Thomas would tell anyone who would listen. Few believed him.

In 1994, Thomas read an article in a newspaper about a young boy, Philip Tepe, who lived in Oklahoma and was dying of AIDS. Philip was a member of a youth basketball team that was scheduled to play in a tournament in Lone Wolf, Oklahoma. When opposing teams voiced concern about having to play with Philip, however, the basketball tournament was canceled. Already distanced from friends and classmates, Philip became even more isolated after his illness caused cancellation of the tournament.

Thomas read about Philip's situation in the newspapers and was determined to help out. He sent Philip tickets to watch a Chiefs' game. On the day of the game, Thomas sent a limousine to pick Philip up. Later, Thomas took Philip golfing and bought him golf clubs and shoes. For Christmas, Thomas gave Philip a football signed by Joe Montana. There was more. When Thomas played in a charity basketball game with Barry Sanders and other pro football stars, he took Philip along and posed for newspaper pictures with Philip.

In March 1994, aware that Philip's condition was worsening, Thomas borrowed a plane from a friend and flew to Oklahoma for a visit. Upon arrival, Thomas handed Philip one of his game-worn Pro Bowl jerseys. Philip died less than forty-eight hours later. To Dorecia Tepe, Philip's mother, Thomas was "a bright light in our life when things felt very dark."

There was nothing unusual about Thomas's concern and compassion for Philip. He routinely engaged in similar acts, willingly and without fanfare. His creativity matched his generosity. Wanting to supplement the food budget of 750 low-income families, Thomas went from locker to locker in the Chiefs' dressing room, insisting that each teammate contribute at least one hundred dollars to the cause. He would wake up early on Saturday mornings and head to a Kansas City library, just so he could show children the joy of reading. He established a foundation, named the Third and Long Foundation, to encourage inner-city kids to read. Upon learning that youthful readers in Kansas City had run up library fines of more than fifty thousand dollars, and knowing that the library sorely needed the funds, Thomas wrote a check to cover the overdue fees. He found ways to pay the college tuition expenses for eighteen financially strapped high school students, even though he had never met them.

Derrick Thomas was a fan of reading and a friend to children. His motivation was simple. "People cared for me," he said, "so now I care back." His goal, he said, was to be remembered as someone who had made a difference.

To Dorecia Tepe, Thomas was more than simply someone who had made a difference. "He was," she said, "like an angel God sent to protect our son."

◆   ◆   ◆

They shine through the darkness, a light for the upright.
—Psalm 112, verse 4.

BETTY SMOTHERS

Betty Smothers was the mother of NFL running back Warrick Dunn. A single parent, Smothers dreamed of being able to buy a home for herself and her six children. She died before she could achieve that dream. A policewoman and part-time security guard in Baton Rouge, Louisiana, Smothers was shot and killed on January 7, 1993, while responding to a robbery attempt. She was thirty-six years old. When Dunn joined the Tampa Bay Buccaneers as a rookie in 1997, he established and funded a foundation, known as Homes for the Holidays, in memory of his mother. Through Homes for the Holidays, Dunn pays the down payment on houses for low-income, single mothers so they can buy their own homes. He also equips the homes for immediate use, provides furnishings, and stocks the refrigerators with food. Since its inception, Homes for the Holidays has enabled more than fifty single mothers to move their families into new homes.

Each year the National Football League awards the Walter Payton NFL Man of the Year Award to a player who exhibits extraordinary concern for and involvement in his community. The Award is named for the Chicago Bears' Hall-of-Fame running back who died in 1999. The League awarded the 2004 Man of the Year Award to Warrick Dunn. At the presentation ceremony, Walter Payton's widow, Connie, lauded Dunn as "truly someone put on this earth to make a difference."

If Warrick Dunn was put on this earth to make a difference, his mother was surely put on this earth to show Dunn how to make a difference. "She gave me the best eighteen years of my life," Dunn says. Betty Smothers died in the middle of Warrick's senior year of high school, before he had decided which college to attend. Though his mother was not around to help Dunn in selecting a college, she had endowed him with the attributes necessary to make a prudent choice. Above all, Smothers taught Dunn to be fiercely independent. Thus it was that he chose to attend Florida State University, instead of playing his college ball in the more familiar environment of nearby Louisiana State University.

Similarly, though Smothers was not around to provide guidance when Dunn began earning big money as a pro, she had left him with a firm set of values to guide him. She had taught him humility and compassion. She had taught him about the nobility of pursuing dreams and sharing with others. Smothers' message to her son was threefold: (1) give back; (2) share; and (3) give others a second chance. So, when Dunn was deciding what to do with his money, Homes for the Holidays was an easy choice.

Betty Smothers was a policewoman, a caring mother, and a giver. She believed in fostering dreams—her own as well as the dreams of others. Her spirit lives on in Homes for the Holidays.

◆   ◆   ◆

Homes are built on the foundation of wisdom and understanding.
—Proverbs 24, verse 3.

REGGIE LEWIS

Reginald "Reggie" Lewis was born in Baltimore, Maryland on November 21, 1965.
He attended Baltimore's Dunbar High School, where he played basketball on a team
that also included future NBA players Reggie Williams, David Wingate, and Tyrone
"Muggsy" Bogues. After high school, Lewis played four years at Northeastern Univer-
sity, averaging twenty-two points and 7.9 rebounds per game. On the strength of his
collegiate career, the Boston Celtics selected Lewis in the first round of the 1987 ama-
teur draft. He played for the Celtics for six seasons, 1987 through 1993. In both
1991–92 and 1992–93, Lewis averaged twenty points per game. He was named to
the 1992 NBA All-Star team. Prior to the 1992–93 season, the Celtics named Lewis
as team captain. He died on July 27, 1993, due to abnormal scarring and enlarge-
ment of the heart. He was twenty-seven years old.

In June 1994, Northeastern University posthumously awarded Reggie Lewis
the honorary degree of Doctor of Humanities. The diploma was inscribed:

> Reginald Lewis, Sr.—Gifted Athlete,
> Generous Philanthropist, Genuine Hero.

As his diploma attests, Lewis was committed to giving back to the community.
He had a particular fondness for making children smile. Once, while Lewis was
walking near a train station in Boston, a group of small boys approached him.
Most of the boys were packing squirt guns. At six feet seven inches tall, Lewis was
an inviting target. Two of the boys posed no threat to Lewis; they lacked squirt
guns and so were ill-equipped for confrontation. The others, however, opened
fire. Within seconds, Lewis was thoroughly drenched. He ducked into a conve-
nience store and emerged minutes later with a newspaper and two squirt guns.
Lewis handed the squirt guns to the two "unarmed" boys, gave them time to load
the guns, and then willingly resumed his role as a target.

The gift of squirt guns was an exception. More commonly, Lewis gave away
turkeys, basketball shoes, sports equipment, and money. Most of all, he gave
away his time. Each year Lewis sponsored the Reggie Lewis-Harbor Point basket-

ball camp at the Boston campus of the University of Massachusetts. He spent hours at camp each day with children, teaching them basketball skills and talking about life. Upwards of 250 children attended each camp session. At the end of camp, each child left with a trophy that Lewis had purchased.

In 1990, Lewis began the practice of giving away turkeys to needy families at Thanksgiving. That year, Lewis personally handed out three hundred turkeys to families in the Boston area. He established a foundation to make the Turkey Give-Away an annual event and promote other charitable projects.

As a result of the generosity and warmth that Lewis displayed during his eleven years in Boston, he became a hero throughout the city. When he died, his body lay in repose on the campus of Northeastern University. At least fifteen thousand people came to pay their respects. More than seven thousand people attended his funeral service. Thousands more lined the route to Lewis's burial site at Forest Hills Cemetery. The public outpouring of sympathy and respect was unprecedented. Jim Calhoun, Lewis's coach at Northeastern, said, "I've lived in Boston fifty years and never saw anything like it."

◆   ◆   ◆

Kindness shown to the poor is an act of worship.
—Proverbs 14, verse 31.

HEATHER FARR

Five-foot-one-inch Heather Farr excelled as both an amateur and professional golfer. She was the American Junior Golf Association's player of the year in 1980 and 1982. Later, as a student at Arizona State University, she was named All-American twice. Farr became a regular member of the Ladies Professional Golf Association tour in 1986 at the age of twenty. In recognition of Farr's golfing prowess and small frame, fellow golfers nicknamed her Mighty Mouse. She had her best season as a professional in 1988 when she finished among the top ten in six tournaments and won $75,821. In 1989, when she was only twenty-four years old, Farr was diagnosed with breast cancer. She died on November 20, 1993.

For Heather Farr, 1993 was the best and worst of times. In March, she married Goran Lingmerth, a former professional football player. Farr assisted in the hospital delivery room as her only sister gave birth to a baby boy in July. Then, in November, Farr began to experience severe headaches and underwent surgery to relieve hemorrhaging in the brain. She passed away less than two weeks later.

On the day of Farr's death, more than two dozen members of the Ladies Professional Golf Tour gathered at the Scottsdale, Arizona hospital where Mighty Mouse was being treated. The players were in town for a weekend pro-am tournament. They quickly developed a routine. After finishing a round at the pro-am, each would go to the hospital to stay with Farr. The players had witnessed Farr's four-year battle with cancer. They marveled at her will to live. They had kept tabs on her as she underwent fifteen-hour back surgery in the spring of 1991 and, in quick succession, a bone marrow transplant and surgery to remove a tumor. After all that, and even after cancerous spots were discovered on her hip, skull, and pelvis, Farr vowed to make it back to the golf course. True to her word, Farr played in a Skins Game in Nashville, Tennessee in the summer of 1992. To the players, Farr seemed not to let anything dampen her spirits.

Farr did more than simply fight cancer. She used her experiences to raise the awareness of breast cancer in young women. She spoke out on the need for early detection and encouraged women to practice breast health every day. Farr also made sure that the message would continue long after her death. In her final days,

Farr expressed her concerns to fellow LPGA golfer Val Skinner. Farr told Skinner, "Young women think they're bulletproof. There are no warning signs." Farr pleaded with Skinner and others, "I need my friends to remember me. If you can help, if you can do anything about it to change it, don't let it go."

Skinner took Farr's words to heart. With Farr as her inspiration, Skinner established a foundation in 2000 that has raised millions of dollars to promote proactive breast cancer health programs.

◆   ◆   ◆

The Lord surrounds you with love and compassion.
—Psalm 103, verse 4.

ALTON GRIZZARD and KERRYN O'NEILL

Lieutenant Alton Grizzard, a football quarterback, and Ensign Kerryn O'Neill, a long distance runner, were two of the finest student-athletes ever to attend the Naval Academy. Grizzard, twenty-four, and O'Neill, twenty-one, died within minutes of each other in the early hours of December 1, 1993, when a deranged man, O'Neill's former fiancé, shot them at close range with a handgun. Grizzard, a native of Virginia Beach, Virginia, was named the 1987 High School Player of the Year for the State of Virginia. In four years at Annapolis, 1987 to 1990, he gained 5,666 total yards, becoming the school's all-time leader in total offense. As a senior, he set a Navy record by passing for twelve touchdowns. At the time of his death, he was an assistant platoon commander with the elite Navy SEAL commando team stationed at the Naval Amphibious Base in Coronado, California. O'Neill, a superb high school track and cross-country runner in her hometown of Kingston, Pennsylvania, had passed up a full athletic scholarship at the University of Hawaii to accept an appointment to the Naval Academy. She went on to win twelve varsity letters at Annapolis, four in cross-country, four in indoor track, and four in track and field. In the process, she set three school track records: best time on the women's cross-country course, and fastest times in five thousand meters, indoor and outdoor. In her junior year, O'Neill was named to the Division II All-American team. After graduating from Annapolis, O'Neill reported to Coronado in October 1993 to begin her career as an oceanographer.

Even by the lofty standards of the Naval Academy, Alton Grizzard and Kerryn O'Neill ranked among the most accomplished of individuals. Talented athletes both, they blessed the world in a way that their families, friends, and colleagues will not forget.

When visitors approached O'Neill's desk at the Naval Amphibious Base facility where she worked, they would quickly notice two things: the jar of candy filled to the brim, that was irresistibly enticing, and O'Neill's ever-present smile. O'Neill loved to rise with the sun in the morning and run with the sun going down in the evening. She used her athletic talents to help motivate others. She would always try to push her teammates to do better. "She was one of the finest people I've ever known," Michelle Montgomery, captain of the 1993 Navy cross-country team, said.

Self-effacing and humble, O'Neill was not very good at talking about herself. Though she had been honored as the 1993 recipient of the William P. Lawrence sword, awarded to the best female athlete at Annapolis, few of O'Neill's colleagues at Coronado were aware of her athletic achievements. In the words of a former teacher, O'Neill "was one of those rare people who apparently had no mirrors in her house because she had no understanding of how outstanding she was."

If Alton Grizzard took the time to look in the mirrors in his house, he would have seen a person described by a friend as "a big teddy bear, everybody's big brother." And when, on the evening of November 30, 1993, O'Neill, apparently in need of a friend, called Grizzard, he would have come immediately to help her, because that's the way he was. "He would always be there if you needed to talk," one of his classmates at Annapolis said. "You could always count on Griz to keep you going."

Jason Van Matre, a tailback on the 1993 Navy football team, remembered Grizzard as "the perfect role model." According to Van Matre, "when he was a senior in 1990 and our current seniors were plebes, he set a shining example on how to act on and off the field."

◆   ◆   ◆

God ended their days abruptly; their years in sudden death.
—Psalm 78, verse 33.

JIMMIE REESE

James Harrison Reese was born on October 1, 1901. He was a career minor leaguer until the age of twenty-eight, when he joined the New York Yankees as an infielder. He enjoyed a stellar rookie season with the Yankees in 1930, batting .346 in seventy-seven games. Reese spent two seasons with the Yankees, 1930 and 1931. During his time with the Yankees, he was best known for being Babe Ruth's roommate. Acknowledging that the Babe was often out on the town, Reese would say that he spent more time with Ruth's suitcase than with Ruth himself. Reese's last season in the big leagues was 1932, when he appeared in ninety games for the St. Louis Cardinals. For the next several decades, he was a player, manager, coach, and scout in the minor leagues. In 1972, the California Angels hired him as a coach. He spent the next twenty-two years in an Angels uniform, gaining a well-deserved reputation as the best fungo hitter in baseball and as a friend to everyone in the ballpark. He took his uniform off for the last time in May 1994, at the age of ninety-two, when it became apparent that he could no longer perform his coaching chores. He died on July 13, 1994.

Jimmie Reese spent seventy-seven years in a baseball uniform. For many of those years, he had the same pregame ritual. He'd grab a handful of candy and some baseballs, wander down to the grandstands in the left-field corner, and hand the candy and baseballs out to the youngest kids he could find. When Reese died, his friend and fellow coach Bobby Knoop said of him, "He was in his nineties, and his best friends were in their twenties." According to former Angels outfielder Gary Pettis, "[Jimmie] always knew a way to make us feel good." Friends would say that his secret to making people feel good was that he viewed every person as being special. Hall-of-Fame pitcher Nolan Ryan was so fond of Jimmie Reese that he named his younger son Reese.

When age and infirmity forced Jimmie Reese to quit his job with the Angels in May 1994, he sat in the locker room and cried. He loved the game of baseball. Baseball loved him back.

◆   ◆   ◆

The just shall bear fruit even in old age, always vigorous and sturdy.
—Psalm 92, verse 15.

CHRISTOPHER REEVE

Christopher Reeve was a tall, versatile actor who appeared in seventeen feature films, twelve made-for-television movies, and 150 stage productions. Reeve studied at Cornell University, majoring in music theory and English, and at the Juilliard School of Performing Arts. He gained stardom with his performance in the title role of the 1978 blockbuster Superman. *He later played the same role in three* Superman *sequels. Reeve was an accomplished pianist and an expert sailor, scuba diver, skier, and equestrian. He was severely injured on May 27, 1995, when he was thrown from his horse, Buck, during a riding competition in Culpeper County, Virginia. Reeve suffered a fractured neck and was paralyzed from the neck down. He died on October 10, 2004, at the age of fifty-two.*

The host of a national television talk show once asked Christopher Reeve and his wife, Dana, how they endured the difficult moments, the times when Reeve's physical limitations would cause them to become discouraged. The responses of both Reeve and his wife were nearly identical. They said that, when life became too difficult, they would always try to find a way to do something to help someone else.

The antidote worked. Reeve and his wife rarely seemed to lose hope. More often than not, they both looked forward eagerly to the next day.

It wasn't always like that. In the days following his accident, Reeve was close to despair. With the help of Dana and his children, however, Reeve found that he had much for which to live.

Reeve and his wife formed the Christopher Reeve Paralysis Foundation to raise money for spinal-cord injury research and improve the quality of life for victims of spinal-cord injuries. Over a period of eight years, the Foundation raised more than forty million dollars for medical research. It was one of many ways in which Reeve used his celebrity status to help others.

Reeve became a prominent and effective spokesperson for the disabled. He taught others the importance of trying to make progress each and every day. He made it clear that his ultimate motivation was someday to walk again. With continued effort, he regained the ability to move his index finger in 2000, a triumph of major proportions. By 2002, he was able to move some of his toes. Later, he gained the ability to feel pin pricks and the touch of others, enabling him to enjoy the special thrill of feeling the hugs of his wife and children.

Before Reeve's accident, the victims of spinal-cord injuries had little expectation of physical improvement. "There was really no hope," said Dr. John McDonald, one of Reeve's physicians. Reeve's efforts changed that. His perseverance brought hope. "I refuse to allow a disability to determine how I live my life," he would tell others.

◆   ◆   ◆

Show me the path I should walk.
—Psalm 143, verse 8.

BROOK BERRINGER

Brook "Last Chance" Berringer burst onto the scene as the starting quarterback for the University of Nebraska during the 1994 football season. When incumbent quarterback Tommie Frazier was sidelined with a blood clot, the six-foot-four Berringer guided the Cornhuskers to seven consecutive wins and a berth in the Orange Bowl against the University of Miami. For the season, Berringer completed over sixty percent of his passes and earned second-team All-Big Eight honors. The following year, he resumed his role as Frazier's backup. Berringer died on April 18, 1996, when a sudden twenty-five-mile-per-hour wind caused the Piper Cub plane that he was piloting to plunge into a field of alfalfa in Raymond, Nebraska. He was twenty-two years old.

After Berringer's exploits during the 1994 season, the quarterback was in constant demand. He made inspirational speeches to high school students and visited patients in hospitals. As important as these activities were, Berringer took special pleasure in what he called his "*Green Eggs and Ham* appearances." He spent hours reading Dr. Seuss to preschool and kindergarten children. Over and over, Berringer would delight his audiences as he recited, "I like green eggs and ham! I do! I like them, Sam-I-am!"

NFL scouts projected Berringer as a top prospect in the 1996 pro draft. Berringer looked forward to accomplishing big things in the professional ranks. Nonetheless, his priorities involved more than football. In September 1995, when Berringer's senior season in college was in full-swing, a friend asked the quarterback what he hoped would happen over the course of the next few years. Berringer's answer was simple. "All I really want," he replied, "is to grow in my relationship with Jesus Christ."

◆   ◆   ◆

Happy are those who find refuge in you, whose hearts are set up on pilgrim roads.
—Psalm 84, verse 6.

265

RODNEY CULVER

Rodney Culver was born in Detroit, Michigan on December 23, 1969. He was an excellent high school athlete and attended the University of Notre Dame on a football scholarship. As a college junior, he led the Irish in rushing. In his senior season, Culver was named team captain, the first African American in Notre Dame history to hold that honor. From 1992 to 1995, Culver played pro football, spending two years with the Indianapolis Colts and two with the San Diego Chargers. He and his wife, Karen, died on May 11, 1996, when ValuJet Flight 592, on which they were flying, crashed into the Florida Everglades.

Rodney Culver was never shy about letting others know his priorities. Whenever he scored a touchdown at Notre Dame, he would point toward the sky, head to the sidelines, and tell his teammates, "God's going to get some ink today! God's going to get some pub!"

In his twenty-six years, Culver made sure that God got plenty of ink. He kept a Bible in his locker and would delight in explaining his Christian beliefs to others. When signing autographs, he would write "Mark 9:23" beneath his name, a reminder that "Everything is possible to one who has faith."

Culver, his younger sister, and two younger brothers grew up in a rough section of Detroit. As a teenager, Culver helped his mother take care of his three siblings. After signing his first pro contract, Culver moved his mother, sister, and brothers to Atlanta with him. During his time in San Diego, Culver raised funds to build a three-story youth center for abused children. After Chargers rookie defensive tackle Don Sasa suffered a serious knee injury in 1995, Culver made a practice of calling Sasa to inquire about his recovery. In an environment where there was little interaction between veterans and rookies, the phone calls were an unexpected source of encouragement for Sasa.

After learning of Culver's death, Chargers general manager Bobby Beathard said, "Rodney was the real McCoy. This is a guy who put everybody ahead of himself." Vinnie Cerrato, who served as Notre Dame's recruiting coordinator during Culver's college career, remembered Culver as "always upbeat and trying to help people, especially the younger guys." His teammates on the Chargers recalled that Culver almost always had a smile on his face. "He wasn't a starter," said defensive lineman Chris Mims, "but he was one of the happiest guys on the team. God was first in his life, and his family, then his career."

◆　　　◆　　　◆

I announced your deed to a great assembly; I did not restrain my lips.
—Psalm 40, verse 10.

PETE SCHNEIDER

"Big Pete" Schneider was a standout six foot four inch tall, 240-pound athlete for Northampton High School in Northampton, Pennsylvania, in the late 1930s. Blessed with long arms, Schneider played even bigger than his listed height. He was a center in basketball, an end in football, and a pitcher in baseball. After high school, Schneider starred in basketball at Muhlenberg College. Following service with the Army Air Corps during World War II, he played pro basketball for Hazleton in the Eastern League. He also played football for the Bethlehem Bulldogs in the American Football League, helping the Bulldogs claim the AFL championship in 1947. When back and knee injuries cut short Schneider's athletic career, he turned to coaching and education. Schneider was a long-time teacher and guidance counselor at Northampton High, as well as head basketball coach and assistant football coach. He also served, for a time, as coach of the girls' junior varsity basketball team and filled several other roles at the school. To students and colleagues at Northampton High, Schneider was "a giant of a man with a heart to match." He died on September 22, 1996, at the age of seventy-seven.

Legend has it that "Big Pete" Schneider raised the finest home-grown toma-toes in all of Northampton, Pennsylvania. The secret, according to Big Pete, was a special formula from Wanko's Farm. And, if Schneider's tomatoes were not the finest, they certainly found their way into more Northampton homes than any-one else's tomatoes. Big Pete made sure of that.

As generous with his time as he was with his tomatoes, Schneider was known throughout Northampton for his willingness to help others.

Schneider was a small-town guy in a big man's frame. He'd been to New York. He'd been to Texas. He had traveled with an elite U.S. Army football team. For Schneider, none of the places he came across in his travels held the same attraction as did his hometown of Northampton. There were a lot of subtle fac-tors working in Northampton's favor, not the least of which was that Schneider's attractive young bride, Dannye, felt at home in Northampton. With Dannye firmly entrenched in the town, every other place was lacking.

Few embraced the role of small-town citizen more passionately than Big Pete. He was moderator of the Northampton spelling bee and coach of the Little League baseball team. He helped neighbors fix their flat tires and shovel snow off their sidewalks. He was a lector at church. When the kitchen sinks of Northamp-ton's widows would become clogged, Schneider would stop by with his toolbox and his plunger. If he accepted any payment at all, it was in the form of a home-cooked meal or dessert.

Schneider ran Northampton's Main Street teen center and taught classes to help students prepare for college admission tests. When Big Pete and Dannye's four children, all athletes, needed a place to play basketball, Pete painted the house of a local paving contractor in exchange for installation of a backyard mac-adam court.

For the better part of four decades, when school was in session, Schneider could be found on the sidelines at Northampton High football and basketball games, imparting his knowledge of Northampton's famed "short-punt" forma-tion, and teaching the importance of technique and positioning. In the summers, he ran Northampton's Newport Playground. The kids at Newport were in equal parts impoverished and hardened, some coming from families so destitute that they could not afford shoes. Other adults avoided working at the Newport Play-ground. Schneider cherished the role—and cherished the kids. He would orga-nize basketball games, swimming competitions, and pie-eating contests. At the end of each day, Schneider would load up his car with playground kids, just so they could experience the thrill of riding in an automobile. The poorest of the

Newport kids would get more than automobile rides. Over the years, Schneider handed out loans to virtually every child he found who was in need.

"Always think about the next guy," Schneider would tell his children. And so Big Pete Schneider continually shared his time and his talents, his money and his energy. The only thing he was reluctant to share was his secret formula from Wanko's Farm.

◆   ◆   ◆

I made no secret of your enduring kindness.
—Psalm 40, verse 11.

REGGIE WHITE

At six feet five inches tall and 305 pounds, Reggie White was a mountain of a man who played defensive end in the National Football League for fifteen seasons. In thirteen of those seasons, he was selected to play in the Pro Bowl. An ordained minister, White was called the "Minister of Defense." He played his collegiate football at the University of Tennessee. White joined the National Football League in 1985 after being drafted by the Philadelphia Eagles. He spent eight seasons with the Eagles and then signed with the Green Bay Packers as a free agent. In January 1997, White led the Packers to a 35–21 victory over New England in Super Bowl XXXI. Considered the most dominant defensive end in the history of the NFL, White retired from football after the 2000 season. He died on December 26, 2004, at the age of forty-three as a result of complications from inflammation of the heart and lungs.

At the end of the 1992 football season, at the height of his athletic career, Reggie White became an unrestricted free agent. White still possessed the speed that allowed him to run forty yards in 4.6 seconds. Several teams, including the Washington Redskins, San Francisco 49ers, and Green Bay Packers, aggressively courted him. A deeply religious man, White told the press that he would go wherever God told him to go.

Shortly after that comment, White found a message on his answering machine that said: "Reggie, this is God. Go to Green Bay."

Although the Packers' coach at the time, Mike Holmgren, disputed any suggestion that he may have tried to impersonate God, the voice on the answering machine sounded suspiciously like Holmgren's. And though it was never confirmed that God necessarily wanted White to play for the Packers, Holmgren certainly had a vested interest in seeing White play in Green Bay.

As things turned out, White did sign with the Packers. He played for Green Bay from 1993 to 1998. His inspired play in the 1997 Super Bowl, during which he recorded three quarterback sacks, helped bring the Super Bowl trophy to Green Bay. While White's contributions to the Packers' success were significant, they paled in comparison to the impact he made in the Green Bay community. In 1997, he and his wife, Sara, founded the Urban Hope Entrepreneurship Center in Green Bay, an organization designed to funnel loans to business-minded individuals in Wisconsin who were having difficulty obtaining start-up funding. Since its establishment, the Urban Hope Center has provided financing for more than four hundred Wisconsin business entities.

The Urban Hope Center developed out of White's conviction that the fundamental purpose of one's existence is to improve the lives of others. Toward that end, White was constantly in search of opportunities to help out. He funded and built a home for unwed mothers, the Hope Palace, on property that he owned in Tennessee. White would walk the streets of the cities in which he played in an effort to find and help homeless individuals. He found jobs for those who were out of work and contributed to scores of charities in Philadelphia, Green Bay, and elsewhere. He also raised funds to rebuild churches that had been burned.

In retirement, White decided that, for his own spiritual development, he needed to take steps to understand the holy scriptures, particularly the Old Testament. He was troubled by conflicting interpretations of the same scriptural passages. He undertook an intense study of the Hebrew language and often devoted eight or more hours a day to the learning process. He visited Jerusalem and read the original scriptures. His goal was to learn as much as he could about the original text and teach others what he had learned.

◆   ◆   ◆

God's law they study day and night.
—Psalm 1, verse 2.

REX BARNEY

Rex Barney was a fireballing right-hander, with a touch of wildness, who pitched for the Brooklyn Dodgers for six seasons. He first joined the Dodgers as an eighteen-year-old in 1943. His best season was 1948 when he won fifteen games, lost thirteen, and had an earned run average of 3.10. That same season he pitched a no-hitter against the New York Giants in a game at the Polo Grounds. Barney closed out his major league career in 1950, with a record of thirty-five wins and thirty-one losses. From 1974 until his death on August 12, 1997, Barney was the public address announcer for the Baltimore Orioles. He would delight those in attendance at games by exclaiming, "Give that fan a contract!" whenever a fan caught a foul ball in flight.

On October 6, 1991, in the last major league game ever played at Baltimore's Memorial Stadium, thirty-nine-year-old Baltimore pitcher Mike Flanagan took the mound in a largely ceremonial relief appearance against the Detroit Tigers. There was one out in the top of the ninth inning. With 50,700 fans in the stands, the anxiety was palpable. After the game, there would be a massive celebration to commemorate the Orioles' thirty-eight seasons at the stadium. Before the Orioles could bat in the home half of the ninth, however, Flanagan had to face Tigers hitters Dave Bergman and Travis Fryman. It would not be an easy task. Having long ago lost miles off his fastball, Flanagan had survived the season on a little bit of "stuff" and a lot of guile.

Two days earlier, long-time Orioles public address announcer Rex Barney had collapsed from dehydration and anemia after announcing a night game at the stadium. Confined to a hospital bed, Barney watched on television as Flanagan took the mound. "Flanny" went to a full count on Bergman. Barney thought two of the pitches that were called balls had been close enough to be strikes. Clearly, the plate umpire, Tim Welke, was not giving Flanagan any help.

Barney looked up to heaven. Pleading Flanagan's case, Barney prayed, "Dear God, please take care of this man. He's the nicest, dearest man I've ever known. Please help him."

Flanagan proceeded to strike out both Bergman and Fryman on sweeping curve balls. With Flanagan's efforts finished, Barney said out loud, "God took care of you, pal."

When Barney wasn't praying for people, he was finding other ways to help. Sam Lacy, sports editor of the *Afro-American Newspaper* in Baltimore, was standing in the Brooklyn Dodgers' clubhouse when Jackie Robinson first arrived at Ebbets Field to play for the Dodgers. Lacy reported that Barney was the first Dodger teammate to offer Robinson a handshake.

At a time when some Brooklyn players refused to acknowledge Robinson and others were circulating anti-Robinson petitions, Barney's handshake conveyed both understanding and acceptance.

◆   ◆   ◆

I stretch out my hands to you.
—Psalm 88, verse 10.

DAN QUISENBERRY

Daniel Raymond Quisenberry pitched in the major leagues for twelve years, most of them with the Kansas City Royals. A sinkerball pitcher with an unorthodox submarine delivery, Quisenberry received the Rolaids Relief Award as the American League's top relief pitcher four times. He retired from baseball in 1990 at the age of thirty-seven. For his career, Quisenberry won fifty-six games, lost forty-six, and had an earned run average of 2.76. In retirement, Quisenberry turned to poetry, publishing a collection of poems in 1998 titled, On Days Like This. *In his poetry, Quisenberry reflected on the final days of his baseball career pitching in the frigid winds of San Francisco's Candlestick Park, the magic of a double play, and the serenity that comes from letting God take control of one's life. Quisenberry died of an inoperable brain tumor on September 30, 1998. He was forty-five.*

In the final stages of his life, when Dan Quisenberry had been weakened by the cancerous brain tumor that would prove fatal, he liked nothing better than to ride in the back seat of an automobile being driven by one of his children, and stick his head out the car window. His ears would flap in the wind, he would say, "like the ears of a dog." Whether in his role as a stellar relief pitcher or as a thoughtful poet, Quisenberry appreciated the simple things in life.

Quisenberry retired in the middle of the 1990 season, at the age of thirty-seven and after twelve years in the major leagues. His poem, *Time to Quit*, provides insight into his reasons for hanging up his spikes. The poem told of a crayoned plea that he had received from his daughter asking him to "come home."

In a poem titled *What If*, Quisenberry wrote of the peace that comes from relying on God. For Quisenberry, trusting in God was the answer, especially when he was scared and lonely.

The poet in Quisenberry relied heavily on his gift of observation. "It's a sin," he told others, "to miss something." Quisenberry took pains not to miss a sunset, a cool breeze, or the twinkle in his daughter's eye. In turn, Quisenberry's gift of observation helped him to keep his baseball career and his fame in perspective. When asked to name the best thing about playing baseball, he said, "No homework."

"Baseball was just a chapter, and a short chapter, of my life," Quisenberry once said. He devoted the other chapters of his life to his family, the homeless, and his poetry. He took rides with his children. He collected food for homeless shelters. He gave public readings of his poetry at local libraries. He encouraged fathers to spend time playing catch with their sons. He loved others. Above all, he trusted in God.

◆   ◆   ◆

Surely the Lord will proclaim peace to his people, to those who trust in him.
—Psalm 85, verse 9.

PAYNE STEWART

William Payne Stewart died on October 25, 1999, when the Learjet in which he was traveling crashed in South Dakota. Stewart, two pilots, and three companions had taken off from Orlando, Florida, and were headed for a business meeting in Dallas, Texas. The plane, flying on automatic pilot, never veered westward toward Dallas after takeoff. Air Force F-16 fighter jets spent several hours tracking the plane at close range. The F-16 pilots reported no signs of life on board. The Learjet finally ran out of fuel and crashed in a field near Mina, South Dakota. At the time, Stewart was forty-two years old and an eighteen-year veteran of the Professional Golf Association tour. His career triumphs included two U.S. Open Championships, one in 1991 and the other in 1999, and a PGA Championship in 1988. In 1986, Stewart finished in the top ten in sixteen tournaments, which was then a tour record. In addition to his excellence on the golf course, Stewart was known for his distinctive attire during tournament play. He competed wearing knee-length knickers, kneesocks, and Scottish-style tam-o'-shanter hats.

One day in 1993, when Stewart was arriving at the Baltusrol Golf Club in New Jersey to play in the U.S. Open, he noticed that a fellow pro had refused a young boy's request for an autograph. The boy was in tears. Stewart approached the boy and said, "Hey, buddy! How are you doing? Why don't you hang out with me?" Stewart then signed an autograph for the boy and continued to acknowledge him throughout the day during his round. That same year, at the Skins Game tournament in Palm Desert, California, Stewart entertained a seventeen-year-old boy from Ohio who was suffering from leukemia.

Stewart was generous with his earnings. In 1987, he collected $108,000 for winning the Hertz Bay Hill Classic in Orlando, Florida. He donated the entire purse to the Florida Hospital Golden Circle of Friends Home, a facility where the families of cancer patients confined to Orlando hospitals stay while their family members receive treatment.

While Stewart was naturally inclined to acts of generosity and caring, he did not always devote the same degree of attention to his spiritual development. As his earnings from golf began to pile up, Stewart would ask his wife, "How much will it take to make us happy?" When Stewart's friend and fellow pro Paul Azinger developed cancer, it caused Stewart to focus more on his faith. "I think Paul getting cancer started me going in a more spiritual direction," Stewart said. "When I saw how he handled the cancer and all the faith he had, I became more spiritual."

In 1998, when the PGA Tour refused to allow golfer Casey Martin, who suffered from the Klippel-Trenaunay-Weber degenerative circulatory disorder, to use a golf cart during tournament play, Stewart spoke out in support of Martin. Stewart stated, "He still has to make the shots, no matter how he gets to them, whether walking or in a cart. Let the guy play."

Together with his wife, Stewart established and funded the Stewart Family Foundation, the goal of which was to make a difference in people's lives. Less than two weeks before his death, the First Orlando Foundation, a community service ministry affiliated with the First Baptist Church, presented Stewart with its annual Legacy Award. The award was in recognition of Stewart's donation of five hundred thousand dollars to build a sports complex for children. When accepting the Legacy Award, Stewart said, "It's not that hard to give something back. I've been blessed with an ability; I think God chose me to play golf, and I use that podium; I use the golf course to give him the praise that he deserves and to make a difference in people's lives."

◆　　　◆　　　◆

You make the clouds your chariot; you travel on the wings of the wind.
—Psalm 104, verse 3.

WALTER PAYTON

Walter Payton was one of the greatest running backs ever to play in the National Football League. He spent thirteen seasons with the Chicago Bears, from 1975 to 1987. When he retired from the game in 1987, Payton had gained a total of 16,726 career rushing yards. At the time, it was the highest career total ever for an NFL runner. During his career, Payton scored 125 touchdowns and had seventy-seven games in which he gained one hundred or more yards. His 275 yards in a game against the Minnesota Vikings in 1977 ranks as one of the top performances ever in the NFL. Payton was selected to play in nine Pro Bowls. He was named to Pro Football's Hall of Fame in 1993. Payton died of a rare disease known as primary sclerosing cholangitis on November 1, 1999.

In 1989, Walter Payton formed the George Halas/Walter Payton Charitable Foundation. Initially, Payton's advisors wanted to call the foundation the Walter Payton Foundation. However, Payton would not agree. He thought it was arrogant to have the foundation named after him. Payton was more receptive to using his name if he could play "second fiddle" to Papa Bear, George Halas. So the George Halas/Walter Payton Foundation came into being. At first, the foundation focused on raising money for inner-city schools. In 1993, Payton decided to branch out into other activities. On Thanksgiving Day 1993, the foundation treated 650 children from various Chicago organizations to dinner at a restaurant in the city. Santa Claus was in attendance, as were Mrs. Claus and Frosty the Snowman.

During the dinner, Payton encountered a small boy who was in tears. "What's wrong?" Payton asked. The boy answered, "I can't believe Santa Claus is here and that Santa would come all the way from the North Pole just to see me." Not well versed in handling such situations, Payton did what came naturally; he started crying too. Collectively, the tears of the little boy and the tears of the former All-Pro halfback gave rise to a new program for the foundation, Wishes to Santa. Payton hoped that, each year, Wishes to Santa could provide a bag of toys at Christmas to all of the thirty thousand children who were wards of the Illinois Department of Children and Family Services.

By 1999, Wishes to Santa was distributing gifts to fifty thousand children. That year, one of the recipients was a fifteen-year-old girl from a group home. Through error, the girl received a bag of gifts intended for a five-year-old. Upon seeing the mix-up, a caseworker called the foundation and requested gifts suitable for a teenager. However, when the replacement gifts reached the group home, the teenager refused to surrender her original bag of toys. "I would rather keep the ones I was given," she said, "because I've never had a toy."

After Payton's passing, his widow, Connie, made a change that was at once both well-intended and contrary to her husband's wishes—she put Walter Payton as the lead name on the foundation. Long after Payton's death, the Walter and Connie Payton Foundation continues the task of bringing toys, smiles—and a few tears—to thousands of children each year at Christmas. The foundation has also launched programs to combat cancer, increase organ donations, and furnish school supplies for needy children.

◆   ◆   ◆

Those who sow in tears will reap with cries of joy.
—Psalm 126, verse 5.

References

Shelby Strother

Terry Frie, "A Sports Columnist Above All," *The (Portland) Oregonian*, 9 March 1991, F1.

Tony Grossi, "Columnist Touched the Heart," *The (Cleveland) Plain Dealer*, 8 March 1991.

Peter Vecsey, "Saying Goodbye to Strother, One of the Best," *USA Today*, 8 March 1991, 10C.

Jerome Brown

Jeff Babineau, "NFL Star's Spirit Lives On In Hometown," *Orlando Sentinel*, 3 July 1992, A1.

Andrew J. Skerritt, "Loss of Sports Hero Hits Home for Brooksville," *St. Petersburg Times*, 2 January 2005, 5B.

Timothy W. Smith, "Mournful, Soulful Hymns for Brown," *The New York Times*, 3 July 1992, B10.

"Jerome Brown Eulogized As Caring Man; 2½-Hour Ceremony Filled With Tears and Gospel Music," (Allentown, PA) *Morning Call*, 3 July 1992, C1.

Derrick Thomas

Thomas George, "Thomas Is Remembered For His Heart and Drive," *The New York Times*, 16 February 2000, D4.

Dan Lebatard, "Thomas Was a Hero to Many; Chiefs' Star Will Also Be Remembered For What He Did Off the Football Field," *The (Montreal) Gazette*, 10 February 2000, C1.

Kathleen Nelson, "Fans Say Goodbye to Thomas in His Final Visit to Arrowhead; 'He Brings Out the Best in Everyone'," *St. Louis Post-Dispatch*, 15 February 2000, C1.

"A Bright Light Goes Dark Too Soon," http://midnightangel308.com/derrick_thomas.html.

"Thomas Is Remembered As A Hero During Memorial in Kansas City; Chiefs' General Manager Hopes Death Proves To Be Reminder About Seat Belts," *St. Louis Post-Dispatch*, 16 February 2000, D2.

Betty Smothers

Warrick Dunn Foundation Vision Statement, http://warrickdunn foundation.org.

"Funeral Scheduled For Slain Policewoman," (New Orleans) *Times-Picayune*, 10 January 1993, B2.

Reggie Lewis

John Eisenberg, "Smiles Flow in Celebration of Reggie's Life," *The (Baltimore) Sun*, 8 August 1993, 1C.

Michael Madden, "His Actions Spoke Volumes," *Boston Globe*, 3 August 1993, 30.

David Nakamura and Christopher B. Daly, "Celtics' Lewis Dies After Collapsing," *The Washington Post*, 28 July 1993, F1.

Windham, Craig. *Reggie Lewis: Quiet Grace*. Winsted, CT: ACTEX Publications, 1995.

Zachary R. Dowdy and Maria Van Schuyver, "Crowds Remember A Man's Giving Soul," *Boston Globe*, 3 August 1993, 1.

Heather Farr

Christine Brennan, "LPGA Players Cherish Memory of Farr's Spirit," *St. Petersburg Times*, 29 November 1993, 1C.

Jimmy Myers, "May God Bless You Heather," *Boston Herald*, 28 November 1993, B15.

Terry Organ, "She Never Won As A Pro, But Heather Farr Was True Champion," *St. Petersburg Times*, 30 November 1993, 4.

David Westin, "Golfer's Work Against Cancer Earns Her Nod," *The Augusta Chronicle*, 7 April 2005, http://augusta.com/masters/stories/040705/aro_3831080.shtml.

Alton Grizzard and Kerryn O'Neill

Brigitte Greenburg, "Grizzard's Murder Cut Short a Bright Future," *Richmond Times-Dispatch*, 10 December 1993, D1.

Isabel Wilkerson, "Murder-Suicide Takes the Lives of 3 Gifted U.S. Navy Officers; Victims and Killer Were Star Athletes, Cream of an Elite Corps," *The (Montreal) Gazette*, 8 December 1993, F10.

"Crime of Passion: Three Bright Futures Snuffed Out in a Moment of Violence," *The Salt Lake Tribune*, 6 December 1993, A1.

Jimmie Reese

Art Thomason, "Reese, An Expert With The Bat, Had Time for Everyone," *The Arizona Republic*, 17 July 1994, D17.

Mark Whicker, "Angels' Reese Was Diamond of a Coach, Friend to All Who Knew Him," *The (Portland) Oregonian*, 17 July 1994, D14.

Mark Whicker, "Legendary Reese Will Be Missed," *Denver Post*, 17 July 1994.

Christopher Reeve

Neville Dean, "Death Of A Real Super Hero," (Newcastle-upon-Tyne, UK) *Journal*, 12 October 2004, 6.

Marilynn Marchione, "From Actor to Activist, Superman in Real Life," *Richmond Times-Dispatch*, 12 October 2004, A1.

Christopher Reed and Ronald Bergan, "Christopher Reeve: Actor Whose Talent and Determination To Fight Quadriplegia Made Him More Than A Superman," *The (Manchester, UK) Guardian*, 12 October 2004, 29.

Carlos Santos, "Reeve Used Power for Good; Encouragement, Surgery Gave Him the Strength to Champion Research For Spinal Injuries," *Richmond Times-Dispatch*, 12 October 2004, A7.

Brook Berringer

Lindsay, Arthur L., and Jan Berringer. *One Final Pass: The Brook Berringer Story*. Grand Island, NE: Cross Training Publishing, 1996.

Rodney Culver

> T.J. Simers, "Culver Portrayed As Picture Perfect; 'He Put Everybody Ahead of Himself,' Says Chargers' Ross of Crash Victim," *Los Angeles Times*, 14 May 1996, 1.

> Leland Stein III, "Friend Laments Loss of Culver To Plane Crash," *Michigan Chronicle*, 29 May 1996, 1A.

> Paul Woody, "Stats Aside, Culver Measured Up," *Richmond Times-Dispatch*, 19 May 1996, D9.

> "Culver Praised in Detroit," *The Grand Rapids Press*, 26 May 1996, B9.

Pete Schneider

> Burian, Evan. *Sports Legends of the Lehigh Valley*. Emmaus, PA: Burian, 2003.

> Recollections of children and friends of "Big Pete" Schneider.

Reggie White

> Ron Borgas, "Remembering a Friend in Reggie White," *Boston Globe*, 2 January 2005, E6.

> Chuck Cavalaris, "White Died While Seeking Purest Form of Religion," *Knoxville News Sentinel*, 6 February 2005, D2.

> George Kimball, "Lamenting the Loss of Green Bay's 'Minister of Defense'," (Dublin) *Irish Times*, 30 December 2004, 19.

> Rob Reischel, "Reggie White: 1961–2004; His Legacy Will Live On; 'Minister of Defense' Dies at 43," *Milwaukee Journal Sentinel*, 30 December 2004, 18.

> Andrew J. Skerritt, "Loss of Sports Hero Hits Home for Brooksville," *St. Petersburg Times*, 2 January 2005, 5B.

> David Waters, "God Seen in Touching Others, Not in Touchdowns," *Knoxville News Sentinel*, 5 February 2005, E8.

> "White Remembered As a Man of Goodness," (Salt Lake City) *Deseret News*, 31 December 2004, D8.

"White Remembered For His Faith, Humor," (Vancouver) *Columbian*, 31 December 2004, B3.

Rex Barney

Barney, Rex with Norman L. Macht. *Rex Barney's Thank Youuuu*. Centreville, MD: Tidewater Publishers, 1993.

Dan Quisenberry

Jeff Miller, "Former Royals Relief Ace Dan Quisenberry, 45, Dies," *The Orange County Register*, 1 October 1998, D1.

Joe Posnanski, "Quisenberry Left Mark With Quick Wit, Pleasantness," *Pittsburgh-Post Gazette*, 1 October 1998, D4.

Joe Posnanski, "Smiles Bid Quiz Fond Farewell," *Kansas City Star*, 6 October 1998, C1.

Quisenberry, Dan. *On Days Like This*. Kansas City, MO: Helicon Nine Editions, 1998.

Payne Stewart

Stewart, Tracey with Ken Abraham. *Payne Stewart*. Nashville: Broadmand & Holman Publishers, 2000.

Walter Payton

Payton, Walter and Don Yaeger. *Never Die Easy: The Autobiography of Walter Payton*. New York: Random House, 2001.

"Walter Payton Dead At 45: NFL's All-Time Rusher Suffered From Rare Liver Disease," *CNN Sports Illustrated*, 2 November 1999, http://sportsillustrated.cnn.com/football/nfl/news/1999/11/01/payton_obit.

2000–2007

2000–2007

Republican George W. Bush narrowly defeated Democrat Al Gore in the presidential election of 2000. The results were in doubt for more than a month after the election, as the Bush and Gore camps battled through a series of lawsuits and appeals.

Shortly after the election, incumbent President William Clinton visited Hanoi. He was the first U.S. president to go to Vietnam since President Richard Nixon visited U.S. troops in 1969, during the height of the Vietnam War.

On September 11, 2001, hijackers funded by terrorist Osama bin Laden piloted two passenger jetliners into the twin towers of New York City's World Trade Center and a third airplane into the Pentagon. A fourth hijacked plane crashed eighty miles outside of Pittsburgh. The official tally of dead and missing from the terrorist attacks was approximately 3,900. In response, U.S. and British air forces attacked Taliban military installations and terrorist training camps in Afghanistan. In 2002, the United States Senate approved the creation of a cabinet-level Department of Homeland Security, combining twenty-two different agencies and one hundred and seventy thousand workers.

The space shuttle *Columbia* disintegrated while returning from a scientific research mission on February 1, 2003. Shuttle pilot Willie McCool, a Navy commander, and the six other crew members perished fifteen minutes before the shuttle was scheduled to land at the Kennedy Space Center in Florida.

The United States launched Operation Iraqi Freedom on March 19, 2003, with aerial attacks on Baghdad and other Iraqi cities. Later that same month, twenty-year-old Army private Jessica Lynch was captured by Iraqi forces during a firefight. Lynch was rescued eight days later.

On April 22, 2004, Army Ranger Pat Tillman, a former safety for the Phoenix Cardinals professional football team, died in Afghanistan after being hit by friendly fire. Also in 2004, an earthquake with a magnitude of 9.0 erupted off the Indonesian island of Sumatra, causing tidal waves that raged across the Indian Ocean at more than five hundred miles per hour. Nearly one hundred and forty thousand people died in a dozen nations in Asia and East Africa. Millions more were left homeless.

Pope John Paul II, the first Polish pope and the first non-Italian pope since 1522, died from Parkinson's disease in 2005. Cardinal Joseph Ratzinger was elected as his successor, taking the name Benedict XVI. Also in 2005, Hurricane Katrina, a category four storm, pounded the southeastern part of the United States, inflicting heavy damage in Louisiana and elsewhere. More than eighty people were killed, thousands lost homes, and millions lost electrical power.

JOHN STEADMAN

John Steadman was a sports columnist and editor in Baltimore for more than fifty years. In his youth, Steadman attended Baltimore's City College, where he played baseball, football, and basketball. After graduating from college, he played minor league baseball in the Pittsburgh Pirates' farm system. Steadman left baseball after one season, taking with him a .125 batting average. He got his start in journalism as a reporter for the Baltimore News-Post *in 1945. He worked for four Baltimore news-papers in all and, at the time of his death in 2001, was writing for* The Sun. *Stead-man was a beloved figure in Baltimore, noted for his fairness, his interest in people, and his passionate attacks on racial injustice in baseball. He won three Freedom Foundation medals, one for writing and two for radio commentaries, and was elected to the National Sportswriters and Sportscasters Hall of Fame in 1999. Steadman died on January 1, 2001, at the age of seventy-three.*

John Steadman used to describe his job in simplistic terms. His challenge as a journalist, he said, was in "taking a blank piece of paper, a mind in the same bar-ren state, and trying to put words together that family and friends might want to read." For fifty years, there were few in Baltimore—friends, family or other-wise—who didn't want to read Steadman's work. "There are positives in this world," said Vi Ripken, the mother of former Baltimore Orioles infielder Cal Ripken, "but without John in Baltimore, we'd never have heard about them."

In a column devoted to pro golfer Gene Littler's battle with cancer, Steadman wrote, "the game of life, like that of golf, doesn't always find you playing in the middle of the fairway. There's rough and bunkers and tough luck all around."

In the days following the assassination of Martin Luther King, Jr., John Stead-man tackled the subject of race relations in his sports column. "It's an indictment upon us all that there was ever a division between the races," he wrote. "Now, more than ever, we must be our brother's keeper."

While Steadman followed sports with interest, his passion lay with people. He spent a lifetime as his "brother's keeper." In the words of one colleague at *The Sun*, Steadman "always stressed the human heart beyond the game." He made visits to every volunteer fire department and senior citizen home in Baltimore, simply to spread smiles and cheer. A long-time friend said of Steadman, "He was the most unselfish, caring person that God could ever have put on this earth."

Steadman regularly served as an usher at the 8:00 AM Sunday service at St. Jude Shrine in Baltimore. Churchgoers at St. Jude's knew Steadman as a devout but subdued worshiper, a man who was always quietly respectful in church. One Sunday, however, after the priest had delivered a sermon urging the parishioners to bring their faith into the streets, Steadman rose from his seat and unabashedly clapped in appreciation.

In addition to being a prolific writer, Steadman was a gifted speaker. He enthusiastically served as master of ceremonies at charitable functions throughout the state of Maryland. Once, at the funeral service of a friend, Steadman was dismayed to find that the minister's sermon contained very few words in memory of his friend. Before the service ended, Steadman strode to the front of the church, took a microphone and said to the assembly, "I don't think we should leave here without saying a few words about Tom White." Steadman then proceeded to deliver a fitting eulogy that lasted twenty minutes.

Steadman once learned of an eight-year-old little leaguer who was fighting cancer. The boy was a devoted fan of Baltimore Orioles outfielder Gene Woodling. As the boy neared his final days, Steadman brought Woodling to Johns Hopkins Hospital to meet the boy.

Such acts gained Steadman a reputation as the champion of underdogs. According to Baltimore legend John Unitas, Steadman "was always a savior for the little guy."

◆   ◆   ◆

My tongue is the pen of a nimble scribe.
—Psalm 45, verse 2.

KOREY STRINGER

Korey "Big K" Stringer, a native of Warren, Ohio, stood six feet four inches tall and weighed 335 pounds. As a collegiate football player at Ohio State University, he was named Big Ten Offensive Lineman of the Year in both 1993 and 1994. From 1995 to 2000, Stringer played offensive tackle for the Minnesota Vikings. He was named to the NFL Pro Bowl team in 2000. Known for his gentle ways, Stringer was a hero to school children in Minnesota. He died on August 1, 2001, of complications from heat stroke. He was twenty-seven years old.

When Korey Stringer was in the third grade at Horace Mann School in Warren, Ohio, his teacher wrote on his initial report card, "I know you're capable of getting A's. I expect you to work harder." Stringer took the message to heart. On Stringer's last report card for the year, his teacher wrote, "I knew you had it in you to be an A-student. You've risen to the challenge."

Korey Stringer made a practice of rising to the challenge. One summer during his grade school years, his parents would not allow him to watch television or play games outdoors, because he had misbehaved. Stringer turned what could have been a tedious summer into an opportunity. He began reading books. The experience changed his life; reading became his passion. According to his wife, Kelci, "That's when he really figured out who he was." Stringer found that reading "freed his mind."

Eager to share his passion for reading, Stringer began visiting Bancroft Elementary School in Minneapolis in 1996. For five years, week in and week out, Stringer spent two hours with students every Tuesday as part of Bancroft's Accelerated Reading program. He would talk to the children, sign autographs, and play games on the playground. Stringer always found a way to steer the conversation to school work. "What have you been reading lately?" he would ask the students. Stringer would tell the children that reading had given him time to be alone and to begin liking who he was. Stringer told the children that reading would help them find out who they are.

Shortly after Stringer's appearance in the 2000 Pro Bowl, he learned that the Little Raiders youth football team in his Ohio hometown was planning to cut twenty-five players, because there were not enough uniforms to go around. Stringer immediately pulled out the ten thousand dollar check that he had received for playing in the Pro Bowl, endorsed the check, and gave it to the Little Raiders' coach. "If you need more money, let me know," he told the coach, "because I don't want any kid cut."

◆   ◆   ◆

I will open my mouth in story, drawing lessons from of old.
—Psalm 78, verse 2.

MIKE WEINBERG

Mike Weinberg played catcher and center field for St. John's University from 1986 to 1989. During his four years at St. John's, Weinberg hit .256 with six home runs and fifty-nine runs batted in. The highlight of his college career came in 1988 when he hit two home runs during the Big East Tournament and earned the tournament's Most Outstanding Player award. After college, Weinberg signed with the Detroit Tigers. He played two years in the Tigers' farm system, but was unable to hit consistently. He batted .238 with Niagara Falls of the New York-Penn League in 1990 and .217 with Fayetteville of the South Atlantic League in 1991. The Tigers released Weinberg midway through the 1991 season. He returned to New York and joined the New York City Fire Department. He also worked as a part-time model. Weinberg died on September 11, 2001, at the age of thirty-four.

On September 11, 2001, Mike Weinberg was on vacation from his duties as a fireman with Engine 1, Ladder 24 in lower Manhattan. He had a 9:08 AM tee time at Forest Park Golf Course in Queens. Minutes before he was to tee off, Weinberg heard that a plane had struck one of the twin towers at the World Trade Center. Weinberg didn't hesitate. He threw his golf clubs into the back of his sports utility vehicle and dashed into lower Manhattan. The members of Weinberg's family were hoping that he would remain at the golf course. Weinberg's coach at St. John's, Joe Russo, had a similar thought. When Russo heard that the towers had collapsed, he said to his wife, "I hope Mike wasn't there."

Mike was indeed there, just as his family knew he would be. Weinberg never passed up an opportunity to help. There were two compelling reasons for him to report to the World Trade Center. First, he was steadfastly loyal to his job and to his fellow firemen. Second, he was devoted to his sister, Patricia Gambino, who worked on the seventy-second floor of Two World Trade Center.

En route to ground zero, Weinberg stopped at his station on West Thirty-first Street. He then drove to the site of the disaster with Father Mychal Judge, the fire department chaplain, and Capt. Daniel Brethel. When the South Tower started to collapse, Weinberg and Brethel took cover under a fire truck, but the truck could not withstand the weight of the falling debris. Weinberg's body was among the first to be pulled out of the rubble.

Muscular and handsome, Weinberg was a featured model in a calendar published by the New York City Fire Department. However, it was his smile that people remember. According to Joe Russo, Weinberg was always smiling. "He was always laughing and made everyone around him feel good," Russo said. "He was just a great person."

Patricia Gambino, who survived by walking down forty-four floors to safety, said of her brother, "People would say he was striking, but he was more beautiful inside."

◆   ◆   ◆

Turn your steps toward the utter ruins, toward the sanctuary devastated by the enemy.
—Psalm 74, verse 3.

SHELBY "BIG FOOT" NJOKU

Shelby Amarachi Njoku was an Honor Roll student at St. Hugh's Grade School in Greenbelt, Maryland, and an altar server at St. Hugh's Church. Known to her teammates as "Big Foot," Njoku was an excellent defender on the Greenbelt Tigers club soccer team. As her nickname would suggest, Njoku was blessed with an exceptionally strong right foot. According to her former coach, when Big Foot was playing the center defender position, it didn't matter who played goalie, because opponents could rarely muster any shots on goal. Njoku died suddenly on November 9, 2001, of viral myocarditis. She was ten years old.

The viral myocarditis struck quickly. Shelby Njoku had a full slate of activities planned for what promised to be a breezy and sunny November weekend in her hometown of Beltsville, Maryland. Njoku and her Greenbelt Tigers teammates would be playing in the 2001 Harvest Classic Soccer Tournament, scheduled for Sunday, November 11. Big Foot never made it to the Harvest Classic. In rapid succession, she was stricken, hospitalized, and died before any of her teammates were even aware she was in trouble. Lying in her bed at Maryland's Laurel Hospital, Njoku sensed her illness was serious. She told her father that if she died, "you'd have to be strong." The remark was typical of the grace under pressure that friends and family had come to expect from Njoku.

Big Foot was a natural defender. As a soccer player, she possessed all of the physical attributes that one would expect in a defensive stalwart. She was aggressive and fast, quick to react, and capable of setting up her teammates with booming passes to midfield. Off the field, Njoku always had a song in her heart and a deep concern for others. She reacted strongly whenever she encountered boorish behavior by others. As the big sister to a brother afflicted with autism, Njoku willingly took on the role of protector when other children would make fun of her brother. With Big Foot around, Shelby's brother, Forbe, never had to worry about what others might say or do. Big Foot was just as quick to come to the defense of others whom she saw being mistreated or bullied. Caring and compassionate, Shelby Njoku showed her classmates and friends how to respond whenever an individual's dignity was threatened.

Graceful under pressure and well-liked by everyone, Njoku moved through life with a clear sense of purpose. She left behind many friends, as well as a poem that offers insight into the way she lived her life:

> My vision is bright
> My vision is clear,
> the sky is blue
> I see where I am going.
>
> —by Shelby, 2001.

◆   ◆   ◆

Be vigilant in my defense.
—Psalm 35, verse 23.

DARRYL KILE

Darryl Andrew Kile pitched in the major leagues from 1991 to 2002, winning 133 games during the course of his career. His best seasons came in 1997, when he won nineteen games and lost seven for the Houston Astros, and in 2000, when he went 20–9 for the St. Louis Cardinals. On June 22, 2002, Kile was scheduled to pitch for the Cardinals against the Chicago Cubs at Wrigley Field, but he never came to the ballpark. Authorities found Kile's body in his hotel room. He had died in his sleep, a victim of coronary atherosclerosis, or narrowing of the arteries. Kile was thirty-three years old. At a memorial service in St. Louis, Dave Veres, Kile's teammate and best friend, described Kile as "an angel."

While playing for the Houston Astros, Darryl Kile rose early one Saturday morning to make a guest appearance at a practice being held by a Little League team. The Little League players had brought bats and baseballs for Kile to sign. As the signing session was winding down, a coach noticed one boy standing reticently behind his teammates. The boy did not appear to have anything for Kile to sign. The coach asked the boy whether he had brought a baseball. The boy said that he had not. Kile took over, telling the coach, "I've got a couple of new balls in my car." Kile motioned to the boy to walk with him to the car. The two, one an established major-leaguer and the other a small boy in need of a baseball, walked together across a span of playing fields, talking and laughing all the way.

Kile was traded to the St. Louis Cardinals at the end of the 1999 season. He enjoyed two excellent seasons with the Cardinals and was working on a third when he died. In his two-and-a-half years in St. Louis, Kile routinely demonstrated both generosity and compassion. A former teammate said of Kile, "He'd do anything he could to help people."

Often Kile's help came in the form of financial assistance. For each St. Louis homestand during the baseball season, he purchased tickets so that groups of children, designated as "Kile's Kids," could attend the games. Kile also provided funds to establish Police Athletic League Memorial Park, a baseball field for St. Louis-area youth. During his days with the Cardinals, Kile would save up the eighty dollars he received each day for meal money when the team was on the road. At the end of the season, he would take the accumulated meal money and quietly give it to a clubhouse worker or other lesser-paid member of the Cardinals' staff.

◆   ◆   ◆

The just are generous in giving.
—Psalm 37, verse 21.

WILLIE McCOOL

William C. McCool finished second among all midshipmen in the Naval Academy's graduating class of 1983. He went on to earn two master's degrees, one in computer science and one in aeronautical engineering. While at the Naval Academy, McCool was a member of the cross-country and track teams. On October 2, 1982, he ran the Academy's cross-country course in 24:27.0, the twenty-sixth fastest time ever by a Navy runner. As a high school student in Guam in 1977, McCool won the Junior Division of the 5.5-mile Mt. Alutom Hill Climb. His record-setting time of thirty-one minutes and five seconds has never been equaled. McCool, a commander in the U.S. Navy, died on February 1, 2003, when the space shuttle Columbia disintegrated while returning from its scientific research mission. He was forty-one years old.

Willie McCool dreamed big. When he was stationed at Whidbey Island in Washington, he bought season tickets to watch Seattle Mariners' baseball games at the Kingdome. His seats were high above the playing field, well out of range of even the most powerful sluggers. Nonetheless, McCool would always bring his baseball glove to the games, ever hopeful of catching a ball on the fly.

From his earliest days, McCool aspired to be a pilot. He completed flight training shortly after graduating from the Naval Academy. After the space shuttle *Challenger* burst into a ball of fire following takeoff on January 28, 1986, McCool participated in the missing-man fly-over ceremony held to honor the shuttle crew members. He was the pilot of the lone plane that peeled off from the formation and flew skyward.

McCool served as a naval test pilot for several years. In 1996, NASA selected him for the space program. On January 16, 2003, McCool piloted the shuttle *Columbia* as it lifted off from its Cape Canaveral launch site. Sixteen days later, the *Columbia* broke up as it reentered the earth's atmosphere, killing McCool and the other members of the crew. Two days before his death, McCool had spoken from space about his hope for the future. "From our vantage point," he said, "we observe an earth without borders, full of peace, beauty, and magnificence. And we pray that humanity as a whole can imagine a borderless world as we see it and strive to live as one in peace."

McCool did his part to bring peace to the world. On Saturday nights at the Naval Academy, when many of the midshipmen would go to parties, McCool spent time tutoring the son of Al Cantello, coach of the Annapolis cross-country team. As a pilot, McCool worked on a program sponsored by the Air Force Association to stimulate interest among grade-school children in aviation, mathematics, and science. When McCool was thirty-one, he was baptized into the Catholic Church. He told Father John Barry, the priest who officiated at his baptism, that he felt he could become a better person "by putting his life more into Christ's hands." At McCool's invitation, Father Barry went to Cape Canaveral to watch the *Columbia* take off. Shortly before the launch, Father Barry heard McCool's confession.

McCool liked to make people happy. At weddings and other celebrations, he often ended up entertaining the little children who were in attendance. According to one of his colleagues, McCool had "the heart of a child and the brain of a genius." Al Cantello recalled him as a perpetually happy person, a rare runner who had a penchant for smiling even during the most grueling cross-country races. "Everyone should meet a Willie McCool in his lifetime," Cantello said.

◆   ◆   ◆

The heavens declare the glory of God; his message goes out to all the world.
—Psalm 19, verse 2.

JIMMY ADAMOUSKI

James "Jimmy" Adamouski, a captain in the United States Army, was one of five soldiers killed on April 2, 2003, in the crash of a Black Hawk helicopter near Karbala, Iraq. Adamouski graduated from Robert E. Lee High School in Springfield, Virginia, where he was an athlete, student leader, and president of his senior class. After high school, Adamouski enrolled at West Point. While at the Military Academy, he played varsity soccer, earning first-team all-conference honors in his senior year. Following his four years at West Point, Adamouski was commissioned as a lieutenant in the Army. Before being assigned to Iraq, he was stationed in Germany and Bosnia. Adamouski was twenty-nine years old at his death.

Nearly nine hundred people attended the funeral service for Jimmy Adamouski. Many of the mourners wore buttons proclaiming the Army captain as "our hero."

Adamouski was an athlete, a scholar, and a leader. To his godfather, Adamouski was "the embodiment of Christian love," a person who constantly put the needs of others before his own needs.

A devout Catholic, Adamouski served as a Eucharistic minister in the church. During his assignment in Bosnia, his fellow soldiers called him "Father Jimmy." The nickname was in recognition of Adamouski's work in bringing Holy Communion to soldiers in the field who could not attend church services.

According to one of Adamouski's West Point classmates, "Jimmy came from love, lived in love, and left love."

◆　　　◆　　　◆

You bring bread from the earth, and wine to gladden our hearts.
—Psalm 104, verses 14–15.

PAT TILLMAN

From 1998 to 2001, Pat Tillman was a hard-hitting safety for the Arizona Cardinals. In May 2002, at the age of twenty-five and at the height of his NFL career, Tillman left football and joined the United States Army. According to friends, his decision to enlist in the Army was prompted by the terrorist attacks of September 11, 2001. Before beginning his pro football career, Tillman excelled as a linebacker for Arizona State University. In 1997, he was named defensive player of the year in the Pacific-10 Conference. He earned his degree from Arizona State in three and a half years, graduating summa cum laude. During the 2000 NFL season, Tillman recorded 224 tackles for the Cardinals, a team record. A veteran of one tour of duty in Iraq, Tillman died on April 22, 2004, when his position came under friendly fire during operations in Afghanistan.

In April 2001, the St. Louis Rams offered Pat Tillman a five-year contract that would pay him nine million dollars. He rejected the offer and instead re-signed with the Arizona Cardinals. His deal with the Cardinals was for one year and paid less than one million dollars.

The next year, the Cardinals offered Tillman a contract that would have paid him $3.6 million for three years. Tillman rejected that offer. Instead, he enlisted in the Army.

So it was that Tillman, holding the rank of Army Specialist Fourth Class, was drawing an annual salary of eighteen thousand dollars in 2004, instead of the $1.8 million he could have earned with the Rams or the $1.2 million he would have received from the Cardinals.

Money was one of many things that held little importance for Tillman. The attention that he might get as a prominent athlete-turned-soldier was another. For publicity purposes, Arizona State University asked Tillman for a photograph showing him in his Army uniform. He politely turned down the request. "The Army thing, it's no big deal," he told the university's sports department.

The Army encouraged Tillman to enroll in its officer training program. Tillman declined. Being an officer was not a big deal either; all he wanted to be was a regular soldier.

Tillman spent his spare time thinking about programs that might help illiterate children learn to read. To him, helping children was a very big deal.

◆   ◆   ◆

I have raised up a hero from the army.
—Psalm 89, verse 20.

JOHN CERUTTI

Left-hander John Joseph Cerutti, a native of Albany, New York, pitched for seven seasons in the major leagues, six of them with the Toronto Blue Jays. The Blue Jays selected Cerutti out of Amherst College in the first round of the 1981 amateur draft. During his major league career, he won forty-nine games and lost forty-three. His best season came in 1987, when he won eleven games for Toronto and lost four. Cerutti was the winning pitcher for the Blue Jays on June 7, 1989, when the team recorded its inaugural victory in the new Toronto SkyDome. When his playing days ended, Cerutti turned to broadcasting. He worked as a television analyst for Blue Jays games from 1997 until his death. Cerutti was also an accomplished golfer and a former club champion at East Lake Woodlands Golf Club in Oldsmar, Florida. He died of cardiac arrest on October 3, 2004, at the age of forty-four.

After learning of John Cerutti's death, television broadcaster Sean McDonough said, "I totally believe there's a heaven, and if John's not there, nobody's going."

In some ways, McDonough considered Cerutti to be an oddity in baseball. McDonough found Cerutti to be polite, mature, and respectful, traits that are not always on display in baseball clubhouses.

Cerutti died in his sleep on the last day of the 2004 baseball season. He had been scheduled to do color commentary for a game between the Blue Jays and the Yankees but failed to appear for the game. Police found him in bed in his room at Toronto's SkyDome Hotel—with his fingers touching the cross that he wore around his neck.

In 1995, four years after his last major league game, Cerutti pitched for the Albany-Colonie Diamond Dogs of the independent Northeast League. On days when he wasn't pitching for the Diamond Dogs, he served as the team's radio broadcaster. To hone his broadcasting skills, Cerutti would diligently listen to tapes of the broadcasts after each game and critique his performance. He displayed a similar diligence in the practice of his faith and in virtually every other aspect of his life. He treated everyone whom he encountered with respect. He always made time for people and would listen earnestly to what they had to say.

When taking leave of friends, he would ask if there was anything he could do for them.

In recognition of Cerutti's gentle nature and his contributions to the game, the Toronto chapter of the Baseball Writers' Association of America established the John Cerutti Award. Each year the honor recognizes a member of the Blue Jays organization who best exemplifies a positive image for baseball.

During his lifetime, John Cerutti did much more than simply present a positive image for baseball; he left a lasting impression on every person he met.

Reporter Kim Lockhart of the *Toronto Star*, who covered the Blue Jays during Cerutti's career, called him "the nicest player I met in four years of hanging around the Blue Jays' clubhouse."

After Cerutti's death, veteran *New York Daily News* sportswriter Bill Madden lobbied for major league baseball to pay public tribute to the pitcher-turned-broadcaster during the 2004 post-season games. Madden described Cerutti as "a loving husband and father of three whose only vice was an infuriating deliberateness in everything he did, from pitching to golfing to eating."

◆   ◆   ◆

Those at peace with God have a future.
—Psalm 37, verse 37.

TEDDY EBERSOL

Edward "Teddy" Ebersol was a youth league pitcher in Litchfield, Connecticut, and a fervent fan of the Boston Red Sox. He was the son of Dick Ebersol, Chairman of NBC Sports, and actress Susan Saint James. Teddy Ebersol died on November 28, 2004, in the crash of a jet airplane that slid off the runway of the Montrose Regional Airport in Colorado during takeoff and burst into flames. Teddy Ebersol was fourteen years old. Mourners at his wake wore Red Sox baseball caps in his memory.

Teddy Ebersol gave the graduation speech at his eighth grade commencement ceremonies. In his speech, he told his classmates, "The finish line is only the beginning of a whole new race." While Ebersol looked forward to the "new race" with great anticipation, it was clear that he had performed well in the race already completed.

Following his mother's lead, Ebersol devoted considerable time and effort throughout his grade school years to helping with the Special Olympics in his hometown of Litchfield. As an eighth-grade student, Ebersol worked full-time for one week with the Litchfield Area Retarded Citizens program. His experience working with the mentally handicapped led him to organize a group of students to perform community service for the Litchfield Area Retarded Citizens. Ebersol also served as an altar server during Masses at his family's local parish, St. Anthony of Padua Roman Catholic Church in Litchfield.

◆   ◆   ◆

Children too are a gift from the Lord, the fruit of the womb, a reward.
—Psalm 127, verse 3.

JOHNNY OATES

Johnny Oates was a catcher in the major leagues for nine full seasons and parts of two other seasons. He played for five teams during his career, mostly in a backup role. Oates was a first-round draft pick of the Baltimore Orioles in 1967. His first full season in the major leagues came in 1972, when he played in eighty-five games for the Orioles and batted .261. His best overall year was 1975, when he split time between the Atlanta Braves and the Philadelphia Phillies, batting .282 with fifteen doubles and one home run. Oates retired as a player in 1981. In 1991, the Orioles named him manager. He went on to manage Baltimore for four years and the Texas Rangers for seven more. Oates led the Rangers to first-place finishes in the American League's West Division in 1996, 1998, and 1999. He died of a brain tumor on Christmas Eve, 2004, at the age of fifty-eight.

Somehow, Johnny Oates came to see his brain tumor as a blessing. He found that the presence of the tumor helped him to simplify his life and focus on the essentials. "Really there's only one day of the week that has any importance," Oates said, "and that's today." He found that he stopped worrying about the future, because "you can't do anything about tomorrow."

Doctors discovered Oates's tumor in 2001. He survived for three more years, living one day at a time. The affliction allowed Oates to focus more on his family and on his priorities in life. He started each day studying the Bible with his wife, Gloria. He took delight in watching the squirrels scamper in his backyard, and he took delight in people as well. He went out of his way to meet others and listen to their views on baseball and life. He attended weekly meetings of the Promise Keepers, a men's Christian group, even when he was experiencing pain from the tumor.

Even before his illness, Oates came across as different. He made time for everyone. He was a humble person, utterly unimpressed with his accomplishments in baseball. As a manager, Oates cultivated personal relationships with both players and sportswriters, an approach that was far from the norm. For pitcher Jeff Zimmerman, who spent more than two years playing for Oates, "he was more like a father figure than a manager." "Just the way he loved life and loved his family was a great example," Zimmerman said.

◆   ◆   ◆

It was good for me to be afflicted, in order to learn your laws.
—Psalm 119, verse 71.

REGGIE ROBY

In his senior season of high school football, Reggie Roby kicked off for Waterloo East High School in Iowa to start its game against Marshalltown High. The football sailed through the goalpost uprights seventy yards away. One onlooker, a college coach on a recruiting trip, turned to a colleague and said, "I believe that's a Division I leg we just saw out there." In fact, what the coach saw was more than a Division I leg—it was a Pro Bowl leg. After high school, Roby took his booming kicks to the University of Iowa. He showed such prowess as a punter that the Iowa coach refused to let him play any other position, for fear he would suffer an injury. At Iowa, Roby led the nation in punting in both his junior and senior years. With his towering spirals, he became a popular pregame attraction. On game days, fans would come out to the stadium early just to see Roby practice his punting. After college, Roby moved on to the Miami Dolphins. For sixteen years, he reigned as one of the best punters in the NFL, averaging 43.3 yards per punt. He was named to the Pro Bowl three times. Roby died on February 22, 2005, at the age of forty-three.

Reggie Roby had high expectations of others, in some cases unrealistically so. A cookie enthusiast, he took it upon himself to bake cookies for team meetings when he played for the Washington Redskins. Oatmeal raisin molasses, triple chocolate walnut, sugar cookies—Roby baked them all. Before leaving home for the meetings, he would bake for several hours, batch up 360 of his best efforts, and bring them to Redskins Park. However, he was always disappointed, for his teammates never took the time to savor his creations. They would devour the cookies in minutes, each player often eating five or six at a time. "I hate that," Roby would complain.

Roby also had high expectations for himself. "My leg will be able to kick forever," he said in 1985, his third season in the National Football League. "Forever" lasted for sixteen years; Roby retired from the game in 1999.

In life after football, Roby was the director of marketing and development for Backfield in Motion, a non-profit group formed to help boys from Nashville's inner-city. More importantly, he was the mentor and father figure for thirty youths who were under the supervision of Backfield in Motion. Roby was also the father of six children born to his wife, Melissa, and himself. The dual role of parent and mentor presented a formidable challenge because Roby took an active interest in the life of each and every child. The end of an academic term brought a staggering number of report cards for Roby to review and numerous parent-teacher conferences that required his participation. Roby prospered under the demands of the job. As Backfield in Motion's chief executive officer once remarked, "it was his calling."

Roby's charitable spirit knew no bounds. Each year during his pro football career, he celebrated Christmas by serving food to the homeless. He would slip away from his house early on Christmas morning and, without fanfare, drive to a local soup kitchen. By design, few knew of his Christmas Day routine; he took pains to make sure that newspapers and TV stations would not publicize his work.

Roby's approach to helping out at soup kitchens was characteristic of all of his charitable efforts. He was quietly effective. According to the founder of Backfield in Motion, "He was just doing it because it was in his heart. He was just a good man."

◆   ◆   ◆

Be generous and share your food with the poor. You will be blessed for it.
—Proverbs 22, verse 9.

BECKY ZERLENTES

Becky Zerlentes was a professor at Front Range Community College in Colorado. She held a Ph.D. in geography, was an avid cyclist, had a brown belt in tae kwon do, and was a Golden Gloves boxer. In 2002, she was the Colorado State Golden Gloves champion in the women's 132-pound weight class. During her amateur boxing career, she won six times in ten fights. Zerlentes died on April 4, 2005, as a result of an injury suffered when she was hit in the head during a bout. She was the first female boxer ever to die during a sanctioned boxing match. At her death, she was thirty-four years old.

Becky Zerlentes was passionate about protecting the environment. When she went out to eat at restaurants, she would carry a Tupperware container in her purse. In the event of leftovers, she would pull out the Tupperware and use it to carry the food home. For Zerlentes, it was a simple act of great import, a way of reducing the consumption of Styrofoam boxes.

Every Tuesday and Thursday, Zerlentes would go for a one-mile walk near her college campus with a fellow professor to pick up litter. She organized group walks to increase appreciation for Earth's simple pleasures and to clean up the environment. She rode her bicycle everywhere and would politely chastise friends who refused to carpool to work. Concerned about the piles of trash resulting from excessive consumption of water in plastic bottles, Zerlentes refused to buy bottled water. Instead, she carried a tiny filtration pump with her to use when drinking water from outdoor fountains.

To promote a better understanding among students of the geographic relationships among countries, Zerlentes would take her classes out to a grassy area, designate each student as a different country, and direct the students to position themselves in the form of a world map.

Zerlentes was a trained massage therapist and would often give massages to friends and colleagues. When people would seek to pay her for the massages, she would decline the money and ask that it be donated to charity.

At her death, a fellow professor described Zerlentes as possessing "a smile and a light in her heart that touched everyone."

◆   ◆   ◆

Truth will spring from the earth.
—Psalm 85, verse 12.

SAM MILLS

Though small for professional football at five feet nine inches tall and 225 pounds, Sam Mills played linebacker in the National Football League for twelve seasons. From 1986 to 1994, he starred for the New Orleans Saints, where he was selected to play in the Pro Bowl four times. He joined the expansion Carolina Panthers in 1995 and quickly became the team's inspirational leader. He was the only player to start every game during the Panthers' first three seasons. When he retired from football after the 1997 season, the Panthers erected a bronze statue outside the team's Bank of America Stadium in his honor. Mills is the only player so honored. He was elected to the Sports Halls of Fame for both Louisiana and New Jersey. Mills died on April 18, 2005, from intestinal cancer. He was forty-five years old.

Sam Mills was never one to make demands on people. But, shortly before he died, he imposed three demands on his family and friends. First, he insisted that his memorial service, now inevitable, be a "celebration." Second, he demanded that those giving eulogies not keep people at the church "too long." His final requirement was that the food served at his reception taste good and have "lots of grease." Fittingly, all three demands concerned the comfort and enjoyment of others.

In the years immediately after Mills graduated from New Jersey's Montclair State University, when it looked like there might not be a spot for him in professional football, Mills took a job as a high school teacher. When the United States Football League began operating in 1983, Mills traded the classroom for the gridiron, but he never stopped teaching.

Mills taught others to persevere. Whether talking about football or life, he encouraged others to "keep pounding." When medical tests revealed that Mills had intestinal cancer, his doctors told him not to expect to live more than a few months. From the date of diagnosis, he lived almost two years.

He taught others to be grateful. Once, when talking about his cancer treatments, he said to reporters, "You have your good days and your bad days. I am just glad I am having days, you know?"

Mills taught teammates and friends to live better lives. He never disparaged the efforts of others. He supported his teammates and coaches and was respectful toward people in the media. He took the time to get to know the names of the individuals with whom he came in contact, whether they were superstars or parking lot attendants. When talking about the way Mills lived his life, former teammate Mike Minter said, "I saw him do it, and I said, 'Man, I want to be like that.'"

Mills taught others to find nobility in the routine of daily life. According to Carolina Panthers general manager Marty Hurney, "the magic of Sam Mills was that every day was the same work ethic, the same discipline, the same routine, and the same competitiveness. So when you're around a person like that and something happens and he's going through a hard time, it's almost like those characteristics kind of go over to you. You see what made him, and you just try to be like him."

On the day after Mills died, Panthers wide receivers Keary Colbert and Drew Carter traveled to a previously scheduled guest appearance at the Brentwood Middle School in North Charleston, South Carolina. The players were asked if it was difficult to follow through with the speaking engagement so soon after Mills's death. "You know what?" Colbert said, "It's actually easier to come out and do something like this on a day like this. We know Sam enjoyed doing these things."

Together with Panthers linebacker Mark Fields, Mills started the Keep Pounding Fund to raise money for the Blumenthal Cancer Center in Charlotte. Mills and Fields sold bracelets with the words "Keep Pounding" for one dollar each. The Keep Pounding Fund has generated almost five hundred thousand dollars for experimental cancer trials and related cancer research.

"I called him Sam Rock," said Kevin Greene, a former Panthers linebacker. "He was not only the physical rock, but he was the spiritual rock and the emotional rock and the leadership rock." According to Marty Hurney, "He made us all better."

◆   ◆   ◆

The teaching of the wise is a fountain of life.
—Proverbs 13, verse 14.

HOLLY CHARETTE

Holly A. Charette was a 2001 graduate of Cranston East High School in Cranston, Rhode Island. In high school, she played field hockey for four years and was a member of the cheerleading squad. After the 2001 terrorist attacks on the World Trade Center and the Pentagon, Charette joined the United States Marine Corps. She was gifted with a smile that was unforgettable—and she used it often. The twenty-one-year-old lance corporal was one of four Marines killed on June 23, 2005, when a suicide bomber in Fallujah, Iraq, attacked a military convoy.

Holly Charette always made time for people. When others were sick, she would bring them ice cream and soup. More than the ice cream and more than the soup, however, there was the smile. Without prompting and even in the most discouraging situations, she took delight in sharing her smile.

Friends and fellow soldiers marveled at Holly Charette's consistently happy attitude. What people marveled at most, however, was her smile. For one friend, it was simply "the biggest smile." Another talked of Charette's "smiling face of hope." For still another, her smile was "a burst of sunshine." According to friends, Charette's smile lit up rooms and changed moods.

Charette once wore a T-shirt embroidered with dragonflies to school. When a teammate on the field hockey team admired the shirt, Charette gave it to the teammate. It was just a way, Charette said at the time, of trying to cheer up someone who was having a rough day. And, of course, along with the T-shirt came Charette's unforgettable smile.

Lance Corporal Holly Charette is gone. Her smile remains visible to many.

◆   ◆   ◆

Smiling faces make you happy.
—Proverbs 15, verse 30.

WELLINGTON MARA

Wellington Timothy Mara, longtime owner, president, and executive officer of the New York Football Giants, was one of the most influential figures in the history of the National Football League. The son of Giants' founder Timothy J. Mara, Wellington Mara joined the Giants organization in 1937 as a part-time assistant. Except for the period during which he served as a Navy officer in World War II, Mara spent his entire adult life with the Giants. He worked in a number of executive positions. A skillful evaluator of talent, Mara led the Giants to prominence in the late 1950s and early 1960s. He was responsible for drafting players such as punter Don Chandler, linebacker Sam Huff, and halfback Frank Gifford. He engineered trades for defensive end Andy Robustelli, quarterback Y.A. Tittle, and cornerback Linden Crow. Mara also led the effort to adopt the NFL's innovative revenue-sharing plan, even though it meant that the Giants would have to sacrifice revenue. Mara viewed revenue-sharing as a necessary device for achieving greater balance among teams in the league and, in turn, a more enjoyable product for the fans. A fervent Catholic, Mara attended Mass daily. He died on October 25, 2005, at the age of eighty-nine.

"I really believe you are the only owner in the NFL whose picture is up in San Quentin," Wellington Mara's administrative assistant once told the Giants' owner. "I can think of worse places," Mara replied.

If Wellington Mara's picture was hanging in San Quentin, it was because he had a soft spot in his heart for all people, whether they were inside San Quentin or outside. He corresponded on a regular basis with prison inmates and anyone else having an interest in football. In a typical month, Mara would receive more than two hundred letters. The letters came from paupers and presidents. Mara answered each and every one—in long hand.

Two months after Mara's death, the *New York Daily News* honored him as the first recipient of its New York Sportsman of the Year Award. When announcing the award, the *Daily News* was quick to explain that it had not selected Mara because he had died, but rather "because of how he lived, and how he treated virtually everyone with whom he intersected."

To his players, Mara was the man who went to the locker room after every game to check on those who had been injured. He was also the man who paid the players' medical bills long after they had retired. To stadium workers, Mara was the man who offered them his hat on frigid days. To prison inmates, Mara was the man who sent gifts to their children at Christmas. To employees in the Giants organization, Mara was the man who would help to pay their rent when their budgets were stretched thin. To the *Daily News*, Mara was simply the man "with the pen and the heart that wouldn't quit."

◆   ◆   ◆

When you give to the poor, it is like lending to the Lord.
—Proverbs 19, verse 17.

MAGGIE DIXON

Six-foot-one-inch Margaret "Maggie" Dixon played four years of varsity basketball at the University of San Diego, captaining the team as a senior. After an unsuccessful tryout in 2000 with the Los Angeles Sparks of the Women's National Basketball Association, Dixon took a job as a graduate assistant with the DePaul University women's basketball team. The U.S. Military Academy named her as head coach of its women's team in October 2005. During the 2005–06 season, Dixon's only year as a head coach, she led the Black Knights to a 20–11 record and a berth in the NCAA Division I tournament. It was the first NCAA tournament appearance ever for the Army women. Dixon died of heart arrhythmia on April 6, 2006. She was twenty-eight years old.

On December 30, 2005, in preparation for a New Year's Eve game against powerhouse University of Connecticut, Maggie Dixon held three separate film sessions for the players on her Army basketball team. At 10:00 PM, Dixon summoned the team to her hotel room for yet a fourth meeting. When the players arrived, they were surprised to find the makings of a party—mounds of ice cream and fruit toppings. The next day, the Black Knights lost by thirty-nine points, bringing their record to 5–7. Dixon responded as only an eternal optimist could. "We're just in the spot where we want to be," she told the team. The Black Knights then went on to win fifteen of their next nineteen games.

Dixon knew how to party and she knew how to win. On the morning after every victory, she would stop at the West Point mess hall for breakfast, stand at a podium in front of all the cadets, and thank them for supporting the team. Dixon made the cadets feel like they had helped the team win—and she made her players feel that they could win. At her death, the West Point athletic director said, "She brought out the best in the team. We had good players here. But I don't think they believed it."

Dixon's message was about more than merely winning. She told her team that victories were meaningless unless they came with compassion, camaraderie, and love. Her coaching style was simple: "always build up the players, never tear them down." When Army lost, she would tell her team, "Keep your heads up. We'll learn from this."

When Army's 2005–06 season ended with a 102–54 loss to the University of Tennessee in the NCAA tournament, Dixon told her team, "You just gave me the best six or seven months of my life." Dixon died three weeks later, the victim of a malfunctioning heart valve and an enlarged heart. On the morning of her death, all eighteen members of her team visited her at Westchester Medical Center, held her hand, and prayed.

Upon learning that Dixon had died, Rob DiMuro, her high school coach in Sherman Oaks, California, said, "What a soul! Salt of the earth in every single dealing I had with her."

◆   ◆   ◆

The Lord surrounds you with love and compassion.
—Psalm 103, verse 4.

EARL WOODS

As a child in Manhattan, Kansas, Earl Woods displayed a talent for playing baseball. He starred as a catcher in high school and attracted the interest of college programs. In 1951, he enrolled at Kansas State University on an athletic scholarship, becoming the first African American baseball player in the Big Eight Conference. When Woods graduated from Kansas State, the Negro League Kansas City Monarchs offered him a contract, but he declined the offer and joined the Army. He made a career of the military, serving two tours in Vietnam and earning the Vietnam Gallantry Cross for heroic conduct. Woods retired from the Army in 1974 as a lieutenant colonel and devoted his spare time to golfing. He passed his love of golf on to his son, Eldrick, better known as Tiger Woods. Earl Woods died on May 3, 2006, at the age of seventy-four.

To Earl Woods, his primary role as a parent was to show his son, Tiger, how to live his life as a caring person. Developing Tiger's prodigious talents as a golfer was subordinate. Earl elaborated on the responsibility he felt as a father in a letter he wrote to Tiger in 1997. The letter read,

> You are my little man. You are my treasure. God gave you to me to nurture and to grow and to develop. I always have had your interests first and foremost in my life, and it always will be. In fact, you mean more to me than life itself. I can remember when I taught you it was OK to cry—that men can cry. It was not a sign of weakness, but a sign of strength. That was part of the education and the legacy that I wanted to leave with you, that sharing and caring for others is a way of life. And it is not taken lightly. I pass on all of my abilities to share and care to you.

Seeing his "little man" achieve greatness in golf was not an essential part of Earl's plan. All he wanted was to raise a good person. Earl accomplished that. He also lived to see his son become widely recognized as the greatest golfer, professional or amateur, in history. The first was "a delight," Earl would say, the second "a bonus."

Earl Woods saw golf as a means of broadening opportunities for young people of all backgrounds. When Tiger rose to golfing prominence, Earl enthusiastically joined him in conducting clinics and exhibitions for inner-city youths. Earl also worked to establish an organization that would help children develop golf and life skills. With Earl as the inspiration and driving force, the Tiger Woods Foundation was established in 1996. The Foundation provides grants in amounts ranging from twenty-five hundred dollars to twenty-five thousand dollars for educational, tutoring, and mentoring programs aimed at disadvantaged youths in urban areas. In February 2006, the Foundation opened a twenty-five million dollar learning center in Anaheim, California.

Earl Woods also wrote books in which he shared with others what he had learned in life. His crowning work as an author, *Start Something: You Can Make a Difference*, has been hailed as "a wise and friendly manual for being a better friend, student, teacher, and community member." In one section of *Start Something*, Earl asks, "Did you help someone today?" In another section, he tells his readers to "notice the kid everyone ignores."

For Earl Woods, sharing and caring came easily.

◆ ◆ ◆

May our sons be like plants well nurtured from their youth.
—Psalm 144, verse 12.

JOHN "BUCK" O'NEIL

From 1938 to 1955, Buck O'Neil was an outstanding first baseman for the Kansas City Monarchs of the American Negro League. In 1946, he led the American Negro League in hitting with a .353 average. He continued his assault on pitchers the next season, batting .358. For his career, O'Neil compiled a .288 average. He was nearly flawless as a fielder, one year committing only one error. Though O'Neil never had the opportunity to play in baseball's major leagues, he competed against major-league players on countless occasions during the off-season and more than held his own. After retiring as a player, O'Neil served as a scout for the Chicago Cubs and was instrumental in signing African American stars such as Ernie Banks, Billy Williams, and Lou Brock for the Cubs. In 1962, O'Neil took a position with the Cubs as an on-field coach, becoming the first African American to coach in the major leagues. In later years, he served as head of the Negro Leagues Baseball Museum in Kansas City, Missouri. O'Neil passed away on October 6, 2006, at the age of ninety-four. In December 2006, President George W. Bush posthumously awarded him the Presidential Medal of Freedom, the nation's highest civil award, for his contributions to baseball and American culture.

As co-founder and head of the Negro Leagues Baseball Museum, Buck O'Neil campaigned tirelessly to have the most notable stars of the Negro Leagues admitted to baseball's Hall of Fame. In February 2006, O'Neil's efforts paid off when a special committee elected seventeen Negro Leaguers to the Hall. To the amazement of baseball experts, O'Neil himself was not elected; he fell one vote short of admission.

When the results of the Hall of Fame voting became public, individuals in and out of baseball felt compelled to praise O'Neil's unique contributions to baseball and to society. Testimonials came in from sources all over the country. O'Neil was genuinely touched. When asked his reaction to being snubbed by the election committee, O'Neil responded in typical fashion. "I have never felt more loved," he said. O'Neil told reporters that not getting into the Hall of Fame allowed him to see more than ever how much people cared about him. There was no hint of bitterness. "I never learned to hate," O'Neil said.

By the time Jackie Robinson integrated the major leagues in 1947, O'Neil was already thirty-five years old and past his prime as a player. Time had passed O'Neil by, or so it seemed. O'Neil, however, never voiced any disappointment at having been denied the opportunity to play in the major leagues. Many suggested that he had come along too early, but O'Neil disagreed. "Waste no tears for me," he wrote in his biography. "I didn't come along too early—I was right on time." If he had come along later, O'Neil said, he wouldn't have had the chance to dance with singer Lena Horne. "What could be better than that?" he asked.

Although he never spent a day as a player in the major leagues, O'Neil became a legend in Kansas City. He worked with every deserving charity that he could find. Children were his special joy. A grammar school girl once told her teacher that O'Neil was a friend of hers. The teacher reacted with disbelief. When O'Neil learned of the teacher's reaction, he accompanied the student to school and introduced himself to the entire class. Under O'Neil's direction, the Negro Leagues Baseball Museum established a charitable fund to raise money for a research and education center for children.

O'Neil loved to sing. He sang for benefits at every opportunity. His particular favorite was "I Believe," a song written in 1952 to lift the spirits of Americans during the Korean War. At event after event, O'Neil would bring the audience to its feet, singing:

> I believe that above the storm
> the smallest prayer will still be heard.
> I believe that someone in the great
> somewhere hears every word.
> Every time I hear a newborn baby cry
> or touch a leaf or see the sky.
> Then I know why I believe.

◆   ◆   ◆

I shall sing of your strength, extol your love at dawn.
—Psalm 59, verse 17.

BRIAN FREEMAN

Brian Freeman, a captain in the United States Army Reserve, was an accomplished athlete who excelled in the bobsled and skeleton luge. Freeman graduated from West Point in 1999. After graduation, he served on active duty with the Army for five years, first at Fort Knox, Kentucky, and later at Fort Carson, Colorado. In 2002, he joined the Army World Class Athlete Program and trained with the United States bobsled and luge teams in Lake Placid, New York. Freeman earned a bronze medal in the four-man bobsled at an America's Cup race in December 2002. He finished sixteenth in the skeleton at the 2003 U.S. National Championships. Released from active duty in 2004, Freeman settled in Temecula, California. The Army recalled him to active duty in the fall of 2005 and assigned him to Iraq. Though trained as an armor officer, Freeman served in a civil affairs unit in Iraq. He was uneasy working in that capacity and expressed his concern to Democratic Senators Christopher Dodd and John Kerry when they visited Iraq in December 2006. Freeman urged the Senators to push for a more thoughtful military strategy in Iraq. "Senator, it's nuts over here," he told Dodd. In January 2007, a group of armed men posing as American military abducted Freeman during a surprise attack in Karbala and later killed him. He was thirty-one years old.

It didn't take Brian Freeman long to ferret out the procedures for bringing Iraqi children to the United States for emergency medical treatment. In April 2006, Freeman learned that an eleven-year-old boy, Ali Abdulameer, was in urgent need of heart surgery. Abdulameer suffered from a debilitating condition that restricted his flow of blood. Without surgery, the condition would be fatal. Freeman learned that it would cost eight thousand dollars to bring the boy to the United States for treatment.

Freeman enlisted the help of Gift of Life International, a nonprofit organization that connects children suffering from heart ailments with hospitals in the United States. He also enlisted the help of his wife, Charlotte, who coordinated assistance efforts in the United States through phone calls and e-mail messages. Over a period of months, Freeman collected Ali Abdulameer's medical records, contacted charity organizations for donations, and applied for U.S. travel visas for the boy and his father. By the middle of January 2007, only the final step, approval of the visas, was lacking.

Freeman didn't live to see the visas issued. He died on January 20, 2007. Hours after his death, the U.S. consulate in Jordan received approval for Ali Abdulameer and his father to travel to the United States. Doctors at a hospital in New York City successfully repaired the child's heart a few weeks later.

Freeman's experiences in helping Ali Abdulameer caused him to rethink his future plans. He talked with his wife and others about forming an organization that would make it easier for Iraqi children to obtain medical care abroad. Freeman planned to call the organization Vets for Kids.

◆   ◆   ◆

Do good, Lord, to those who are upright of heart.
—Psalm 125, verse 4.

DAMIEN "DEE DEE" NASH

"Dee Dee" Nash was a five-foot-eleven, 215-pound running back for the Denver Broncos. A native of St. Louis, Nash starred at the University of Missouri. He was a fifth-round draft pick of the Tennessee Titans in 2005 and signed with the Broncos as a free agent before the 2006 season. Denver promoted Nash from the practice squad to the active roster late in the 2006 season. He started for the Broncos on November 19, 2006, against the San Diego Chargers and gained eighty-eight yards from scrimmage, including a run of twenty-six yards. Nash died of natural causes on February 24, 2007, after playing in a charity basketball game. He was twenty-four years old.

Dee Dee Nash went out a winner. In the last hours of his life, he hit four jump shots from beyond the three-point arc. More significantly, his efforts that day raised $1,200 for heart-transplant research.

Nash organized the charity basketball game in honor of his older brother, Darris, who had received a heart transplant a year earlier. The proceeds went to the Darris Nash Find A Heart Foundation, which collects funds for heart-transplant research.

After the game, Dee Dee Nash proudly held his infant daughter, Phaith, and displayed his engaging smile. He collapsed and died a short time later.

In his brief life, Nash made a profound impact on others—with his irrepressible smile, his enthusiasm for helping out, and his concern for family and friends. He had played in Denver for only a short time, but left a big impression. His smile, which he would often reveal at the most unexpected moments, brought fun to otherwise tedious scrimmages. According to Broncos coach Mike Shanahan, no other player had ever made a more positive impact on the team in one year than did Dee Dee Nash.

◆   ◆   ◆

Guard your heart, for in it are the sources of life.
—Proverbs 4, verse 23.

ERNIE "BIG CAT" LADD

Ernie "Big Cat" Ladd played eight years as a defensive tackle in the American Football League. He was the largest football player of his time, standing six feet nine inches tall and weighing 315 pounds. Ladd attended Grambling State University on a basketball scholarship. He began his pro football career with the San Diego Chargers in 1961 and remained with the Chargers until 1965. He spent the 1966 season with the Houston Oilers and then closed out his career as a member of the Kansas City Chiefs. From 1970 to 1986, Ladd was a regular on the professional wrestling circuit. He is a member of both the American Football League Hall of Fame and the World Wrestling Entertainment Hall of Fame. Big Cat died of colon cancer on March 10, 2007, at the age of sixty-eight.

As a professional wrestler, Ernie Ladd invariably took on the role of villain. He felt he had no option, because he dwarfed his opponents. "I was too big to get sympathy," he said.

In real life, Ladd was anything but a villain. He was warm and outgoing, a man dedicated to helping others. He used his fame and influence to combat the effects of racism. After arriving in New Orleans for the 1965 American Football League All-Star Game, Ladd found that local taxi drivers were refusing to transport African American players. He organized his fellow all-stars and successfully pressured the league to move the game to Houston. After his playing days, Ladd worked with former Houston Oilers lineman John L. White to operate Project P.U.L.L., an organization that arranged for athletes, teachers, doctors, and lawyers to serve as mentors for minority youths in the Houston area.

When his wrestling career ended, Ladd became the pastor of a church congregation in Franklin, Louisiana. Despite knee problems that forced him to use a wheelchair, he frequently visited prisons in Louisiana to talk about football and wrestling and spread the word of God. When Hurricane Katrina struck in 2005, Ladd spent his time raising money for victims of the disaster.

Ladd was an incurable optimist, even as he neared death. His optimism stemmed from a confidence that God had everything in order. "I'm in the Master's hands now," Ladd told friends in his final days.

◆   ◆   ◆

Reach out your hand from on high; deliver me from the many waters.
—Psalm 144, verse 7.

EDDIE ROBINSON

Eddie Robinson, "Coach Rob" to those who knew him, became the head football coach at Grambling State University in Louisiana in 1941 when he was twenty-two years old. Success came quickly and lingered long. At age twenty-three, Robinson coached Grambling to an undefeated season in which the team did not give up a single point. Years later, when Robinson was seventy-five, he led Grambling to a share of the Southwestern Athletic Conference championship, and was named the Conference's coach of the year. Overall, Robinson's teams won 408 games and produced more than two hundred future National Football League players. Robinson died on April 3, 2007. He was eighty-eight.

For the first twenty-five years of his coaching career, Eddie Robinson and his players were prohibited by law from drinking out of the "whites only" water fountains in Louisiana or using the "whites only" restrooms. The blatant discrimination did not trouble Robinson. He was confident that better times were coming. He would tell his players that if they blocked better and tackled better, racial barriers would come down. Robinson played a significant role in bringing down those barriers. His record at Grambling left no doubt that blacks could excel in the coaching profession. His success paved the way. Hundreds of other African American football coaches followed.

Robinson claimed to be the quintessential American. "For over fifty years," he would say," I've had one job and one wife. I don't believe anyone can out-American me." Few could outwork him either. In his early years at Grambling, Robinson mowed the football field and marked the yard lines before games. To compensate for Grambling's lack of a weight room, Robinson filled coffee cans with cement so that his players could work out with "weights." Robinson also coached the men's and women's basketball teams at Grambling.

Robinson was a teacher and friend, coach and mentor. He demanded that his players work as hard in the classroom as they did on the football field. He carried a record of his players' grades with him in his briefcase, and was quick to prod them if their academic performance needed improvement. He taught his players to become good Americans first, then good football players. "Life is bigger than just you," he told his players, "it's about others."

◆   ◆   ◆

Patience brings peace.
—Proverbs 15, verse 18.

KEVIN MITCHELL

Six-foot-one, 260-pound Kevin Mitchell was a ten-year veteran of the National Football League. Mitchell was born and raised in Harrisburg, Pennsylvania. In his teens, he was a standout football and basketball player for Harrisburg High. He attended Syracuse University on a football scholarship, where he played both linebacker and nose guard. In 1992 and 1993, Mitchell was named first-team All-Big East. He recorded eight tackles and two quarterback sacks in the 1993 Fiesta Bowl, earning the Most Valuable Defensive Player award. The San Francisco 49ers drafted Mitchell in the second round of the 1994 collegiate draft. He went on to enjoy a successful pro career, playing four seasons with the Forty-Niners, two with the New Orleans Saints, and four with the Washington Redskins. Overall, Mitchell appeared in 144 games as a professional and recorded 222 tackles. He retired prior to the 2004 season and settled in Ashburn, Virginia. In recognition of Mitchell's stellar college career, Syracuse University named him to its All-Century team in 1999. Mitchell died in his sleep on April 30, 2007. He was thirty-six years old.

The tributes for Kevin Mitchell began pouring in the day after his death. From Harrisburg and Syracuse and Ashburn and points beyond, people felt compelled to remember Mitchell in their own special way. He was, they said, "the best." He had "the warmest smile," "the loudest laugh," and "the most cheerful attitude."

To children, "K-Mitch" was the biggest teddy bear. To his Syracuse University philosophy teacher, he was the most respectful student. To flight attendants who worked the Redskins' charter planes, he was the most joyful football player, owner of the least-inflated ego. To his college coach, he had the biggest heart. To his brother, Chris, he was the best of friends. To college teammates, Mitchell was the most genuine person. To football fans in San Francisco, New Orleans, and Washington, he was the most patient of autograph signers. To the salesclerks in a Virginia retail store, he was the most gracious of customers.

The kind words accurately reflected different facets of Mitchell's personality. None of the tributes, however, captured the essence of Kevin Mitchell as perfectly as the words spoken by friend Eddie Mason, a former Redskins teammate. To Mason, K-Mitch was simply "the best daddy I'd ever seen in my life."

Mitchell was a loving husband and a loving daddy. To him, those responsibilities took priority. And so, on the last night of his life, Mitchell did what came naturally. He read bedtime stories to his two children, four-year-old Jonathan and two-year-old Kayla, and tucked them in for the night. Then he spent time with his wife, Denise, discussing their plans to return to Harrisburg and start a home-remodeling business. It was, Denise said, "a great day."

Denise Mitchell and her children laid K-Mitch to rest in Harrisburg on Saturday, May 5. The next day, Sunday, turned out to be another great day for Denise. Upon returning to the family home in Virginia, she learned that she was again pregnant. She ran through the house "like a little kid, screaming." It is, Denise Mitchell says, one more piece of her husband to keep.

When K-Mitch wasn't spending time with his family or planning his future in home remodeling, he could be found working with young children and teenagers at the football clinics and speed camps conducted by MASE Training. He developed an easy rapport with kids. It helped that he was a lovable teddy bear. More importantly, he treated all of the children as if they were his own, imparting in equal measure football techniques, tips on building character, and spiritual guidance.

At Mitchell's memorial service, images from his life flashed on an overhead video screen. There was a picture of him wearing number fifty-five for the Redskins. There was a picture of him on his wedding day. And, fittingly, there was a picture of him feeding one of his babies.

To the end, K-Mitch was the best daddy.

◆   ◆   ◆

As a father has compassion on his children, so the Lord has compassion on the faithful.
—Psalm 103, verse 13.

JUSTIN SKAGGS

Justin Skaggs was a veteran Arena Football League player. He starred at wide receiver and linebacker for the Utah Blaze and was commonly acknowledged as one of the team leaders. Skaggs played collegiately at Evangel University in Springfield, Missouri. Before joining the Arena Football League, Skaggs spent time with the Washington Redskins, San Francisco 49ers, and Tampa Bay Buccaneers of the National Football League. He caught fifty-two passes for the Blaze in 2006 and followed that up with twenty-one more during the first thirteen weeks of the 2007 season. His last appearance for the Blaze came against the Orlando Predators on May 25, 2007, a game in which he made three tackles from his linebacker position. Days later, he experienced numbness in his arms and hands and severe headaches. An MRI revealed abnormalities and swelling on his brain, raising the suspicion of cancer. On June 8, Skaggs learned that he had two inoperable brain tumors. He died on June 15, 2007. He was twenty-eight years old.

Shortly after Justin Skaggs died, his five-year-old son, Jake, asked his mother, "Will Daddy ever play football again?" Tara Skaggs wasted no time in responding. "Yes," she said, "Daddy will play football again—in heaven."

Doctors began performing medical tests on Skaggs on June 1. He died two weeks later. In the intervening span of fourteen days, Skaggs did a lot. He bolstered the morale of his teammates, gave media interviews, celebrated his daughter's birthday, hugged his children, and attended a performance by Tim McGraw and Faith Hill in Salt Lake City. He also endured terrible pain.

Skaggs knew he was facing a formidable opponent. Yet even after doctors confirmed the worst, he remained upbeat and positive. He reacted to the news of his cancer with equanimity.

"I have a lot of faith," he told reporters. He felt fortunate to be with the Blaze. "I could not have better teammates or be in a better place to have this," he said.

Teammates said they learned a lot about Skaggs merely by peering into his locker. The items that Skaggs displayed most prominently in his cubicle were pictures of Tara, Jake, and three-year-old daughter Abbie.

Teammates also learned a lot about Skaggs by the things he did after he took sick. The Blaze's head coach, Danny White, first told the team that Skaggs's condition was potentially serious on June 1. When making the announcement, White told the players not to expect to see Skaggs back in the locker room. Three days later, Skaggs showed up to visit his teammates before they were to play the Colorado Crush. "The team really had our heads down," Blaze lineman Hans Olsen said. "We were told we would not see him. But ten or fifteen minutes before the game, in walks Justin. Chills went up my spine."

On June 11, three days after doctors confirmed the existence of the brain tumors, Skaggs and his wife went to the Tim McGraw/Faith Hill concert with a group of teammates and their spouses. When Tim McGraw broke into his hit song, "Live Like You Were Dying," Robin Konopka, wife of Blaze lineman Steve Konopka, couldn't help but watch Skaggs. "Justin's eyes got real big, and he sang every word," Robin Konopka said. "It was so emotional, but he never stopped."

Skaggs was fond of Tim McGraw. He was fond of his teammates. He loved his wife and children. He had faith in God.

◆   ◆   ◆

I shall sing of your strength, extol your love at dawn.
—Psalm 59, verse 17.

References

John Steadman

Jay Apperson, "A Monumental Farewell Tribute: Baltimore Residents and Others Turn Out to Say Goodbye to Sports Columnist John Steadman and to Remember How He Touched Their Lives," *The (Baltimore) Sun*, 6 January 2001, 1B.

Gregory Kane, "Steadman Leaves Us A Legacy of Fairness," *The (Baltimore) Sun*, 10 January 2001, 1B.

Mike Klingaman, "A Baltimore Legend, Champion of Underdogs, Sportswriter: A Man of Grace and Humor, He Told the Stories of the Greats and the Little Guys of Maryland Sports For More Than A Half-Century: John Steadman: 1927–2001," *The (Baltimore) Sun*, 2 January 2001, 1A.

Michael Olesker, "'Didn't We Have Some Great Times?' John Steadman: 1927–2001," *The (Baltimore) Sun*, 2 January 2001, 1B.

"Baltimore's Best in Sports John Steadman: Hall of Fame Sportswriter Reflected What Was Good in Local Athletics," *The (Baltimore) Sun*, 3 January 2001, 10A.

Korey Stringer

Thomas George, "At Stringer's Funeral, Tributes Mingle with Tears and Poetry," *The New York Times*, 7 August 2001, D4.

Rusty Miller, "Stringer Recalled As Fun-Loving," *Milwaukee Journal Sentinel*, 9 August 2001, 19.

Aaron Portzline, "Huge Crowd Says Goodbye to Stringer," *Columbus Dispatch*, 7 August 2001, 1C.

Patrick Reusse, "Final Goodbyes: An Ohio Town Gathers To Praise and To Mourn," (Minneapolis) *Star Tribune*, 7 August 2001, 1C.

"Korey Stringer: He Was An All-Pro, On and Off the Field," *Columbus Dispatch*, 8 August 2001, 8A.

Mike Weinberg

Kay Hawes, "September 11 Attacks Had A Unique Impact On a Nation of Student-Athletes," *The NCAA News*, 11 November 2001, http://ncaa.org/news/2001/20011119/active/3824n30.html.

"Ex-Tiger Farmhand Victim of WTC Attack," *The Michigan Daily*, 20 September 2001.

Shelby "Big Foot" Njoku

Recollections of Megan Shaffer, friend and teammate.

Darryl Kile

Stephen Cannella, "Kile Found Dead in Chicago Hotel Room," *Sports Illustrated*, 23 June 2002, http://sportsillustrated.cnn.com/baseball/news/2002/06/22/cards_kile_ap.

R. B. Fallstrom, "A Family's Farewell; Teammates, Relatives and Fans Honor the Cardinals' Darryl Kile," *South Florida Sun-Sentinel*, 27 June 2002, 6C.

Rick Hummel, "'We Love You and We Miss You'; Kile's Friends Remember The Man, The Athlete and The Practical Joker; Players and Fans Say Goodbye," *St. Louis Post-Dispatch*, 27 June 2002, D1.

Joe Strauss, "Kile A Most Unlikely Star," (Albany, NY) *Times Union*, 2 July 2002, C1.

"Kile Remembered As Gamer, Team Leader," 25 June 2002, http://sportsillustrated.cnn. com/baseball/news/2002/06/22/kile_profile_ap.

"Memorial On the Mound; Kile's Friends Fondly Recall the Good Times," *Houston Chronicle*, 27 June 2002, 3.

Willie McCool

David Brown and Nelson Hernandez, "'Up in the Stratosphere,' But 'One of the Guys'," *The Washington Post*, 2 February 2003, A30.

Warren Cornwall and Craig Welch, "William McCool; Co-Pilot Had Been Stationed at Whidbey Base, Fell In Love With the Olympic Mountains," *Seattle Times*, 2 February 2003, A9.

Stephanie Desmon, "Space Shuttle Voyage Was Co-Pilot's Lifelong Dream; Friends in Lubbock, Texas, and Annapolis Remember 'All-American Guy' McCool," *The (Baltimore) Sun*, 3 February 2003, 9A.

William Gildea, "The Perfect Place to Honor a Hero," *The Washington Post*, 2 November 2003, E3.

Eric Sorensen, "Whidbey Salutes Pilot, Astronaut; Brave, Spirited McCool Also Was 'Regular Guy',"*Seattle Times*, 8 February 2003, A12.

"'Columbia Is Lost'; A Generous Family Man," *Los Angeles Times*, 2 February 2003, A9.

Jimmy Adamouski

David Cho and Steven Ginsberg, "'Now You Soar With Your God'; Back-to-Back Funerals Honor Three Lost to War in Iraq," *The Washington Post*, 25 April 2003, B7.

Monica Davey, "Plans for Families, Degrees and Careers Come to Abrupt End in Iraq," *The New York Times*, 13 April 2003, B12.

Pat Tillman

Chris Dufresne, "Tillman Always Special," *The Ottawa Citizen*, 26 April 2004, C14.

Bob Padecky, "Tillman Left Us Wondering What Was Next," *The (Santa Rosa, CA) Press Democrat*, 4 May 2004, C1.

Lisa Olson, "Tillman Tribute Reflects the Man," *New York Daily News*, 4 May 2004, 76.

Doug Robinson, "Tillman Took a Different Path, Always," (Salt Lake City) *Deseret News*, 3 May 2004, D1.

Gary Smith, "Remember His Name," *Sports Illustrated*, 11 September 2006, 86.

Rick Telander, "Replacing Heroic Tillman Is Impossible," *Chicago Sun-Times*, 3 May 2004, 106.

John Cerutti

Matt Michael, "ESPN Announcer Loses Best Friend; Those Who Knew Former Chiefs Pitcher Are Stunned By His Death," *The (Syracuse) Post-Standard*, 5 October 2004, D1.

Wayne Scanlan, "Human Qualities Set Cerutti Apart From Rest," *The Ottawa Citizen*, 5 October 2004, D3.

"Baseball Might Have Mentioned Cerutti," *Toronto Star*, 24 October 2004, E5.

Teddy Ebersol

Owen Canfield, "A Special Family With A Special Touch," *Hartford Courant*, 4 December 2004, B4.

Jane Gordon, "Litchfield Remembers Teddy Ebersol," *The New York Times*, 5 December 2004, 14CN.

Joe McGurk, "Pals Mourn Ebersol Son," *New York Post*, 9 December 2004, 35.

Katie Melone, "Teddy Ebersol's Spirit Celebrated at Service," *Hartford Courant*, 17 December 2004, B7.

Johnny Oates

Vic Fulp, "Faith, Family, Friends Inspired Oates; Former Prince George Star Enjoyed Successful Major League Career," *Richmond Times-Dispatch*, 29 December 2004, E2.

Joe Gross, "Even In Tough Times, Oates Was A Shining Light," (Annapolis) *Capital*, 26 December 2004, C13.

Hank Kurz Jr., "Rangers' Oates Dies at Age 58; Former Manager Who Had Brain Tumor Led Texas to First Postseason Berths in Franchise History," *Beaumont Enterprise*, 25 December 2004, C1.

Reggie Roby

Candy Sagon, "Cookies To Please A Pro," *The Washington Post*, 16 March 2005, F4.

Armando Salguero, "Reggie Roby, 1961–2005; Booming Kicks 2nd to Charitable Spirit," *Chicago Tribune*, 23 February 2005, 2.

"Reggie Roby; Retired NFL Punter," *Pittsburgh Post-Gazette*, 24 February 2005, A19.

Becky Zerlentes

Bill Briggs, "Inspiration Not Confined to Ring; Boxing Was One of Many Success Stories for Becky Zerlentes, Who Died at 34 on Sunday After a Bout," *Denver Post*, 6 April 2005, D1.

Bill Briggs, "Boxers Mourn Golden Gloves Star; A Ring of Sadness, Silence," *Denver Post*, 7 April 2005, A1.

Bill Briggs, "Mourners Celebrate Boxer's Life," *Denver Post*, 10 April 2005, B11.

Sam Mills

Charles Bricker, "The Mouse That Roared: Former Linebacker Sam Mills Showed That Perseverance Can Overcome Size," *South Florida Sun-Sentinel*, 24 April 2005, 13C.

Rick Flores, "He Treated Everyone The Same," *Northwest Florida Daily News*, 22 April 2005, B1.

Gene Sapakoff, "Panthers Day at Brentwood Middle School," *The Post and Courier*, 20 April 2005, C1.

"Mills' Service Is What He Wanted," *Chicago Sun-Times*, 22 April 2005, 143.

"Mills Remembered For Class On, Off Field; Former Linebacker Planned His Own Service," *The Grand Rapids Press*, 22 April 2005, E4.

Holly Charette

Alice Gomstyn, "Holly Charette—Buried With Honor; 'She's Our Sister,' Says One Retired Marine, 'And That's Why We're Here'," *The Providence Journal*, 3 July 2005, A1.

Elizabeth Gudrais, "Roll Call for Holly," *The Providence Journal*, 2 July 2005, A3.

Michael Levenson, "R.I. Kin Mourn Cheerleader Turned Marine," *Boston Globe*, 26 June 2005, B1.

Jennifer Levitz, "'All I Can Think of Is That I Hope You Felt No Pain'," *Providence Journal*, 27 June 2005, http://projo.com/news/content/projo_20050626_hollyc.23f3380.html.

Jamie Wilson, "One Woman's Death Brings Iraq War Home to Small-Town America," *The (London, UK) Guardian*, 4 July 2005, 15.

Wellington Mara

Dave Anderson, "Remembering a Giant; Wellington Mara, The Heart of His Team," (Paris) *International Herald Tribune*, 29 October 2005, C2.

Ron Borges, "Man of Vision Saw It All in NFL," *Boston Globe*, 30 October 2005, C11.

Wayne Coffey, "Well Suited for Honor; *Daily News* Tabs Mara as Sportsman of the Year," *New York Daily News*, December 18, 2005, 102.

Gordon Forbes, "Mara Was A Giant Man of Class and Influence: Beloved NY Owner 'Brought Dignity to Everyone He Touched'," *USA Today*, 26 October 2005, C11.

Dave Goldberg, "There Will Never Be Another Wellington; Giants' Owner Was The Classiest of Class Acts," *St. Louis Post-Dispatch*, 30 October 2005, D1.

"Thousands Turn Out for Mara," (Annapolis) *Capital*, 29 October 2005, C2.

Maggie Dixon

Lisa Olson, "She Commanded Respect; Dixon Left Mark on Army," *New York Daily News*, 12 April 2006, 66.

Selena Roberts, "Dixon's Civility Lightened Load At West Point," *New York Times*, 16 April 2006, 8.

"Army Coach Dixon Mourned By 1,200 In L.A.," *Chicago Sun-Times*, 12 April 2006, 105.

"Mourners Remember Dixon; Player, Brother Praise Army Coach For Her Inspiration," *Houston Chronicle*, 12 April 2006, 2.

Earl Woods

Bill Hutchinson, "He Raised a Tiger and Now He's Gone: Cancer Kills Earl Woods, Golf Great's 'Best Friend'," *New York Daily News*, 4 May 2006, 7.

Bob Keisser, "Earl Woods Gave Golf to Tiger," (Long Beach, CA) *Press-Telegram*, 3 May 2006.

Jim Litke, "Woods Has Become the Man His Father Wanted Him to Be," *The Augusta Chronicle*, June 1, 2006, C2.

Ed Sherman, "Earl Woods, Tiger's Father, Dies at 74," *Knight Ridder Tribune News Service*, 3 May 2006, 1.

Woods, Earl and Tiger Woods Foundation (co-author). *Start Something: You Can Make a Difference*. New York: Simon & Schuster, 2006.

Woods, Earl. *Playing Through: Straight Talk on Hard Work, Big Dreams, and Adventures with Tiger*. New York: Collins, 1998.

Woods, Earl. *Training a Tiger: A Father's Guide to Raising a Winner in Both Golf and Life*. New York: Collins, 1997.

Curtis Zupke, "Earl Woods, Tiger's Father and Best Friend, Dies at 74," *Knight Ridder Tribune News Service*, 3 May 2006, 1.

Website for the Tiger Woods Foundation, http://tigerwoodsfoundation.org.

John "Buck" O'Neil

Ken Burns, "Good Job, Buck," *Chicago Tribune*, 15 October 2006, 7.

O'Neil, Buck with Steve Wulf and David Conrads. *I Was Right On Time*. New York: Simon & Schuster Paperbacks, 1996.

Joe Posnanski, "Buck O'Neil Remembered: Farewell, Old Friend," *Knight Ridder Tribune News Service*, 14 October 2006, 1.

Matt Stearns and Steve Penn, "Buck O'Neil Awarded Presidential Medal of Freedom," *Knight Ridder Tribune News Service*, 7 December 2006, 1.

Doug Tucker, "O'Neil Remembered For His Dignity, Love," *The Vancouver Sun*, 16 October 2006, D5.

Brian Freeman

Ernesto Londoño, "Quest to Heal Iraqi Boy Became a Final Mission," *The Washington Post*, February 15, 2007, A1.

Damien "Dee Dee" Nash

Mike Klis, "Broncos' Nash Death Cause Not Determined," *Denver Post*, 9 May 2007, D6.

Lee Rasizer, "'Everybody Was Proud'; In His Hometown, Family, Friends Pay Tribute to Dee Dee," *Rocky Mountain News*, 5 March 2007, 6.

Lee Rasizer, "'I Don't Understand Why He's Gone'; Nash's Family, Friends, Broncos Bid Goodbye to 24-Year-Old Athlete," *Rocky Mountain News*, 6 March 2007, 20.

Ernie "Big Cat" Ladd

Frank Litsky, "Loomed Large Over Gridiron, Ring," *Toronto Star*, 19 March 2007, E7.

Mike Mooneyham, "Ladd's Legacy Extends Beyond Ring and Gridiron," *The (Charleston, SC) Post and Courier*, 18 March 2007, C12.

Eddie Robinson

Eric Prisbell, "Coach Broke Ground and Records," *The Washington Post*, 5 April 2007, A1.

Joseph Schiefelbein, "Robinson Will Always Be Around," (Baton Rouge) *Advocate*, 12 April 2007, 1.

Michael Wilbon, "Grambling's 'Coach Rob' Did It All," *The Washington Post*, 5 April 2007, E1.

Kevin Mitchell

Rod Frisco, "Mitchell's Game Had An Elegance," *The (Harrisburg, PA) Patriot-News*, 4 May 2007, T20.

Mark Maske, "'Terribly Shocking': A Linebacker and a Family Man Leaves Behind a Legacy of Love," *The Washington Post*, 23 June 2007, E1.

James Phillips, "Kevin Mitchell, 1971–2007; 'He Always Had A Smile On His Face'," *The (Harrisburg, PA) Patriot-News*, 1 May 2007, T3.

Ford Turner, "Kevin Mitchell, 1971–2007; Former NFL Player's Hometown Says Goodbye," *The (Harrisburg, PA) Patriot-News*, 6 May 2007, B1.

Recollections of Eddie Mason, friend, colleague, and former teammate.

Justin Skaggs

Loren Jorgensen, "Stunned Blaze Learn That Teammate Skaggs Is Ailing," (Salt Lake City) *Deseret News*, 2 June 2007, D1.

Loren Jorgensen, "Skaggs Faces New Battle," (Salt Lake City) *Deseret News*, 12 June 2007, D1.

Loren Jorgensen, "Blaze Family Pays Tribute to Skaggs," (Salt Lake City) *Deseret News*, 19 June 2007, D1.

Steve Luhm, "'Just a Class Individual'," *The Salt Lake Tribune*, 16 June 2007, 1.

Steve Luhm, "Utah Blaze: Skaggs Memorial Heavy on Emotion," *The Salt Lake Tribune*, 19 June 2007, 1.

Steve Luhm and Baxter Holmes, "'A Really, Really Good Guy'," *The Salt Lake Tribune*, 16 June 2007, 1.

Brad Rock, "Skaggs, Fisher, Sloan Inspire," (Salt Lake City) *Deseret News*, 17 June 2007, D1.

"Blaze Mainstay Undergoes Emergency Brain Surgery," *The Salt Lake Tribune*, 15 June 2007, 1.

"Remembering Utah Blazeman Justin Skaggs," *The Salt Lake Tribune*, 17 June 2007, 1.

Epilogue

When you look up at the sky at night, since
I'll be living on one of them, since I'll be
laughing on one of them, for you it'll be as
if all the stars are laughing. You'll have stars
that can laugh.

—*The Little Prince*, Antoine de Saint-Exupéry, 1943

The idea of stars that are capable of laughing was a fitting complement to Al McGuire's distinctly whimsical view of the world. Perhaps McGuire identified with the forlorn little prince. Whatever the reason, McGuire took great delight in giving copies of *The Little Prince* to friends and colleagues. One of the lessons to be gleaned from the lives of the "Dream Teamers" is that the gift of a small book about a little prince can bring joy to others. There are other lessons as well:

Spreading joy takes little effort. To paraphrase Johnny Unitas, it takes so little to make people happy. Kerryn O'Neill shared candy. Jimmie Reese shared baseballs. Art Rooney passed out ice cream money. Holly Charette shared her smile. Each in their own way brought joy to others. Using the words of philosopher Pierre Teilhard de Chardin, each found a different way to "harness for God the energies of love."

The human heart sings for many reasons. Walter Payton's heart sang—and his tears flowed—when he was able to bring Santa Claus to disadvantaged children. Jerome Brown loved to break out in song at high school graduations. Buck O'Neil was moved to sing whenever he heard a newborn baby cry or touched a leaf or saw the sky. Shelby Strother and Ernie Harwell sang to cheer up a dying man. Just days after doctors confirmed the presence of inoperable tumors in his brain, Justin Skaggs sang country songs with Tim McGraw.

Finding one's way can be a lengthy journey. The process of spiritual growth takes time. Before committing his life to the cause of social justice, Paul Robeson was, for years, a detached and apolitical performer. Saul Rogovin drifted for nearly twenty years before finding his calling; Chief Yellowhorse drifted even longer. And if Buck O'Neil was "right on time," Mickey Mantle was almost a tad late, waiting until the "ninth inning."

Prayers do get answered. Joe Collins prayed for the success of Moose Skowron. Moose went on to enjoy a successful fourteen-year career in the big leagues. Rex Barney prayed that aging left-hander Mike Flanagan would escape difficulty in the last inning of the final game at Baltimore's Memorial Stadium. Flanagan proceeded to strike out both of the batters he faced. Alan Ameche asked for the ability to help others, even if only a single individual. He ended up helping scores of children throughout the cities of Baltimore and Philadelphia.

Miracles do happen. Some miracles are spectacular, others more subtle. From out of nowhere, a seagull landed on Eddie Rickenbacker's head, saving his life. Ella Lane retrieved "Baby Night Train" from a trash bin and found a place for him in her heart and home. Maura O'Donnell, a tiny woman with a big heart, started a "Super Dance" that has become an annual tradition and has raised more than $2.5 million for the Cystic Fibrosis Foundation. In the last year of her life and her only season as a head coach, Maggie Dixon led the West Point women's basketball team to heights it had never before reached.

Perhaps it is easier, as Pier Giorgio Frassati and Ken Hubbs surmised, to experience the presence of God at higher altitudes. However, God is also clearly present in the valleys, on the open seas, and everywhere else. Pete Maravich found God in the middle of a sleepless night. Dan Quisenberry seemed to experience God's presence precisely during those moments when he was scared and lonely. John Cerutti clutched the cross in his final moments. Each, in his own way, found a source of comfort.

We must condition our hearts. Not only did the Dream Teamers work hard to perfect their athletic skills, they conditioned their hearts to show compassion and work for justice. The relationship between teammates Jackie Robinson and Pee Wee Reese provides a useful example. Reese had joined the Brooklyn Dodgers in 1940 and quickly established himself as the team's regular shortstop. The Dodgers signed Robinson, a shortstop by trade, in the latter part of 1945, and brought him to the majors for the 1947 season. Robinson's presence led to a series of challenges for Reese. Initially, there was talk that Robinson might take over as the Dodgers' shortstop, leaving Reese without a position. Though concerned about his future, Reese did not allow either resentment or anger to set in. "If he's good enough to take my job, he deserves it," Reese told himself. Later, Reese was asked to sign a petition being circulated by some members of the Dodgers who wanted

Robinson off the team. Reese refused to sign. "I don't care if this man is black, blue, or striped," Reese said. Still later, when Reese could not tolerate the epithets being hurled at Robinson by fans, he left his shortstop position, walked over to first base, and placed his arm around Robinson's shoulders. "This man is my teammate," Reese declared to all the world. Reese's actions required the heart of a man committed to compassion and justice. The impact of those actions upon Robinson, the game of baseball, and race relations in the United States was extraordinary.

We are all teammates. There was a reason that Mickey Mantle's "ninth inning" was a vast improvement over his previous eight. When Mantle received his liver transplant, the donor was not one of Mantle's former Yankee teammates or even one of his friends. The liver came from an anonymous individual who had made the decision to give a precious gift to a fellow human being. The transplant caused Mantle to realize—perhaps for the first time—that he was a member of a team that extended far beyond baseball's twenty-five man roster. It was the same realization that prompted Johnny Unitas to go out of his way to shake the hands of the homeless. Similarly, all of the Dream Teamers, sooner or later, came to the startling realization that their *true teammates* were not merely the players on their own squad, but included their competitors, their fans, the individuals making up their communities, the people in their nation, and the inhabitants of the entire world. The whole human family, whether wealthy or indigent, whether living in a castle or homeless, became their *teammates.*

A "borderless" world is not out of reach. Looking out through the window of the space shuttle *Columbia,* Willie McCool had a vision of "an earth without borders, full of peace, beauty and magnificence." If we accept the notion that each person in the world is our teammate, a borderless world becomes possible. Geographic boundaries intended to confine people become unnecessary. Divisions between countries cease to exist.

The lives of the Dream Teamers can serve as a guide. The Dream Teamers not only survived in this life, they flourished. Each individual demonstrated a knack for responding to the needs of others, making the right decisions at the right time, injecting hope into situations that seemed hopeless, and making the world a better place. Without exception, the Dream Teamers proved to be humble, gentle, and caring individuals. In short, when God placed others in their way, the

Dream Teamers came up big. In doing so, the Dream Teamers have shown us how to live this life to its fullest.

We all have the opportunity to be stars. On the football field, Derrick Thomas was a star. Off the field, he was one of the "Thousand Points of Light." To Dorecia Tepe and her son Philip, however, Thomas was simply "an angel." We, too, have the opportunity to be remembered as stars, if not angels, by those whose lives we touch.

About the Author

Fred Day is a lawyer and inveterate sports fan. He maintains a law practice in Falls Church, Virginia. He is a graduate of Providence College in Providence, Rhode Island. He holds a master's degree in political economics from the University of Albany, State University of New York, and a law degree from George Washington University. His previous books include *Clubhouse Lawyer: Law in the World of Sports* (2004), *Sports and Courts: An Introduction to Principles of Law and Legal Theory Using Cases from Professional Sports* (2005), and *Regulation of Wireless Communications Systems* (1997).

About the Artist

Vinn Truong began exhibiting his work in galleries at the age of thirteen. He graduated with a Bachelor of Fine Arts degree from George Mason University in 1999, with a major in painting and sculpting. To this point, he has done more dreaming about art than actual work in the field. *Dream Team* marks his first credited work. He works as an illustrator in Alexandria, Virginia.

Index

978-0-595-45406-8
0-595-45406-2

Printed in the United States
96530LV00005B/4-6/A

9 780595 454068